1986

W9-AEE-684

Invitation to MODULA-2

by Stuart B. Greenfield

PETROCELLI BOOKS
Princeton, New Jersey

Composition by Backes Graphics

Library of Congress Cataloging-in-Publication Data

Greenfield, Stuart B.
    Invitation to MODULA-2.

    Bibliography: p.
    Includes index.
    1. Modula-2 (Computer program language)
I. Title.
QA76.73.M63G74   1985   005.13'3   85-12186
ISBN 0-89433-273-2

To the memory of my Father,
Abraham Greenfield,
And to my Mother,
Helen Greenfield;

———

Both of whom taught me
The value of education
And provided me with
The means for
Obtaining it.

Contents

Preface

At present, the art of programming has centered on the use of structured programming principles. Over the past decade, Pascal has become the most widely used high-level language embodying many of those principles. Through the experience gained using Pascal, along with the recognition of the need for coding facilities offered by other languages (for example, the programming language C), the first half of the 1980s has seen the emergence of two new and important general-purpose, high-level languages, Ada and Modula-2. This pair of languages represent the next step in the implementation of structured programming principles. Ada and Modula-2, in effect, reflect present-day thinking with regard to not only programming structure but the needs of the emerging discipline of software engineering. Both support the concepts of modularity, separate (but dependent) compilation, data abstraction, and concurrency. Furthermore, they create an appropriate environment for the application of an object-oriented design philosophy.

This book describes the second of those two languages, Modula-2. Its primary goal is to allow you to quickly "come up to speed" with Modula-2. Additionally, it is hoped that this book will set the stage for you to move on to further study in the areas of structured program design and software engineering. The book is intended to serve, as its name states, as an invitation to Modula-2. If, indeed, through this book, you are stimulated to read further in the computer science literature and begin coding in Modula-2, it will have served its purpose well.

This book is suitable for anyone with at least an introductory level of understanding of one computer language (preferably Pascal). This group may include introductory level computer science students, serious computer hobbyists, and advanced high school students. Additionally, this book should be of interest to the computer professional who wishes to obtain quick and easy access to information about Modula-2, whether he or she be a programmer, manager, or engineer.

An informal style of presentation is used throughout the book. There are over 50 complete Modula-2 programs including a number of small case studies. The source listings are used as the main vehicle for presenting basic Modula-2 principles. All programs have been written, compiled, and executed using the Modula-2 implemented by Volition Systems of San Diego, California, on an Apple II computer, with a few being run on a Stride Micro 420. This Modula-2 is used in conjunction with the p-system operating system, which is reflected in some of the code dealing with files. Although the programs have been developed on a particular system, care has been taken not to write implementation-dependent code whenever possible. Thus, the programs, with little or no change, can be used with virtually any Modula-2 implementation.

After a first reading of many books, they remain on the reader's bookshelf as a reference. It is hoped that this book will play such a role as well. With this in mind, you will find in the appendices lists of Modula-2's reserved words and standard identifiers and the ASCII character code, along with a list of all the code listings developed in the book, indicating the name of each program and the topic(s) that it exemplifies. The last appendix is a short bibliography which directs the uninitiated and the curious toward further readings.

There are many people who either explicitly or implicitly contribute to the writing and production of any book. By proclaiming thanks to a listed few, an author runs the risk of omitting someone important to the endeavor. Yet I will take that chance, since my desire to thank outweighs my fear of omission.

I say thanks:

To Richard Wiener for the many suggestions he made in his technical review of the manuscript which has turned into this book; for his contagious enthusiasm for Modula-2 and computer science; and for the friendship we have nourished for over two decades.

To Volition Systems for providing the computing public with a fine implementation of Modula-2 with which to work.

To Orlando Petrocelli and his staff for providing the means through which this book has been brought to you.

To my former colleagues, Shirley Aronson and Ed Trunk, for their years of unfailing friendship and encouragement.

And finally, to my wife, Judith Greenfield, for her timely advice and assistance during the composing of this book and for her constant faith in my capabilities.

Stuart B. Greenfield
Stone Ridge, N.Y.

1

Some Introductory Notions

Modula-2 is a high-level, general-purpose computing language suited for both scientific and business applications. It can be used and enjoyed by not only the professional programming expert at work but also the serious home computer enthusiast because of its small size which allows it to be implemented on microcomputers all the way up to mainframe computers. Thus, with Modula-2 and its capabilities, virtually any programmer can have at his or her fingertips implementations of many of the latest high-level programming concepts up to now found only on large computing systems.

A programmer using Modula-2 composes a program text not directly understood by any computer hardware. Rather, the programmer's creation is saved in a text file (referred to as the source code) and placed electronically on some external memory storage device, such as a floppy disk. To execute the program, the source code must first be translated into the language that can be understood by the computer being used. This task is accomplished by another computer program called a compiler whose output is the object code of the Modula-2 program. The object code is the version of the program which can be executed by the computer hardware. It is also saved on an external memory storage device so that it can be re-executed whenever a user wishes.

In this book, you will be introduced to the fundamentals of the instructions and syntax of Modula-2, structured programming concepts, and a number of Modula-2's capabilities which set it apart from most of the earlier programming languages in common use today.

1.1 A Short History and Overview of Modula-2

Modula-2 is the most recent language designed by Niklaus Wirth of the ETH Technical Institute of Zurich, Switzerland. Around 1970, Wirth defined the first of his important languages and called it Pascal. So successful has that endeavor been that there is hardly a college computer science program today that has not embraced Pascal as its premier computing language. Furthermore, Pascal has been well received as an industrial general-purpose language.

In the mid-1970s, Wirth designed Modula, a special-purpose language used for programming real-time control systems. Out of the experience of the development of these two languages, Modula-2 emerged in 1980.

Wirth's philosophy was to develop a small, efficient language that would provide for the programmer only primitive computing operations close to the machine level. All I/O routines (for example, writing to the screen or a file device, reading from the keyboard or a file device, allocating memory storage, and scheduling of processes) would be programmed in Modula-2 and stored in a standard library.

Wirth developed a small, efficient language that would support large software system design as well as machine-level programming. In effect, he took Pascal and expanded it both upwards and downwards, along with improving its syntax.

The concept of structured programming (block structure), along with virtually all other aspects of Pascal, are incorporated into Modula-2 so that a Pascal programmer will find that he or she can very quickly begin to write Modula-2 programs. The improved syntax of Modula, along with its module structure, low-level machine access, and multiprocessing capabilities, have been built into Modula-2.

In particular, in Modula-2 we have the ideas of the module concept, separate compilation, and module libraries to aid in the development of large software systems—programming projects that will be developed by a sizable team of programmers. We also have the capability, to some extent, of replacing assembly language programming because of the ability, under controlled circumstances, to relax data-type checking and the capability of directly accessing machine memory words and addresses.

1.2 Looking at a Simple Modula-2 Program

We will begin by looking at a simple Modula-2 program. The task of our first program will be to allow the user of the program to enter, at the computer keyboard, any integer number. Then this number is to be squared, with the result being displayed on the computer screen. To make the program "user friendly," appropriate prompt lines and/or messages should appear on the screen.

Listing 1.1 shows the program that will perform the task along with the output that appears on the computer screen when the program is executed (and the user enters the number 34 followed by a carriage return). (The line numbers are not part of the program but have been placed there only for identification purposes during our discussion of the program text.)

```
1    MODULE SquareAnInteger;
2    (*a program for squaring an integer*)

3    FROM InOut IMPORT WriteString,WriteLn,ReadInt,WriteInt;

4    VAR number,answer:INTEGER;

5    BEGIN
6        WriteString ("Enter an integer you wish to square: ");
7        ReadInt (number);
8        WriteLn;
9        answer:=number*number;
10       WriteInt (number,5);
11       WriteString (' squared equals ');
12       WriteInt (answer,5);
13   END SquareAnInteger.
```

screen output:

Enter an integer you wish to square: 34
   34 squared equals 1156

LISTING 1.1

The first thing we see (line 1) is that every Modula-2 program must start with a program heading which begins with the reserved word MODULE followed by at least one space. Note that this reserved word is in capital letters, as are all reserved words in Modula-2 (refer to Appendix A for a listing of all Modula-2 reserved words). Other words used in Modula-2 programs can have both upper and lowercase letters. (Modula-2 is what is called *case sensitive,* so care must be taken when composing programs.)

Next, in the program heading, we must place an identifier—any name we wish to call our program. In our example we have named the program SquareAnInteger. Identifiers can contain any number of letters and digits but they cannot have spaces, punctuation marks, or other special characters and they cannot begin with a digit.

Note that the program heading ends with a semicolon. You will see that in Modula-2 the semicolon is used quite frequently. It is used to separate one statement or instruction from the next. It is almost always necessary.

Line 2 of the program is a comment—a remark written into the program text, usually to explain something about the program. The beginning of a comment is signified by the contiguous pair of characters (* while the end is signified by *). Comments can appear virtually anywhere in a Modula-2 program and are ignored by the compiler. Furthermore, comments can be nested. That is, we may construct comments within comments as shown below:

(* outer (* inner *) comment *)

Besides being useful as a way to put down, in English, what a code segment may be accomplishing, comments can be used as an aid during *program debugging,* the process of correcting a program's logic.

As was mentioned in the previous section, only primitive operations are available in Modula-2. For us to read from the keyboard and write to the screen easily, someone must program these routines in Modula-2 (we will refer to routines as procedures). The job has been done for us and the resultant *module* of input and output routines has been placed, among other modules, in a standard library which is included as part of every Modula-2 system. The module which includes these routines (some of which we need for our first program) is called InOut. To make the InOut module available for use in our program we must *import* the module. This is accomplished through the use of an import list. One such list is written as line 3 of our program. In that line we are calling for the importation of four specific objects from InOut, namely, WriteString, WriteLn, ReadInt, and WriteInt. With the inclusion of that import list in our program, we can write out strings of characters to the screen, cause a carriage return to be executed, and read and write integer numbers from the keyboard and to the screen, respectively.

With this in mind, let us look at the *body* of SquareAnInteger which is the text found between the reserved words BEGIN and END.

Line 6 invokes the WriteString procedure and has it place the literal string of characters found between the quotation marks on the screen. (Single quote marks could as well be used in this case.) This literal string is referred to as a string parameter. The WriteString procedure expects one string parameter to be placed between the opening and closing parentheses. Note the inclusion of a semicolon at the end of line 6 to separate the instructions of lines 6 and 7.

Line 7 instructs the computer to wait for a user to enter a quantity at the keyboard. This quantity should be a set of digits followed by the carriage return. If other than digits are typed, the computer will be quick to note the error. If an error-free entry is made, the computer stores the entered number in part of the computer's memory—RAM— under the name of number. The word "number" is an identifier that we have chosen to call the memory area where the entered quantity has been stored. It is referred to as a *variable* and all variables in Modula-2 must be declared before being used in a program. In line 4 we have complied with this requirement. There we see a variable declaration list. To signify such a list, the reserved word VAR is used, followed by a space after which the variables are listed along with their corresponding data types. (We will discuss data types shortly.)

In our program we have declared two variables—one for the user-entered number and one for the calculated result. Both are listed in our variable declaration list separated by a comma. The colon indicates the end of the variables being listed of a particular data type. The reserved word which follows the colon is the name of the type of data that the variables represent. In our example, the two variables are of type INTEGER. (More will be said of this type in the next section.)

The WriteLn instruction follows (line 8) and is used when a carriage return is desired. Note that the WriteLn has no parameters and is, as you might expect by now, followed by a semicolon.

In line 9, the computer carries out the job of squaring the entered integer value. The algorithm used (the method of carrying out the computation) is to multiply the number by itself. The result is stored in another memory area which we have called "answer", and has already been declared as an integer variable. Line 9 is what is called an assignment statement. We are, in effect, assigning to the variable answer the results of the computation indicated on the right-hand side of the statement. The assignment of a value to a variable is indicated by the pair of characters ":=". Line 9 should be read as follows: "answer is assigned the value of number times number".

Now that the computation has been completed, the final task is to write out the result on the computer screen. Lines 10 through 12 perform the job. Since both number and answer are integer values, we can write them on the screen by using the WriteInt procedure. This procedure has two parameters, the first being the integer value to be written and the second being the number of columns on the screen that are to be reserved for writing out that value. Note that if more than one parameter is needed for a procedure, the parameter values are separated by a comma. The number being written to the screen is right justified.

In line 11, once again a literal string is to be written on the screen. In this case we have used single quote marks to indicate the string—that was our choice; double quote marks could just as well have been used.

Line 13 indicates the end of the body of our program. After the reserved word END along with a space is typed, the name of the program must appear followed by a period. The period indicates that the end of the program text has been reached.

One final comment should be made before we move on. The word END, in part, serves the same function as the semicolon. So, we could actually have written line 12 without the semicolon at its end. But to have it placed there does not cause any problems, so it's up to you whether in your programs you wish to include it or not. In our sample programs in this book, we will consistently have the semicolon appear.

1.3 Predefined Data Types and their Declarations

All variables in Modula-2 must be declared in a VAR declaration. Both an identifier and its *data type* must be declared for each variable, as was done in line 4 of Listing 1.1. The data type associated with a particular variable establishes the format of the data to be stored in that variable and the range of possible constants (values) for that data.

Modula-2 recognizes six elementary data types which can be used by the programmer, namely, INTEGER, CARDINAL, REAL, CHAR, BOOLEAN, and BITSET. We will study the first five of these elementary data types at this time. The sixth, BITSET, has to do with set theory (in particular sets of integers), so we will leave that type for a later discussion when we look at how sets are represented in Modula-2 (Section 4.5).

Although there are six elementary data types, many other types can be constructed by the programmer. These data types are usually constructed from the elementary types and must be defined for the Modula-2 compiler through an appropriate *type declaration*. A discussion of these programmer-defined types and their declarations will be deferred until Chapter 4.

As for now, we will look at each of the five data types to be considered here.

INTEGER data type

An integer is any whole number, either positive, negative, or zero. The data type INTEGER is used when we need to use integers in our Modula-2 programs. On any computer, we cannot represent all the possible whole numbers, so the range of possible integer values must be established. A common range is from -32768 up through 0 on to +32767. (Although this range seems rather arbitrary, it makes sense when you look at the way in which integers are stored in the computer's memory.)

As we have noted before, INTEGER variables are declared through a VAR declaration. As an example, consider that we wish to establish a variable which keeps track of a golfer's deviation from par. We might declare

```
VAR StrokesFromPar:INTEGER;
```

since a golfer may be above, below, or at par.

If there is an occasion to declare more than one integer variable then each variable could be either declared separately or they all can be declared together, as was done in Listing 1.1.

As we have already seen in our first program, if integer numbers are to be read from the keyboard or written to the screen, then the standard library module InOut must be imported into the program. Then we can use the ReadInt and WriteInt procedures.

CARDINAL data type

A cardinal number is much like an integer number except its range of values is limited to all the non-negative whole numbers. In Modula-2, the predefined data type CARDINAL allows us to represent a sizable range of cardinal numbers. Commonly, the range is from 0 to +65535. Why have such a data type when we already have type INTEGER? It allows the programmer to explicitly indicate that a variable must be positive or zero and it yields a greater range of available positive values for any given computer implementation.

Variables of type CARDINAL are declared as you might expect. For example, in a program developed for a farming operation, we might declare

```
VAR CowCount:CARDINAL;
```

(Although CowCount could be declared as type INTEGER it makes more sense to declare it as type CARDINAL since one does not expect to have a negative number of cows in a herd.)

To execute I/O operations with cardinal numbers at the keyboard and screen, you must import into any program you compose the objects ReadCard and WriteCard from module InOut.

REAL data type

The number representations thus far discussed fall quite short of covering our numeric needs as programmers. We may need to represent quantities that cannot be described by whole numbers, such as a student's test average, maybe 92.6, or the circumference of a circle whose diameter is 2, approximately 6.28318. Furthermore, we may need to represent very large and very small numbers, such as the electric charge (in Coulombs) found on an electron, which is 1.6×10^{-19}.

The data type REAL is used to represent such numbers. But care must be taken when writing them into a Modula-2 program or typing them when responding to a program prompt line. For example,

```
92.6   6.28318   1.6E-19   -52.0   8.025E5   37.   0.0
```

would be correctly formatted real numbers, whereas,

```
5E-3   1.6e-19   -52   0
```

would be incorrectly formatted.

You might wonder why a distinction has been made between real numbers and integer/cardinal numbers. Well, their internal representations are different—real numbers need more memory for their representation. Also, the computer low-level instructions for arithmetic operations on real numbers are different and slower than those for whole numbers.

As was true for whole numbers there is an upper and lower limit on the sizes of real numbers. These limits depend on your computer implementation. You might check out these limits for yourself.

As an example of how variables of type REAL are declared, consider the following. Suppose we wish to rewrite our first program, SquareAnInteger, so that we could square any real number. For that version of the program (which we might rename SquareAnyNumber) we would declare

VAR number, answer: REAL;

(Of course, there are other things that would have to be changed in SquareAnInteger as well.)

If you intend to use type REAL in a program, and real numbers are to be read from the keyboard or written to the screen, then you must import into your program the standard library module RealInOut (see Chapter 7). In some Modula-2 implementations, library module RealInOut does not exist. For such implementations, type REAL I/O operations are included in library module InOut. (See your Modula-2 user's manual for details.)

Although values of types CARDINAL, INTEGER, and REAL are all numeric in character, it should be understood that Modula-2 does not allow the programmer to mix these types except through the explicit use of data type conversion and transfer functions. This philosophy of essentially no data-type mixing is referred to as *strong typing*. Strong typing helps enforce good programming logic and can prove to be quite helpful at times during the debugging phase of a program's development.

CHAR data type

Modula-2 has a standard set of characters associated with it. The set is comprised of the upper and lowercase English alphabet, the ten digits 0 through 9, a number of punctuation marks and special characters, along with 33 nonprintable control characters. (See the ASCII code, Appendix B.) This set constitutes the range of values for the CHAR data type.

It is allowable for a variable name to consist of merely one character in Modula-2. On the other hand, the same character may be used as a CHAR value. For example, if we write x in a program, is it the character x or is it the variable identifier x? To relieve this possible ambiguity, all CHAR values will be placed in single or double quote marks, so that the character x will be written as "x" or 'x'. Other examples of characters are, "A", 'O', '+', "p", "?".

As you might expect, variables of type CHAR are declared as follows:

VAR ch:CHAR;

Furthermore, CHAR I/O operations can be accomplished by importing into a program the Read and Write procedures from the InOut standard module.

BOOLEAN data type

There are occasions within a program where it would be useful to have a predefined data type whose only possible values are TRUE and FALSE (referred to as Boolean values). Such a predefined data type is provided for us in Modula-2, and is referred to as type BOOLEAN. As an example, consider that a meteorological program makes reference to whether it is raining or not at some location. A variable Raining could be declared as follows:

```
VAR Raining:BOOLEAN;
```

If it's raining, then Raining is TRUE; if not, then Raining is FALSE.

Boolean values cannot be read directly from the keyboard or written directly upon the screen.

All of the above described elementary data types will be widely used in examples throughout this book, during which times you will see them in action.

Before we leave this section, it should be noted that the reserved word VAR need only appear once for any group of variable declarations as the example below indicates.

```
VAR Howmany:CARDINAL;
    i,j:INTEGER;
    Test1,Test2,Average:REAL;
    DoAgain:BOOLEAN;
    ch,z:CHAR;
```

1.4 The Assignment Statement, Arithmetic Operators and Expressions

Besides being able to enter values from the keyboard for variables of type INTEGER, CARDINAL, REAL, and CHAR as described in the preceding section, we can assign values to those variables (along with type BOOLEAN variables) through the use of the assignment statement. For example, in Listing 1.2, we have a set of legitimate assignments being made to a number of variables. (We will assume they have all been appropriately declared.)

```
1  StrokesFromPar:=-3;                    (*INTEGER*)
2  a:=41762;                        (*a & b CARDINAL*)
3  b:=a;
4  CowCount:=37; BullCount:=3; (*CARDINAL or INTEGER*)
5  BovineCount:=CowCount+BullCount;
6  Celsius:=5.0*(Fahrenheit-32.0)/9.0;    (*REAL*)
7  Raining:=FALSE;                      (*BOOLEAN*)
8  Grade:="A";                            (*CHAR*)
```

LISTING 1.2

Here are a few points concerning Listing 1.2. Note that if an assignment statement is used to assign a value to a variable, then the assignment operator, ":=", is employed.

We are not confined to assigning actual values to a variable through
an assignment statement, but we can (as in line 3) assign a variable
the value associated with another variable, as long as both variables
are of the same type, or are what are called *assignment compatible*.
Furthermore, as seen in lines 5 and 6, a variable may be assigned a
value which is the result of evaluating an expression consisting of
variables and/or values whose data types are assignment compatible
with the data type on the left side of the assignment statement.

In general, we can say the data type of the variable on the left side
of an assignment operator must be compatible with the data type of
the variable, value, or expression on the right side of the operator.
The simplest form of assignment compatibility is where the data type
on each side of the assignment operator are one and the same. But
this need not be the case for all appropriate uses of the assignment
statement! A more detailed look at assignment compatibility will be
deferred until section 4.8 of Chapter 4, after we have considered the
topics of enumerated types, subranges, and structured data types.

Before we leave Listing 1.2, note that in line 4 we have written two
statements. This is perfectly all right, as the Modula-2 compiler
doesn't care if you have included any carriage returns in a program or
not. For readability, it is a good idea to usually have only one instruction per line in a program, but it's all up to you!

An arithmetic expression is, in general, composed of variables and
constants of one of the numeric data types and a number of arithmetic
operators. The arithmetic operators available in Modula-2 are listed
in Table 1.1. Each operator can be used with all three numeric data
types unless otherwise noted in the table.

Table 1.1. Arithmetic operators.

+	addition	
–	subtraction	
*	multiplication	
/	division	(for REAL type only)
DIV	division (quotient)	(for INTEGER and CARDINAL types only)
MOD	division (remainder)	(for INTEGER and CARDINAL types only)

In Modula-2, arithmetic expressions are constructed just as in mathematics. For example, we might wish to evaluate the expression in line 6 of Listing 1.2 when the Fahrenheit temperature is 90.5 degrees. (Note that each term in our expression is of type REAL.) Then,

```
Celsius:= 5.0*(Fahrenheit-32.0)/9.0
         5.0*(90.5-32.0)/9.0
         5.0*58.5/9.0
         292.5/9.0
         32.5
```

Note the order in which the operations were performed. In general, multiplications and divisions are performed before additions and subtractions. If there is a set of parentheses, then all operations within are performed first. Otherwise, computations are performed from left to right.

A few short examples dealing with INTEGER/CARDINAL division should ensure your understanding.

```
  5   DIV   3 = 1    (quotient)
  5   MOD   3 = 2    (remainder)
-87   DIV   9 =-9
 87   DIV  (-9)=-9
```

What about negative numbers with the MOD operator? We cannot use them since the MOD operator is only defined for positive values.

We will conclude this section with an example (see Listing 1.3) which employs a good number of assignment statements and arithmetic expressions.

```
1   MODULE WhatCoins;
2   (* for printing out an amount of money in coin denominations *)

3   FROM InOut IMPORT WriteString,WriteLn,WriteCard;
```

```
4     FROM RealInOut IMPORT ReadReal,WriteReal;

5     VAR Amount:REAL;
6          Cents,Quarters,Dimes,Nickels,Pennies:CARDINAL;

7     BEGIN
8        WriteString("Enter amount of money: $");
9        ReadReal (Amount);
10       WriteLn;
11       Cents:=TRUNC(100.0*Amount);
12       Quarters:=Cents DIV 25;
13       Cents:=Cents-Quarters*25;
14       Dimes:=Cents DIV 10;
15       Cents:=Cents-Dimes*10;
16       Nickels:=Cents DIV 5;
17       Pennies:=Cents MOD 5;
18       WriteLn;
19       WriteString('The coins that make up this amount are:');WriteLn;
20       WriteLn;
21       WriteCard(Quarters,3);WriteString(' quarters');WriteLn;
22       WriteCard(Dimes,3);WriteString(' dimes');WriteLn;
23       WriteCard(Nickels,3);WriteString(' nickels');WriteLn;
24       WriteCard(Pennies,3);WriteString(' pennies');WriteLn;
25    END WhatCoins.
```

Screen output:

Enter amount of money: $12.87

The coins that make up this amount are:

```
 51 quarters
  1 dimes
  0 nickels
  2 pennies
```

LISTING 1.3

We would like to point out just a few things about Listing 1.3. Note that since we are using real numbers, we have imported library module RealInOut (line 4). (Remember, ReadReal and WriteReal may be found in module InOut in some Modula-2 implementations.) In line 11, we have used a type conversion function named TRUNC to assign a REAL number to a variable of type CARDINAL. (The multiplication by 100 preserves the values of the two decimal places.)

The mixing of data types in expressions is not allowed in Modula-2, so TRUNC is not the only type conversion function available. FLOAT is a type conversion function that can be used to assign a CARDINAL number to a variable of type REAL.

Now is a good time to mention type transfer functions. If a given data type occupies the same RAM memory space as a second data type, then the given type's internal representation can be interpreted anew as if it was a value of the second data type. For example, both data types CARDINAL and INTEGER occupy the same memory. If we wish to change a variable—card—of type CARDINAL to type IN-TEGER, then the statement INTEGER(card) will perform the desired type transfer.

As additional examples, consider that the following declarations have been made:

```
i,j,:INTEGER;
a,b,c,d:CARDINAL;
x,y:REAL;
```

Then we make the following type transfers and conversions:

```
i:=INTEGER(a)+j; (* transfer CARDINAL to INTEGER *)
b:=CARDINAL(j)+a; (* transfer INTEGER to CARDINAL *)
c:=TRUNC(x); (* convert REAL to CARDINAL *)
y:=FLOAT(d); (* convert CARDINAL to REAL *)
```

1.5 Constants and Constant Expressions

Constants—values that are fixed for the entire program—can be explicitly declared in a CONST declaration. The format of the constant will dictate the data type of the constant. For example, we might declare the following constants:

```
CONST PI=3.14159;          (* REAL *)
      MaxOccupancy=150;    (* CARDINAL*)
      FirstLetter='A';     (* CHAR *)
```

At times, it is convenient to declare a constant defined by an expression. Modula-2 has included such a capability, each term in the expression must be a constant itself. For example, in a program dealing with magnetic effects we may declare

```
CONST PI=3.14159;
       PermeabilityOfVacuum=4.0*PI*1.0E-7;
```

Additionally, a character string may be declared as a constant. For example, we may declare,

```
CONST question="Answer yes or no";
```

1.6 Representing Numbers in Different Bases

Modula-2 allows us a choice as to how we wish to represent CARDINAL or INTEGER type numbers within our programs. We can represent a number in base 10, base 8, or base 16; that is, in decimal, octal, or hexadecimal form, respectively.

For example, the number of eggs in a dozen can be described simply as 12 in decimal, 14B in octal, or 0CH in hexadecimal. Note that if a B (capitalized) follows a string of appropriate digits (0 through 7), those digits will be interpreted as an octal number. Similarly, if an H (capitalized) follows a string of appropriate digits (0 through 9, A through F), those digits will be interpreted as an hexadecimal number. (It should be further noted that if the leftmost digit of an hexadecimal number is in the range A through F, it must be preceded by the digit 0.) A decimal number is indicated by having no letter appended to it.

In Listing 1.4, a short program is shown which employs some of the above ideas. The screen output, upon execution of the program, is also included.

```
MODULE DifferingBases;

FROM InOut IMPORT WriteInt,WriteCard,WriteLn;

VAR i, j,k:INTEGER;
    a,b,c:CARDINAL;

BEGIN
  i:=12;
  j:=-14B;
  k:=-0AH;
```

```
        WriteInt(i,10);
        WriteInt(j,10);
        WriteInt(k,10);
        WriteLn;WriteLn;
        a:=13;
        b:=14B;
        c:=6CH;
        WriteCard(a,10);
        WriteCard(b,10);
        WriteCard(c,10);
END DifferingBases.
```

Screen output:

```
    12      -12     -10
    13       12     108
```

LISTING 1.4

2

Decision-Making and Repetition

So far in our programming, we have composed programs where instructions are carried out in the same sequence in which they are written. But programming languages need more capabilities than just that—they must offer the programmer the opportunity for the sequence of execution to be altered depending on variable values or values of expressions, both of which are not known beforehand. Furthermore, the decision of what instructions should be executed next may depend on the response from the keyboard by a user.

There are two decision-making structures which give us the capability we need, namely, the IF statement and the CASE statement. They will be presented in this chapter. But before we present these constructs, we will spend a little time on Boolean expressions and Boolean operators.

One of the most important capabilities of a computer is its ability to repeatedly execute a sequence of instructions. In Modula-2 this "looping" capability comes to us in four different forms, namely, FOR-DO, REPEAT-UNTIL, WHILE-DO, and LOOP-EXIT. The difference between these four constructs is in the manner in which the computer exits from the repeated loop of code. Each time the computer passes through the loop, a test of some kind must be made to determine whether the computer should terminate the looping operation or not.

In addition to the decision-making structures, this chapter will develop each of the aforementioned looping constructs and indicate when each of them should be used. At the end, a short programming example will be presented for which we will write four solutions, each solution using a different construct.

2.1 Boolean Expressions and Operators

Boolean expressions evaluate to either of the two Boolean values TRUE or FALSE. So, for example, if an INTEGER variable n has a

17

value of 4, then the Boolean expression $n = 4$ is TRUE, whereas $n = 6$ is FALSE. The use of the equal sign in the Boolean expression $n = 4$ asks the computer to compare the value of the variable n to the value 4. If they are equal then the value of $n = 4$ is TRUE. If they are unequal then the value of $n = 4$ is FALSE.

The equal sign is just one of six relational operators that can be used to form Boolean expressions. Table 2.1 lists each of the six with a description of their meaning. Note that the "not equal" operator can be constructed two different ways from the Modula-2 character set.

Table 2.1. Relational operators.

Operator	Use	Description (a and b are variables or constants)
=	a = b	a IS EQUAL TO b
>	a > b	a IS GREATER THAN b
<	a < b	a IS LESS THAN b
> =	a > = b	a IS GREATER THAN OR EQUAL TO b
< =	a < = b	a IS LESS THAN OR EQUAL TO b
<>, #	a <> b, a # b	a IS NOT EQUAL TO b

More complex Boolean expressions can be formed from the simple Boolean expressions described above in conjunction with Boolean operators. There are three Boolean operators for our use, namely, NOT, OR, and AND. These operators are listed in Table 2.2 with an explanation of each. Note that the ampersand—&—can be used in place of AND.

As with arithmetic operators there exists a precedence order for Boolean operators. When you encounter an expression, evaluate any NOTs first, followed by ANDs, then finally by ORs. As with arithmetic expressions, the evaluation of anything in parentheses takes precedence over all.

Table 2.2. Boolean operators.

Operator	Use	Description (p and q are Boolean values or terms)
NOT	NOT p	if p is TRUE then (NOT p) is FALSE; (if p is FALSE then (NOT p) is TRUE)
OR	p OR q	if p or q or both are TRUE then (p OR q) is TRUE; (if both are FALSE then (p OR q) is FALSE)
AND,&	p AND q p & q	if both p and q are TRUE then (p AND q) is TRUE; (if either or both are FALSE then (p AND q) is FALSE)

A few examples may be helpful. Assume that the following variable declarations have been made:

```
x,y:INTEGER;
Raining:BOOLEAN;
Temp(*Temperature*),Avg(*Average*):REAL;
s, t,u,v:BOOLEAN;
i,j:CARDINAL;
```

Next, consider that the following values are assigned to these variables:

```
x:=10;y:=-5;
Raining:=FALSE;Temp:=92.5;
Avg:=86.7;
s:=TRUE; t:=FALSE;u:=TRUE;v:=FALSE;
i:=0;j:=20;
```

If these variables are used in Boolean expressions, as shown below, then, upon evaluation, they will either be TRUE or FALSE as indicated:

```
(x=10) OR (y<-5)                                <–TRUE
NOT Raining AND (Temp>85.0)                      <–TRUE
(Avg>=80.0) & (Avg<90.0)                         <–TRUE
(x=10) AND (y<-5) AND (Temp>95.0) AND (Avg=86.7) <–FALSE
((s OR t) AND u) AND v                           <–FALSE
s OR ((t AND u) AND v)                           <–TRUE
(i#0) & (j DIV i = 10)                           <–FALSE
```

If you have some programming experience, you may think this last example may have a problem. If indeed i=0, then might not there be a "divide by zero" error signaled by the computer? The answer is no! In Modula-2, if the left-hand argument of an operation (either AND or OR) alone can determine the result, then the right-hand argument is not evaluated. So, in our last example, if i = 0 then j DIV i is not evaluated. The same story holds true in the case of our first example. Since x is indeed equal to 10 then there is no need to check whether y is less than –5—and Modula-2 doesn't perform the check.

This process of not evaluating a condition when its value will not affect the result is referred to as *short-circuiting* a Boolean expression. In general, the short-circuiting occurs at any point within the expression when the Boolean result of that expression has been un-questionably determined. Consider the fourth expression above. The evaluation of that expression takes place from left to right. Since the condition $(y < -5)$ evaluates to FALSE, the last two conditions are short-circuited. If the second condition is changed to read $(y < 0)$ which evaluates to TRUE, then, indeed, the third condition, $(Temp > 95.0)$, would be found to be FALSE, and the last condition would be short-circuited. Only under the condition that the first three conditions were TRUE would all four conditions actually be checked.

In the two examples dealing with the Boolean variables, s, t, u, and v, note that the use of parentheses can indeed change the outcome of the evaluation. You should check them for yourself.

Now we are ready to use Boolean expressions in the next section dealing with the IF statement.

2.2 The IF Statement and its Extended Forms

The basic form of the IF statement is:

```
IF < Boolean expression > THEN
  < statements >
END;
```

The Boolean expression can be either simple or complicated—the only requirement is, of course, that the result of its evaluation be either TRUE or FALSE. If it is TRUE then the statements which are bracketed by the reserved words THEN and END are executed. If the expression result is FALSE then the computer moves on to execute the first state-ment following the END. As a few examples, consider,

```
IF x < 0 THEN WriteInt(x,6);END;
IF (Average >=80.0) & (Average < 90.0) THEN
  Grade:='B';
  GradePoint:=3.0;
END;
IF Raining THEN WriteString('Stay home and read a good book.');END;
```

(In these examples and all those yet to come in this book we will assume all variables have been appropriately declared.)

In the first example, no parentheses are needed around the single Boolean term. In the second example, parentheses are needed as shown. Also note that the THEN part of the construct consists of two statements.

The question may arise as to why parentheses are needed in the second example. (This same question could have been asked during the discussion on Boolean expressions and operators of the previous section.) It is due to the fact that the AND (&) operator has a higher priority order than any of the relational operators. Thus, if parentheses were missing from the second example, the right-hand operand associated with the & operator would be the value of Average rather than the value of Average < 90.0, thus causing a logical error in the evaluation sequence as well as a syntax error.

This need for parentheses whenever a Boolean expression is other than simple holds true for all cases with but one exception. If an operand associated with a Boolean operator is itself Boolean then parentheses need not be placed around that operand.

We have discussed three sets of operators up to this point, namely arithmetic, relational, and Boolean. The priority order in which evaluations of expressions employing these operators are to be done is given below where the top line of operators has the highest priority and the bottom line has the lowest. Note that the unary operators + and − have been included and are different from the addition and subtraction operators, although the same characters are used for their designation.

+(unary), −(unary), NOT

*, /, DIV, MOD, AND(&)

+, −, OR

=, < > (#), < , > , < =, > =

In the final example, we see that if the Boolean expression contains a Boolean variable, then, since that variable's value itself is either TRUE or FALSE, we need not (and should not) write, IF Raining= TRUE THEN . . . . Furthermore, note that if there is but one statement to be executed in the THEN part of the IF statement, we will usually write the entire construction on a single line, as has been done in the first and last examples.

An IF statement can include an ELSE part. The form is:

```
IF < Boolean expression > THEN
  < statements >
ELSE
  < statements >
END;
```

For example,

```
IF NOT Raining AND (Temperature > 85.0) THEN
   WriteString("Go for a swim.");
ELSE
   WriteString("Read a good book.");
END;
```

In this IF-THEN-ELSE-END construct, if the Boolean expression is TRUE, the THEN part is executed. If it is FALSE, the ELSE part is executed. In either case, after the appropriate statements are executed, the computer moves on to the statement just following the END of the IF statement.

Now let's turn our attention to the following programming problem. We are to categorize student averages as A, B, C, D, or F in the usual manner; A, if the average is 90 or above, B, if it is 80 or higher but less than 90, etc.

We could do the job by simply using the IF-THEN-END construct as shown below:

```
IF Avg>=90.0 THEN Grade:='A';END;
IF (Avg>=80.0) & (Avg<90.0) THEN Grade:='B';END;
IF (Avg>=70.0) & (Avg<80.0) THEN Grade:='C';END;
IF (Avg>=60.0) & (Avg<70.0) THEN Grade:='D';END;
IF Avg<60.0 THEN Grade:='F';END;
```

But the above coding is not very efficient nor is it elegant. No matter what the student's average is, even if it is 90 or higher, the computer will have to go through all five IF statements—the last four to no avail.

A more efficient approach to the problem is to use the IF-THEN-ELSE-END construct in a nested fashion. The result is:

```
IF Avg>=90.0 THEN
   Grade:='A'
ELSE
   IF Avg>=80.0 THEN
      Grade:='B'
   ELSE
      IF Avg>=70.0 THEN
         Grade:='C'
      ELSE
         IF Avg>=60.0 THEN
            Grade:='D'
```

```
      ELSE
        Grade:='F';
      END;
    END;
  END;
END;
```

Now that's more efficient since once a THEN part is executed, the remainder of the construct is skipped over—but its syntax is a bit awkward! So, Modula-2 has a better solution syntactically without giving up efficiency. We can use an ELSIF part in our IF statements. Using the ELSIF yields the following code:

```
IF Avg>=90.0 THEN
  Grade:='A'
ELSIF Avg>=80.0 THEN
  Grade:='B'
ELSIF Avg>=70.0 THEN
  Grade:='C'
ELSIF Avg>=60.0 THEN
  Grade:='D'
ELSE
  Grade:='F';
END;
```

This version is obviously more compact, syntactically pleasing, and probably promotes easier understanding of the code. You might write a program to test each of these solutions for yourself.

2.3 The CASE Statement

In the last section, we saw that the IF-THEN-ELSE-END construct can be used to choose between two courses of execution on the computer. Expanding that line of thought to the IF-THEN-ELSIF-. . .-ELSE-END construct gives us a way to choose one of many possible courses of execution. But in some cases this latter construct is not the most efficient. If the variable being selected is of type INTEGER, CARDINAL, CHAR, or BOOLEAN (along with enumerated types and subranges, to be discussed in Chapter 4), then we can employ the CASE statement.

The structure of the CASE statement is best shown by presenting a few examples. Suppose a different message is to be printed to the screen depending on the INTEGER value of the variable *n*. Using a CASE statement, our code might look like this:

```
CASE n OF
   1:WriteString('Hello');|
   2:WriteString('Goodbye');|
   3:WriteString('Tomorrow is');
     WriteLn;
     WriteString('another day');|
   4:WriteString('Hasta Luego');
END;
```

The values 1 to 4 are called case labels and need not be in ascending order. Each case label is followed by a colon. Then follow the statements to be executed under that label. The use of the vertical bar character indicates the end of the statements under that particular case label. Note that the last entry under the CASE statement should not be followed by a vertical bar since the reserved word END signals the end of the entry as well as the end of the CASE statement.

What would happen if for some reason the variable *n* had a value other than in the range 1 to 4 in our example? The computer would signal an error. If we wish to avoid this we could add into our CASE statement an ELSE part. An ELSE part can be used as a catchall as shown in our rewritten program segment below.

```
CASE n OF
   1:WriteString('Hello');|
   2:WriteString('Goodbye');|
   3:WriteString('Tomorrow is');
     WriteLn;
     WriteString('another day');|
   4:WriteString('Hasta Luego')
ELSE
     WriteString('n outside of defined range');
END;
```

In Listing 2.1 we offer you a complete program dealing with a pair of dice and the probabilities associated with each possible value that may be rolled. See if you can follow the logic. Note the job of displaying the probability is done twice—first using a CASE statement and second using an appropriate IF construct. Which would you rather use?

Note that a number of variable values can be used as a case label by merely separating them by commas.

```
MODULE DiceProbability;

FROM InOut IMPORT WriteString,WriteLn,WriteCard,ReadCard;
FROM RealInOut IMPORT WriteReal;

VAR Value:CARDINAL;

BEGIN
    WriteString('Enter dice value: ');
    ReadCard(Value);
    WriteLn;
    WriteString('The probability of rolling a ');
    WriteCard(Value,2);
    WriteString(' is:');WriteLn;
    CASE Value OF
        2,12:WriteReal(1.0/36.0,11);|
        3,11:WriteReal(1.0/18.0,11);|
        4,10:WriteReal(1.0/12.0,11);|
        5,9:WriteReal(1.0/9.0,11);|
        6,8:WriteReal(5.0/36.0,11;|
        7:WriteReal(1.0/6.0,11);
    ELSE
        WriteString('IMPOSSIBLE VALUE!');
    END;
    WriteLn;
    IF (Value=2) OR (Value=12) THEN
        WriteReal(1.0/36.0,11)
    ELSIF (Value=3) OR (Value=11) THEN
        WriteReal(1.0/18.0,11)
    ELSIF (Value=4) OR (Value=10) THEN
        WriteReal(1.0/12.0,11)
    ELSIF (Value=5) OR (Value=9) THEN
        WriteReal(1.0/9.0,11)
    ELSIF (Value=6) OR (Value=8) THEN
        WriteReal(5.0/36.0,11)
    ELSIF Value=7 THEN
        WriteReal(1.0/6.0,11)
    ELSE
        WriteString('IMPOSSIBLE VALUE!');
    END;
END DiceProbability.
```

LISTING 2.1

If contiguous values of the variable, say 5 through 9, are to be used as a case label in a case statement then they can be indicated as 5. .9. Also, a case label can be composed of a constant expression. Our last short illustration shown below codes these additional concepts.

```
CONST k=19;
        .
        .

CASE n OF
    1:<statements>|
    2. .8:<statements>|
        .
        .

    2*k-1:<statements>
END;
```

2.4 The FOR-DO Construct

The basic form of the FOR-DO loop is,

```
FOR <index variable> :=<lower value> TO <higher value> DO
    <statements>
END;
```

The index variable must be of type INTEGER, CARDINAL, CHAR, or BOOLEAN, or an enumerated type or subrange. The statements to be repeated are placed between the reserved words DO and END. As each repetition is completed, the index variable is incremented and is compared to the higher value. If it is not greater than the higher value, the sequence is executed again. If the index variable value exceeds the higher value, the computer moves on to the instruction just beyond the END of the FOR-DO loop.

The FOR-DO construct is used when it is known how many times the code sequence is to be executed prior to the execution of the loop. For example, a misbehaved pupil may be given an assignment to hand in the sentence, "I won't put a tack on the teacher's chair.", written out 100 times. With a computer at home and a self-serving interpretation of "written out" to mean "printed out," this pupil might use the FOR-DO loop shown below to produce the completed assignment.

```
FOR i:=1 TO 100 DO
    WriteString("I won't put a tack on the teacher's chair.");
END;
```

Both the "lower value" and the "higher value" of the FOR-DO loop may be in the form of expressions. In this case, the Modula-2 compiler cannot determine the exact number of iterations of the FOR-DO construct. This does not pose a problem since the number of iterations need only be determined just prior to the execution of the loop during run-time of the program.

A FOR-DO loop may not even execute at all, if the lower value is greater than the higher value. This feature of the FOR-DO construct is shared with the WHILE-DO construct which will be discussed in section 2.6.

There is one additional capability that we have when using the FOR-DO construct. We can instruct the computer to increment the index variable by other than one unit, as illustrated in the following example which lists for us the odd digits.

```
FOR k:=1 TO 9 BY 2 DO WriteCard(k,1);END;
```

Here are a few more examples.

```
FOR ch:='a' TO 'z' BY 2 DO Write(ch);END;
screen output:   acegikmoqsuwy
FOR I:=10 TO -20 BY -3 DO WriteInt(I,3);END;
screen output:     10   7   4   1 -2 -5 -8 -11 -14 -17 -20
```

Note that even with a CHAR index variable, the BY option uses integer values. This use of integer values for the BY option is true no matter what type of index variable is being used. Further note that in order to index through descending values, the BY option should be negative.

2.5 The REPEAT-UNTIL Construct

The FOR-DO loop is fine if the number of repetitions of the code sequence is determined before the loop is entered. But there are instances when the number of repetitions are determined only after the loop has been entered. For example, consider the job of counting the number of Es, both upper and lowercase, in a text entered by a user sitting at the keyboard. To end the text entry, the user will be asked to type the asterisk. The code segment to be repeated would be

```
Read(ch);
IF (ch='e') OR (ch='E') THEN INC(eCount);END;
```

where ch is a CHAR variable, eCount is a CARDINAL variable initialized to zero, and the INC instruction takes the value of eCount and increments it by one.

We cannot use a FOR-DO construct for the above code segment since we do not know at what point the user will terminate the text by entering an asterisk. Therefore, we need a different looping construct, and the REPEAT-UNTIL will do the job for us.

The form for the REPEAT-UNTIL loop is,

```
REPEAT
   <statements>
UNTIL < Boolean expression > ;
```

To exit a REPEAT-UNTIL construct, a test must be passed. The test checks whether a Boolean expression is TRUE or not. Note that the code segment to be repeated is executed at least once since the test takes place at the end of each repetition of the loop. In the example at hand, the test will be whether or not the user typed an asterisk.

Listing 2.2 presents a program for letter-counting in its entirety (along with a sample output) showing the use of the REPEAT-UNTIL construct.

```
MODULE LetterCounter;

FROM InOut IMPORT Read,WriteString,WriteLn,WriteCard;

VAR ch:CHAR;
    eCount:CARDINAL;
BEGIN
   eCount:=0;
   WriteString('Enter some text, ending with an "*":');
   WriteLn;WriteLn;
   REPEAT
     Read(ch);
     IF (ch='e') OR (ch='E') THEN INC(eCount);END;
   UNTIL ch='*';
   WriteLn;WriteLn;
   WriteString("The number of E's in the text is: ");
   WriteCard(eCount,2);
END LetterCounter.
```

screen output:

Enter some text, ending with an "*":

The following sentence is false.
The preceding sentence is true.

The number of E's in the text is: 12

LISTING 2.2

2.6 The WHILE-DO Construct

Testing as to whether repetition should continue or not at times is desired at the beginning of a loop. The WHILE-DO construct fulfills this desire. With the WHILE-DO, it is possible to not execute the code sequence to be repeated, even once.

The form of the WHILE-DO construct is,

```
WHILE <Boolean expression> DO
   <statements>
END;
```

As an example of its use, suppose we wish to develop a program which will sum up the first n terms of an harmonic series of order $p = 2$, whose nth term is $1/(n*n)$. Listing 2.3 is one possible solution.

```
MODULE pSeriesSum;

FROM InOut IMPORT WriteString,WriteLn,ReadCard;
FROM RealInOut IMPORT WriteReal;

VAR n:CARDINAL;
    nReal,Sum:REAL;
BEGIN
   Sum:=0.0;
   WriteString('Enter the no. of terms in the p series');WriteLn;
   WriteString('to be summed: ');
   ReadCard(n);WriteLn;
   WHILE n #0 DO
      nReal:=FLOAT(n);
      Sum:=Sum+1.0/(nReal*nReal);
      DEC(n);
   END;
   WriteString('Sum of terms is: ');
   WriteReal(Sum,12);
END pSeriesSum.
```

LISTING 2.3

Note that if the user enters 0 in response to the prompt, entry is not made into the loop and we avoid the consequences of dividing by zero. Since the value of *n* is decreased by one with the DEC instruction, we see that eventually *n* will be reduced to zero and program execution will move beyond the WHILE-DO loop. Finally, since the formulation of each term calls for a REAL division, the previously introduced function FLOAT has been used to convert *n* into the REAL variable nReal.

Care must be taken to always define any values needed to initially evaluate (prior to loop entry) the Boolean expression employed by a WHILE-DO loop.

2.7 The LOOP-EXIT Construct

The LOOP-EXIT construct basic form is:

```
LOOP
   <statements>
   <EXIT statement>
   <statements>
END;
```

The EXIT statement contains the test as to whether execution moves to the instruction just following the loop or the looping should continue. Thus we see that the LOOP construct allows us to test anywhere within the loop (usually somewhere in the middle). The EXIT statement could appear even at the beginning of the loop or at its end, but for those occasions you should use the more readable, more natural WHILE-DO or REPEAT-UNTIL constructs, respectively.

As an example, consider the following code segment:

```
LOOP
   ReadReal(value);
   IF value=0.0 THEN EXIT;END;
   Result:=10.0/value+1.5;
END;
WriteString("Divide by zero - will take corrective measures");
```

To avoid unscheduled termination of the program due to a divide by zero error, testing for value=0.0 must be done—but only after the value has been read. The LOOP-EXIT construct allows us to set up the looping code segment easily.

It is possible to have two or more EXIT statements in a LOOP-EXIT construct, as illustrated in the program of Listing 2.4.

```
MODULE LoopWith2Exits;
(* set up a chart of X & Y values *)

FROM InOut IMPORT WriteString,WriteInt,WriteLn,ReadInt;

VAR X,Y:INTEGER;

BEGIN
    WriteString('Enter starting integer: ');
    ReadInt(X);
    WriteLn;WriteLn;
    WriteString('X        Y'; (* column headings *)
    WriteLn;WriteLn;
    LOOP
        WriteInt(X,4);
        IF X=0 THEN EXIT;END;
        Y:=ABS(1000 DIV X);
        IF Y<10 THEN EXIT;END;
        WriteInt(Y,10);
        WriteLn;
        INC(X);
    END;
END LoopWith2Exits.
```

LISTING 2.4

Note that in Listing 2.4, after an integer is entered by the user, a table of values is developed for X and its corresponding Y values by the entrance into a LOOP-EXIT construct. Exiting from the loop occurs if X equals zero. If X is not equal to zero, then Y can be calculated without the possibility of a "divide by zero" error.

Y will always be a non-negative quantity since the absolute value of (1000 DIV X) is assigned to Y through the use of Modula-2's ABS built-in function. Next, the second chance for exiting from the loop occurs, this time if Y falls below 10.

It is even possible to have no EXIT statements. Under what conditions might this be reasonable? Suppose a computer is being used to continuously monitor an alarm system. As long as no alarm condition occurs, we want continuous looping. If an alarm does occur, then indeed the computer may execute some corrective code. Upon completion of this code, monitoring should pick up where it left off and looping should continue.

2.8 A Last Word on Looping with an Example

There are coding problems where the choice as to which looping construct to use is up to you. That is, a problem may arise where you can use any of the four constructs. As an example, consider the following programming problem:

A variable is initialized at –1000. We are to divide this variable by 2 and then add 2 to form its new value. Next, the value should be written out to the screen, and finally, the variable value should be incremented. This process should continue until the variable value is found to be greater or equal to zero.

Four different solutions to this little programming job can be found in Listing 2.5, each using a different looping construct.

```
MODULE Repetition;

FROM InOut IMPORT WriteInt,WriteLn,Write;

VAR J:INTEGER;
    I:CARDINAL;

BEGIN
  J:=-1000;
  FOR I:=1 TO 8 DO (* note that the value 8 must be known a priori *)
    J:=J DIV 2 + 2;
    WriteInt(J,4);Write(',');
    INC(J);
  END;
  WriteLn;

  J:=-1000;
  WHILE J < 0 DO
    J:=J DIV 2 + 2;
    WriteInt(J,4);Write(',');
    INC (J);
  END;
  WriteLn;

  J:=-1000;
  REPEAT
    J:=J DIV 2 + 2;
```

```
        WriteInt(J,4);Write(',');
        INC(J);
    UNTIL J>=0;
    WriteLn;

    J:=-1000;
    LOOP
        J:=J DIV 2 + 2;
        WriteInt(J,4);Write(',');
        IF J>=0 THEN EXIT;END;
        INC(J);
    END;

END Repetition.
```

LISTING 2.5

3

Procedures and Function Procedures

Programming experience over the past few decades has clearly pointed out the shortcomings of some of the earlier popular languages. If sizable programs are to be written, then consideration of program composition must hold a high priority. To be successful, new programming languages must address themselves to the problems of program development and general program maintenance, which includes debugging and future modifications.

Large programming projects are often developed by a team of programmers. Each programmer will be in charge of some portion of the overall project, so a programming language must be capable of being broken into distinct parts. Furthermore, attention must be given to having a programming language where it is easy to localize any "bugs" so they can be successfully removed by the original programmer or any other member of the project team. In the future it may be likely that the program developed by the team may have to be modified. Again, the language should have the facilities for making that job both easy and efficient.

Modula-2 has all the capabilities to deal with large programming projects. The procedure concept is the first of these capabilities to which we will now turn our attention. A *procedure* is an independent programming unit which has its own heading, declarations, and executable code. (The declarations are optional.) In effect, a procedure allows you to define new programming instructions.

Modula-2 is certainly not the first language which has embraced the procedure concept in some form or other. BASIC has a rudimentary procedure in its use of subroutines. FORTRAN has its more sophisticated subroutines, and Pascal has virtually the identical procedure structure as has Modula-2. Other languages have procedural capabilities as well.

In the next section, we will pose a programming task and solve it in the same manner in which we have solved tasks over the past two chapters. Then, to illustrate the use of Modula-2's procedure concept, in the section to follow we will approach the same programming task anew—using the procedure concept.

3.1 A Program without Procedures

Suppose we wish to develop a program made up of three output screen pages. The first screen will indicate the title and author of the program, the second will display a food menu which will offer the user a choice of meals, and the final screen will display a computer response to the selection that the user made from the menu. Our version of the particular program we have in mind is shown in Listing 3.1.

We will scan the text of MODULE Dinner and make a number of comments. Line 3 calls for the importation of a library module called Strings. From this module we are importing the object STRING which is not the same kind of object that all our previous importations were. For example, the objects WriteString, WriteLn, ReadReal, etc., are really the kind of objects that we will be discussing in this chapter— they are procedures. On the other hand, STRING is a programmer-made data type. It allows us to declare variables of type STRING which can have up to 80 alphanumeric characters. How is such a data type constructed? The answer to that question will be forthcoming in the next chapter. All we have to note at this time is that in line 5, a variable of type STRING has been declared.

```
1    MODULE Dinner;

2    FROM InOut IMPORT WriteString,Write,WriteLn,Read;
3    FROM Strings IMPORT STRING;

4    CONST delay=5000;
5    VAR message:STRING;
6        ch:CHAR;
7        i,j:CARDINAL;

8    BEGIN
9       Write(CHR(12));
10      FOR i:=1 TO 8 DO WriteLn;END;
11      WriteString('                    DINNER');WriteLn;
12      WriteLn;
13      WriteString('                        by')WriteLn;
14      WriteLn;
15      WriteString('              S. Greenfield');
16      j:=0;
17      FOR i:=1 TO delay DO INC(j);END;
```

```
18      Write(CHR(12));
19      WriteLn;
20      WriteString('Would you like to have...');WriteLn;
21      WriteLn;
22      WriteString('1—> steak and potatoes,');WriteLn;
23      WriteLn;
24      WriteString('2—> franks and beans,');WriteLn;
25      WriteLn;
26      WriteString('3—> corned beef and cabbage?');WriteLn;
27      WriteLn;WriteLn;
28      WriteString('Enter appropriate number: ');
29      Read(ch);
30      CASE ch OF
31         '1':message:='Steak and potatoes';|
32         '2':message:='Franks and beans';|
33         '3':message:='Corned beef and cabbage';
34      ELSE
35         WriteLn;WriteLn;
36         WriteString("You didn't enter an appropriate number.");
37         HALT;
38      END;
39      Write(CHR(12));
40      WriteLn;
41      WriteString("I'm so glad you chose what you did.");WriteLn;
42      WriteString(message);
43      WriteString(' are my absolute');WriteLn;
44      WriteString('favorites!');
45   END Dinner.
```

LISTING 3.1

Continuing our scan down the text of MODULE Dinner we come to the beginning of the executable portion of the program. In lines 9, 18, and 39, we see a rather cryptic instruction. Its purpose is to clear the computer screen.

Lines 10 through 15 place the "title page" on the screen. Since we want the title page to remain on display for a few seconds, we have included a short routine which causes a time delay (lines 16 and 17). This routine just acts as busy work for the computer while the user reads the title page. Note that the "higher value" of the FOR-DO construct has been created as a constant (line 4). This is an example of good programming practice as it allows us to easily change this value by looking at the top of the program.

The second part of the program places the "menu" on the screen and asks the user to enter his or her choice (lines 18 through 38). The only new bit of code in that program segment is the use of the HALT instruction (line 37). When invoked, a program is terminated.

After the user enters a response and if that response is either 1, 2, or 3, then the third part of the program, the computer's "retort," is executed (lines 39 through 44).

Although the program does the job for us, it does not make use of the procedure concept. Using procedures would make the program more understandable, less prone to errors during the development stage, and more easily modified at a future time. In the next section, we will reorganize MODULE Dinner using the procedure concept.

3.2 The Procedure Concept

We can view our programming task, the writing of MODULE Dinner (which for this version we will rename MODULE DinnerWithProcedures), as being composed of three subtasks or subprograms which we can name TitlePage, Menu, and Retort. These three names will act as the identifiers of the three procedures which we will develop for the program. These procedures will be "called," that is, they will be invoked from what we will refer to as the "main program" or "main body" of the program.

An example of a procedure heading is:

PROCEDURE TitlePage;

Note that the heading starts with the reserved word PROCEDURE followed by at least one space, an identifier, and lastly a semicolon.

To invoke such a procedure from some part of a program we merely write the procedure's identifier at the appropriate points in the text. For example, if we wish to call TitlePage, we would write:

TitlePage;

With this procedure concept in hand, we can construct a main program as follows:

MODULE DinnerWithProcedures;

BEGIN (* main program or main body, your choice *)
   TitlePage;

```
      Menu;
      Retort;
END DinnerWithProcedures.
```

But the computer will not understand what is meant by the identifiers TitlePage, Menu, and Retort. In fact, the compiler will note that these identifiers have not been declared, that is, they have not been defined before they have been used in the text of the program. Developing the text of each of these procedures and placing it above the main program is what is necessary for the computer to fully understand what code those identifiers are to represent.

In Listing 3.2 (lines 53 to 57), our main program appears at the end of the complete program text. This is the portion of the program where execution commences. Note that in this case, the main program merely consists of the three procedure calls. The code for each of the three procedures has been properly constructed and placed above the point where the procedure is invoked.

```
1     MODULE DinnerWithProcedures;

2     FROM InOut IMPORT WriteString,Write,WriteLn,Read;
3     FROM Strings IMPORT STRING;

4     VAR message:STRING;

5        PROCEDURE TitlePage;
6        CONST delay=5000;
7        VAR i,j:CARDINAL;
8        BEGIN
9           Write(CHR(12));
10          FOR i:=1 TO 8 DO WriteLn;END;
11          WriteString('                    DINNER');WriteLn;
12          WriteLn;
13          WriteString('                        by');WriteLn;
14          WriteLn;
15          WriteString('            S. Greenfield');
16          j:=0;
17          FOR i:=1 TO delay DO INC(j);END;
18       END TitlePage;

19       PROCEDURE Menu;
20       VAR ch:CHAR;
21       BEGIN
22          Write(CHR(12));
23          WriteLn;
```

```
24        WriteString('Would you like to have...');WriteLn;
25        WriteLn;
26        WriteString("1-> steak and potatoes,');WriteLn;
27        WriteLn;
28        WriteString('2-> franks and beans,');WriteLn;
29        WriteLn;
30        WriteString('3-> corned beef and cabbage?');WriteLn;
31        WriteLn;WriteLn;
32        WriteString('Enter appropriate number: ');
33        Read(ch);
34        CASE ch OF
35           '1':message:='Steak and potatoes';|
36           '2':message:='Franks and beans';|
37           '3':message:='Corned beef and cabbage';
38        ELSE
39           WriteLn;WriteLn;
40           WriteString("You didn't enter an appropriate number.");
41           HALT;
42        END;
43     END Menu;

44     PROCEDURE Retort;
45     BEGIN
46        Write(CHR(12);
47        WriteLn;
48        WriteString("I'm so glad you chose what you did.");WriteLn;
49        WriteString(message);
50        WriteString(' are my absolute');WriteLn;
51        WriteString('favorites!');
52     END Retort;

53  BEGIN (* main program *)
54     TitlePage;
55     Menu;
56     Retort;
57  END DinnerWithProcedures.
```

LISTING 3.2

When TitlePage is invoked, program control is transferred from the main program at line 54 to the beginning of PROCEDURE TitlePage (line 5), and TitlePage is executed (lines 5 to 18).

Note that PROCEDURE TitlePage has a heading, a declaration section, and a beginning and ending of its own executable code. You should note that the end of a procedure, unlike the end of a main program, is followed by a semicolon.

Upon completion of TitlePage, program control is transferred back to the statement just after the procedure call, viz., to line 55.

Next, PROCEDURE Menu is invoked with control being passed to it. Upon completion, control reverts back to the calling part of the program (the main program, in this case), and PROCEDURE Retort is invoked, after which the program is terminated.

If you follow the order of execution of the instructions in Listing 3.2, you will find that, in effect, it corresponds exactly to the order of execution found in Listing 3.1, outside of the calling of the three procedures. Therefore, we should expect that the two versions of the program should execute in an identical manner. And they do!

But there are some differences between the two versions which are rather important. In version 1 (Dinner), all the declarations (CONST and VAR) were made at the top of the program. These declared objects are actually usable any place within the program and therefore are referred to as global declarations. But notice that, in actuality, the only portion of the program where, for instance, the two CARDI-NAL variables are needed is in the first part of the program—the title page. It is desirable to make objects, such as i and j, available to only those portions of a program where they are needed.

In version 2 (DinnerWithProcedures), having used procedures to define subtasks, we can declare objects locally so that they are only visible and only exist within the procedure in which they are declared. Since the constant delay and the variables i and j are only needed in PROCEDURE TitlePage, that is where they have been declared.

Thus we see that in going from version 1 to version 2 we have reduced the global declaration list down to just message (because it is used in two procedures), and all other declarations have been declared locally within the procedures that make exclusive use of them.

What are the benefits of localizing declarations? Those localized objects cannot be used or altered inadvertently outside of their scope (the procedure in which they are declared). In fact, they do not exist outside of their scope so the memory space that they have occupied can actually be used for other things during program execution. On the other hand, if an object is to be used across a number of procedures or within the main program, then it must be globally declared.

It should be noted that when a procedure is invoked, memory space is allocated for all constants and variables declared locally within the activated procedure. Deallocation of that same declaration memory space takes place upon completion of the activated procedure. As stated above, the released memory space can be used later within the program, possibly during the activation of some other procedure. All this memory allocation and deallocation takes place "automatically" due to the work of the Modula-2 compiler being used, although it is important for the programmer to understand the process since it indeed can be useful information during program design.

The programming structure which uses the procedure concept is often referred to as *block structure*. A block consists of the declarations and statements following a procedure or program heading. For example, an entire program constitutes the outermost block. Each procedure, in our example, constitutes a block nested within the outermost block. It is useful to use indentation to indicate the nesting of blocks, as has been done in Listing 3.2.

The scope of the declarations associated with each block is the block itself and includes all nested blocks within. On the other hand, the scope does not include portions of the program which are outside its block. For example, if we wrote a statement such as WriteCard(j,5) and placed it, say, in the main program or in PROCEDURE Menu in Listing 3.2, the compiler would note an error because j is not visible. It doesn't even exist in those parts of the program.

As you move on through this book, the aforementioned ideas should become clearer with each new programming illustration.

3.3 Procedures with Parameters

Consider that we are composing a program in which two or more procedures are to share the same variable. According to the discussion in the last section, that variable must then be declared globally. As an example where such a situation occurs, look at Listing 3.3a, which is a short program that performs a simple computation.

```
MODULE Computation;
FROM InOut IMPORT WriteInt;
VAR a,b,result:INTEGER;

    PROCEDURE Compute;
    BEGIN
        result:=a+3*b;
    END Compute;

    PROCEDURE Calculate;
    BEGIN
        a:=68; b:=4;
```

```
        Compute;
        WriteInt(result,5);
    END Calculate;

BEGIN (* main program *)
    Calculate;
END computation.
```

LISTING 3.3a

Note that since variables a, b, and result are shared by both PRO-CEDURE Compute and PROCEDURE Calculate, those variables have been declared globally and are accessible within the block of the entire program. But these declarations need not be made globally if we extend our knowledge of the procedure concept to include *parameter passing*.

A *parameter* is just a variable that is declared, not in a VAR list, but within a procedure's heading. An example of a procedure heading with two parameters is:

```
PROCEDURE CompareTwoNumbers(x,y:REAL);
```

Such a heading might be used for a procedure which takes two numbers, compares them and indicates which of the numbers is larger.

A procedure with parameters is invoked by typing its identifier, followed by a set of parentheses within which values or variable identifiers must be placed, separated by commas. The correct number of parameters must be used, and they must be in the proper order and be of the proper data type. So, if we wish to call up PRO-CEDURE CompareTwoNumbers so that the numbers 3.1 and 5.78 can be compared, then we would type

```
CompareTwoNumbers(3.1,5.78);
```

in our program text.

With regard to MODULE Computation, we could pass the two values, a and b, without the need to declare them globally. Instead, we can declare them locally in the procedure from which they are coming (Calculate) and declare a pair of what are called *pass by value* parameters in the procedure to which they are going (Compute). In Listing 3.3b, a second version of MODULE Computation is shown, this time with a and b being localized. Note that now, only result must be declared globally.

It should be further noted that the identifiers used in a procedure's parameter list need not have the same names, as the variable identifiers used when the procedure is called. As stated before, only the correct number, order, and data types must be strictly adhered to. Furthermore, as seen in Listing 3.3b, when passing by value, either a variable identifier or an actual value can appear in the parameter list.

```
MODULE Computation;
FROM InOut IMPORT WriteInt;
VAR result:INTEGER;

    PROCEDURE Compute(x,y:INTEGER);
    BEGIN
       result:=x+3*y;
    END Compute;

    PROCEDURE Calculate;
    VAR a,b:INTEGER;
    BEGIN
       a:=68; b:=4;
       Compute(a,4);
       WriteInt(result,5);
    END Calculate;

BEGIN (* main program *)
    Calculate;
END Computation.
```

LISTING 3.3b

The variable result can also be passed by a parameter and therefore does not have to be declared globally. But in this case, it is desired to pass back to the calling procedure, Calculate, the calculated value of result. This can be accomplished by what is called, *passing by reference.* When a variable is passed by reference the variable identifier must be used when calling the procedure.

To distinguish passing by reference from passing by value, the reserved word VAR, followed by a space, precedes the variable in the procedure heading (see Listing 3.3c).

In our example under discussion, note that we are not passing a known value of the variable, result, from the calling procedure

(Calculate) to the invoked procedure (Compute), but rather just the variable identifier. The invoked procedure's task is to assign an appropriate value to result and pass it back to the calling procedure.

Although it appears that there are only two ways in which to pass parameters from a calling part of a program to a called procedure, in actuality we can really identify three ways.

The first is passing by value as we described above. A parameter passed in this manner can be referred to as an "in" parameter in that it is passed into the called procedure.

Our second passing technique, passing by reference, really encompassing two rather distinct parameter passing modes in one. We can either have (as we do in the program of Listing 3.3c) a variable identifier passed up to the invoked procedure which is to be assigned a value by that procedure and passed back to the calling procedure, or we can have a variable which already holds a given value passed up to the invoked procedure. After the invoked procedure appropriately uses and possibly modifies the passed variable value, that value is passed back to the calling part of the program.

A parameter using the first of the two variations in passing by reference may be referred to as an "out" parameter, while the second variation, where a value is passed up to the called procedure as well as passed back, may be referred to as an "in out" parameter.

The programming language Ada makes such a distinction between parameter passing modes. Alas, it would have been nice if Modula-2 did the same.

```
MODULE Computation;
FROM InOut IMPORT WriteInt;

    PROCEDURE Compute(x,y:INTEGER;VAR answer:INTEGER);
    BEGIN
        answer:=x+3*y;
    END Compute;

    PROCEDURE Calculate;
    VAR a,b,result:INTEGER;
    BEGIN
        a:=68; b:=4;
        Compute(a,4,result);
        WriteInt(result,5);
    END Calculate;
```

```
BEGIN (* main program *)
   Calculate;
END Computation.
```

LISTING 3.3c

It might be helpful to summarize the ideas we have presented concerning the passing of parameters and picture them in another way before we move on. Assume that we have two procedures, P1 and P2, and we wish to pass parameters from P1 to P2.

PASSING BY VALUE: It's like a one-way street! Only a copy of a variable is passed from P1 to P2. The copy can be changed in P2 but the variable keeps its original value in all other parts of the program. The actual parameter appearing on the parameter list, when P2 is called, can either be the variable identifier or a value of the variable. But, if it's a variable identifier, that variable must hold an appropriate value as its contents, since the intent is to pass it as an "in" parameter.

PASSING BY REFERENCE: It's like a two-way street! Only the identifier of a variable, which either has a value associated with it or not, can be passed by reference from P1 to P2. The actual variable value (not just a copy) is passed. If the variable passed by reference is changed, then that change will hold true for all parts of the program where that variable is visible. If the parameter is intended to be an "out" parameter, then the actual variable value passed can be considered undefined, whereas if the intention is to pass the parameter as an "in out" parameter, then the variable must be assigned an appropriate value before passing.

Why not test your understanding of parameter passing by considering the program shown in Listing 3.4. Can you predict the values that i, j, and a will have when printed on the screen?

```
MODULE Passing;
FROM InOut IMPORT WriteInt,WriteLn;
FROM RealInOut IMPORT WriteReal;

   PROCEDURE P2(VAR c:INTEGER;d:INTEGER;VAR e:REAL);
   BEGIN
      INC(c); INC(d); e:=e+1.0;
   END P2;

   PROCEDURE P1;
```

```
    VAR i,j:INTEGER;
        a:REAL;
    BEGIN
        i:=5; j:=7; a:=2.1;
        P2(i,j,a);
        WriteInt(i,3); WriteLn;
        WriteInt(j,3); WriteLn;
        WriteReal(a,11);
    END P1;

BEGIN (* main program *)
    P1;
END Passing.
```

LISTING 3.4

Check out your analysis of MODULE Passing? The three values written out to the screen will be 6, 7, and the equivalent of 3.1 in scientific notation.

A RETURN statement may appear in one or more places within a procedure. If a RETURN statement is executed, program control is returned to the calling part of the program. Such a premature termination of a procedure is usually saved for exceptional conditions. For example, if characters were to be processed and the question mark flagged an exceptional condition having occurred, the following code might be written:

```
PROCEDURE ProcessChar;
BEGIN
    Read(ch);
    IF ch="?" THEN
        WriteString('Question');
        RETURN;
    END;
    Process1;
    Process2;
END ProcessChar;
```

3.4 Function Procedures

We can develop a type of procedure—called a *function procedure*—which returns to the calling part of the program a value of some data type. Function procedures can have declarations and both pass-by-value and pass-by-reference parameters just as regular procedures do.

They are invoked through the use of an assignment statement or by writing the result returned to the computer screen (or any other output device).

An example of a function procedure heading is:

PROCEDURE F1(a:REAL;d:REAL) :REAL;

Note that the heading starts with the reserved word, PROCEDURE, has an identifier and a parameter list just as regular procedures have. In addition, since it is to return a value of some data type, the function procedure also has a data type of the returned value in its heading just after a colon.

Examples of the invocation of PROCEDURE F1 are:

```
    value:=F1(x,y);
or WriteReal(F1(x,y),11);
```

where it is assumed that x and y have been properly initialized.

As a complete example consider Listing 3.5, a factorial function program for integers between 0 and 8. Note that the function procedure F, (or any function procedure), must have at least one return statement. But unlike the return statement that might be found in a regular procedure, the return statement in a function procedure must have an explicit value associated with it of the proper data type, since that value will be the actual value returned to the calling part of the program. Furthermore, since the process of executing the RETURN statement passes control immediately back to the calling part of the program, all code to be executed within the function procedure must be executed prior to reaching the RETURN statement.

```
MODULE Factorial;

FROM InOut IMPORT WriteString,WriteLn,WriteCard,ReadCard;
    PROCEDURE F(x:CARDINAL):CARDINAL;
    VAR result:CARDINAL;
    BEGIN
       result:=1;
       WHILE x#0 DO
          result:=x*result;
          DEC(x);
       END;
```

```
        RETURN result;
    END F;

VAR n:CARDINAL;

BEGIN
    WriteString('Enter an integer less than 9: ');
    ReadCard(n); WriteLn;
    IF n < 9 THEN
        WriteCard(n,1);
        WriteString('!=');
        WriteCard(F(n),5);
    END;
END Factorial.
```

LISTING 3.5

One additional observation should be made concerning the code in Listing 3.5. The declaration of the global variable *n* has been made just prior to the body of the main program. This is a logical place for it to appear—near where it is first used in the program code. But it could have been declared between the import list and the heading of PROCEDURE F just as well, as far as the Modula-2 compiler is concerned.

A function procedure can have a number of parameters on its parameter list, or none. Regardless of whether its parameter list is loaded or empty, both its formal heading and invocation statement must include a set of parentheses. For example, say a function procedure G has an empty parameter list and returns a value of type CHAR. Then its heading should be written as

PROCEDURE G():CHAR;

and the call to G might appear as follows:

ch:=G( );

where ch has been declared as a variable of type CHAR.

Before closing this section, it should be noted that ordinarily, in order to minimize side-effects in other parts of a program, usually all parameters passed to function procedures are passed by value, and within its code no global variables are altered. But it should be noted that there are carefully thought-out exceptions to such a rule.

3.5 Built-in Standard Procedures

The Modula-2 compiler recognizes a number of predeclared standard procedures, both of the regular and function kind. We have already seen a few of these standard procedures in the programs that we have written over the first three chapters of this book. For a complete view of these procedures, see Table 3.1 for study and for future reference.

Table 3.1. Modula-2 standard procedures.

Identifier and Parameter List	*Kind of Procedure*	*Description*
ABS(x)	function	Absolute value; x:INTEGER or REAL; RETURN type:same as x
ODD(x)	function	Determines if x is odd; x is INTEGER/CARDINAL expression; RETURN type:BOOLEAN
ORD(x)	function	Ordinal value of x; x:CHAR,INTEGER, CARDINAL, or enumeration type; RETURN type:CARDINAL
CHR(x)	function	Character associated with x; x:CARDINAL; RETURN type:CHAR
VAL(T,x)	function	Generalized inverse of ORD; Value with ordinal number x and type T; x:CARDINAL; RETURN type:T, (CHAR, INTEGER, CARDINAL, or enumeration type)
TRUNC(x)	function	Truncates x; x:REAL; RETURN type:CARDINAL
FLOAT(x)	function	Converts x to floating point number; x:CARDINAL; RETURN type:REAL
INC(x)	regular	Equivalent to x:=x+1; x:CHAR, INTEGER, CARDINAL, memory addresses, subranges, and enumeration type
DEC(x)	regular	Equivalent to x:=x-1; x:(same as for INC(x))
INC(x,n)	regular	Equivalent to x:=x+n; x:(same as for INC(x)); n:expression compatible with x
DEC(x,n)	regular	Equivalent to x:=x-n; x,n:same as for INC(x,n)
HALT	regular	Terminates program execution
HIGH(A)	function	Upper index bound of 1-dimensional ARRAY; A:ARRAY; RETURN type:CARDINAL
CAP(x)	function	Converts character to uppercase; x:CHAR; RETURN type:CHAR
INCL(s,e)	regular	Include(add) element e, in set s; s:any set base type; e:element or expression compatible with s
EXCL(s,e)	regular	Exclude(remove) element e, from set s; s,e:same as for INCL(s,e)

| NEW(p)∗ | regular | Sets p to point to a new memory area; p :pointer type |
| DISPOSE(p)∗ | regular | Disposes of memory area pointed to by p; p :pointer type |

∗Can have additional parameters (due to employment of record variants).

3.6 Recursion

One of the most important capabilities that a high-level language can have for the development of solutions to programming problems is that capability in which a subroutine can, as part of its code, call itself. Such a notion goes under the name of *recursion.* Modula-2 supports recursion. Within a procedure or function procedure a call can be made to itself, but it should be understood that each recursive call to a subroutine will be independent of the previous calls. That is, if a subroutine calls itself, after the newly invoked call is completed, then the original invocation of the subroutine is completed.

As a simple example, let us rewrite the illustrative example of section 3.4 where a program was developed to calculate the factorial of a small range of cardinal values (see Listing 3.5). The resultant program is illustrated in Listing 3.6 where PROCEDURE F is recursive.

```
MODULE Factorial; (*with recursion*)

FROM InOut IMPORT WriteString,WriteLn,WriteCard,ReadCard;

    PROCEDURE F(x:CARDINAL):CARDINAL;
    VAR result:CARDINAL;
    BEGIN
      IF x=0 THEN
        result:=1;
      ELSE
        result:=x*F(x-1);
      END;
      RETURN result;
    END F;

VAR n:CARDINAL;

BEGIN
    WriteString('Enter an integer less than 9: ');
    ReadCard(n);WriteLn;
    IF n<9 THEN
```

```
        WriteCard(n,1);
        WriteString('!=');
        WriteCard(F(n),5);
    END;
END Factorial.
```

LISTING 3.6

In order to write a recursive procedure or function procedure two points must be kept in mind. First, you must include a way for the subroutine to conclude. Second, each recursive call of the subroutine should bring you closer to the execution of the call that concludes the subroutine.

To illustrate these ideas, look at the example of Listing 3.6 in which we have the code segment

```
IF x=0 THEN
    result:=1;
ELSE
    result:=x*F(x-1);
END;
```

The first point from above is satisfied by the case when $x = 0$ since no further call to **PROCEDURE F** is made. The second of our points is met by the ELSE clause of the IF-THEN-ELSE statement, where we see that each succeeding call to F will reduce the argument (the parameter value) of F by one, eventually becoming zero.

Is the use of recursion a desirable way to design a solution to a programming problem? Not often! If an iterative solution can be found (the types of solutions we have been presenting thus far), it is usually preferred since it will no doubt prove to be more efficient than a recursive solution in terms of memory use and speed of execution. So why use recursion? Sometimes it provides us with a very simple and readable solution to a problem or even the only viable solution.

For example, the famous Towers of Hanoi problem (which can be found in many books on Pascal and data structures) has a rather elegant (essentially), four-line solution using recursion, whereas its iterative counterpart will be many dozens of lines of code which will prove difficult to read and therefore to understand.

So, the trade-off of memory use and speed of execution when using recursion may be worth it to obtain a simpler and more readable solution to a given problem.

4

More on Data Types

Modula-2, like its predecessor Pascal, allows the programmer to be very expressive in his or her code writing. Part of this capability is due to the fact that the language does not limit us to just the elementary data types we have already studied. A programmer can define new data types from the very simple on up to data types which are structured as collections of simple and/or structured data types, as we will see as this chapter progresses. Additionally, Modula-2 provides us with the capability to place variables in particular memory areas within the RAM memory. This feature will be addressed in the last section of this chapter.

4.1 Enumerated Data Types

Although Modula-2 provides us with the five predefined basic data types discussed previously—CHAR, INTEGER, CARDINAL, REAL, and BOOLEAN—at times they may be inadequate for describing what we want in a program. Modula-2 gives us the ability to invent our own types which we will refer to as programmer-defined data types or just *enumerated types*.

As an example, say we are interested in writing a program dealing with the days of the week. For such a program, we can enumerate a new data type which we will call DaysOfWeek and whose constants—that is, values—are the following:

Mon   Tue   Wed   Thu   Fri   Sat   Sun

Once we define the above as the constants for our new programmer-defined data type, they become the only possible values for that data type as used in that program.

Each basic data type which we have studied earlier, with the exception of type REAL, has an ordinal number associated with each constant of the data type. For example, the ordinal values for FALSE

53

and TRUE, the constants of type BOOLEAN, are 0 and 1, respectively. The ordinal value associated with the character "A" is 65 (see Appendix B for the ASCII code). In fact, if the ORD function procedure (see Table 3.1), is invoked for any of the elementary data types we have studied (except for REAL), the result returned will be the ordinal number associated with the particular constant used. Just as for those elementary data types, enumerated types also have an ordinal number associated with each of its constants.

Enumeration types must be explicitly declared in a program. Since it is a new type that is being declared, then a TYPE declaration should be used. As an example of such a declaration, let us declare the programmer-defined data type DaysOfWeek. We would declare

```
TYPE DaysOfWeek=(Mon,Tue,Wed,Thu,Fri,Sat,Sun);
```

Note that the reserved word TYPE must appear and be followed by at least one space. Then follows a TYPE identifier of our choice, an equal sign, and a list of the allowable constants placed between parentheses, after which the usual semicolon appears. The order in which the constants are placed sets the ordinal values for those constants. In our example, the ordinal value of Mon is 0, Tue is 1, all the way up to Sun which is 6.

If we wish to use this newly declared data type, then an appropriate VAR declaration must be written in the same manner in which we have been writing them all along. For our example, we might declare

```
VAR Day:DaysOfWeek;
```

On the other hand, we could combine the two declarations (TYPE and VAR) and just declare

```
VAR Day:(Mon,Tue,Wed,Thu,Fri,Sat,Sun);
```

But we will avoid using this shortcut in this book.

In Listing 4.1, we have a complete programming example which uses our newly defined data type DaysOfWeek.

```
1    MODULE WorkAndRest;

2    FROM InOut IMPORT WriteCard,WriteString,WriteLn;

3    TYPE DaysOfWeek=(Mon,Tue,Wed,Thu,Fri,Sat,Sun);
```

```
4    VAR Day:DaysOfWeek;

5    BEGIN
6       FOR Day:=Mon TO Sun DO
7          CASE Day OF
8             Mon:WriteCard(ORD(Mon)+1,2); WriteString(' Monday');|
9             Tue :WriteCard(ORD(Tue )+1,2); WriteString(' Tuesday');|
10            Wed:WriteCard(ORD(Wed)+1,2); WriteString(' Wednesday');|
11            Thu :WriteCard(ORD(Thu )+1,2); WriteString(' Thursday');|
12            Fri :WriteCard(ORD(Fri )+1,2); WriteString(' Friday');|
13            Sat :WriteCard(ORD(Sat )+1,2); WriteString(' Saturday');|
14            Sun :WriteCard(ORD(Sun )+1,2); WriteString(' Sunday');
15         END;
16         IF Day < Sat THEN
17            WriteString(' is a work day.')
18         ELSE
19            WriteString(' is a rest day.');
20         END;
21         WriteLn;
22      END;
23   END WorkAndRest.
```

screen output:

```
1   Monday is a work day.
2   Tuesday is a work day.
3   Wednesday is a work day.
4   Thursday is a work day.
5   Friday is a work day.
6   Saturday is a rest day.
7   Sunday is a rest day.
```

LISTING 4.1

Note how an enumeration type (DaysOfWeek) can be used as the running index in a FOR-DO construct (line 6). Since each constant of an enumeration type has an ordinal number associated with it, values from Mon to Sun are essentially the same as numbers from 0 to 6, as far as the computer is concerned.

The same can be said about the use of enumeration types in CASE statements (line 7) where the variable in the statement is the enumerated type with the case labels being constants of that type. In particular, note the details of the code associated with the case labels (lines 8 through 14). A cardinal number is formed and written out to the screen from the addition of 1 to the ordinal value of each enumeration constant. So, for example, if Wed is the constant, then 3 is written out to the screen.

Finally, depending on the value of the Boolean expression in the IF statement (line 16), one or the other of two statements appears on the screen. Again, note that the computer, in effect, is evaluating the Boolean expression based on the relative values of the ordinal numbers associated with the DaysOfWeek type.

4.2 Subrange Types

Sometimes we only really need to use a subset of all the possible constants associated with a data type. For example, we might be interested in developing a program that will average exam scores when the scores are integer values from 0 to 100. Instead of declaring a variable for the scores of type CARDINAL, we can use a *subrange type* where the base type is type CARDINAL. The declarations would be as follows:

```
TYPE Score=[0..100] ;
VAR ExamScore:Score;
```

or, using our shortcut technique,

```
VAR ExamScore:[0..100] ;
```

Note that the base type of our subrange type is implicitly indicated since the range of constants for the subrange type are a portion of the constants associated with type CARDINAL. The syntax for declaring a subrange is to place the lower and upper limits of the subrange being used in square brackets separated by two periods.

Since it seems to be easier to use an already existing data type (CARDINAL in this case), the question might be asked: Why bother using a subrange type? There are two good reasons. First, it helps to make the program more readable. For example, from the program declaration using type Score, we would see that exam scores should only fall in the range from 0 to 100. Our second reason is that the use of subrange types can often be used as a debugging tool. An execution error will be announced by the computer if, in our example, an exam score falls outside the subrange 0 to 100.

Consider the averaging of exam scores. Let us assume that all exam scores are cardinal values and that cardinal division of the total of all the exam scores divided by the number of exams is good enough as the average. Then a program to perform the averaging might appear as in Listing 4.2.

The comments within the program should be sufficient for your understanding so we need not discuss the details of the text except to bring to your attention the use of the sentinel 999. A sentinel is a value which signals that something should occur at that point in the program. Our use of a sentinel in Listing 4.2 signals that there are no more exam scores to be entered and that program control should move beyond the REPEAT-UNTIL construct.

```
MODULE Averaging;

FROM InOut IMPORT WriteString,WriteLn,ReadCard,WriteCard;

TYPE Score=[0..100] ; (* subrange type declaration *)
VAR ExamScore,Average:Score; (* subrange variables *)
     Mark,TotalScore,k:CARDINAL;
     Finished:BOOLEAN;

BEGIN
     WriteString('Enter exam scores followed by <cr>:');WriteLn;
     WriteString('(Enter 999 to end entry)'); (* announce to user *)
     WriteLn;WriteLn;                          (* what the sentinel is *)
     Finished:=FALSE;
     TotalScore:=0;
     k:=0; (* k counts the number of exams entered *)
     REPEAT
         ReadCard(Mark); (* cannot use a subrange of CARDINAL with ReadCard *)
         IF Mark=999 THEN (* test if sentinel entered or not *)
            Finished:=TRUE;
         ELSE
            INC(k);
            ExamScore:=Mark;
            TotalScore:=TotalScore+ExamScore;
         END;
     UNTIL Finished;
     Average:=TotalScore DIV k;
     WriteLn;WriteLn;
     WriteString('The average of the scores is:');
     WriteCard(Average,4);
END Averaging.
```

LISTING 4.2

We can make subrange types from programmer-defined data types. As an example, let us define a subrange of the enumeration type that we developed in the last section, namely, DaysOfWeek. We could declare,

```
TYPE DaysOfWeek=(Mon,Tue,Wed,Thu,Fri,Sat,Sun);
     WorkDays=[Mon..Fri] ;
VAR Days:DaysOfWeek;
    WorkWeek:WorkDays;
```

Other possible useful subranges are:

```
TYPE Letters=['A'..'Z'] ;
     Digits=["0".."9"] ;
     NegativeNumbers=[-32768..-1] ;
```

4.3 Structured Data Types

So far, we have studied simple data types. The variables of these types can only take on one single constant value of that type at a time. There is no higher level relationship or structure possible between variables of the same type.

Structured data types are higher-level types built up from collections of the simple data types (or of structured data types themselves). They contain or imply some relationship among the elements of the simple data type (referred to as the base type) of which they are composed.

We have three such structured data types in Modula-2 which are predefined in the language, namely, arrays, sets, and records. These three types will be the subjects of the next three sections of this chapter.

4.4 Arrays

An *array* is a collection of memory locations called elements into which values will be placed. These elements can hold either a simple or structured data type. In any case, the values must be of the same type.

To declare an array, we should use a TYPE declaration followed by a VAR declaration. An example of such a pair of declarations is,

```
TYPE Gamma=ARRAY[-5..10] OF CHAR;
VAR photon:Gamma;
```

or we could declare, in short,

```
VAR photon:ARRAY[-5..10] OF CHAR;
```

Note the use of the two reserved words, ARRAY and OF, as well as the square brackets in the TYPE declaration. Inside the square brackets appears the array's *index type*—a subrange of an implied simple type, whether predefined or enumerated. In this case at hand, a subrange of type INTEGER has been implied since the index runs from -5 to 10. Thus we have a total of 16 elements in this array type. The type that is designated after the word OF, the array's *base type,* indicates what type of values are to be placed in the 16 elements. In this case, the type is CHAR.

An assignment statement would be used to place a value in an array element. In the example being considered, we might write

```
photon[-2] :="q";
```

where we are assigning the -2th element the character q. Reading a value of an array element can be simply accomplished by using an assignment statement or writing the value out to an output device such as the screen. For our example, we might write

```
ch:=photon[5] ;
or Write(photon[0] );
```

where it is assumed that ch has been appropriately declared as a CHAR variable.

The previous example dealt with a one-dimensional array, but in Modula-2 we can also declare arrays of two, three or more dimensions. For example, we may be asked to develop an array structure to hold a baseball player's yearly totals of hits, runs, home runs, and runs batted in from 1975 to 1984. We can do the job by developing a two-dimensional array structure as shown below:

```
TYPE Statistics=(Hits,Runs,HomeRuns,RunsBattedIn);
     YearlyStats=ARRAY[1975..1984] ,Statistics OF CARDINAL;
VAR player:YearlyStats;
```

With the above declarations having been made, we can, for example, assign 17 home runs for the year 1981 by writing

```
player[1981,HomeRuns] :=17;
```

and if the player batted in 79 runs in 1977, we would write

```
player [1977,RunsBattedIn] :=79;
```

To write out these same statistics to the screen, we would write

```
WriteCard(player[1981,HomeRuns],3);
WriteCard(player[1977,RunsBattedIn],5);
```

or if we wish to assign these statistics to a pair of variables, we would write

```
Stat1:=player[1981,HomeRuns];
Stat2:=player[1977,RunsBattedIn];
```

where Stat1 and Stat2 are CARDINAL variables.

An entire array may be assigned to another array of the same type through the simple use of an assignment statement. For example, if we declare another variable, namely LeftFielder, of type YearlyStats, then we could write

```
LeftFielder:=player;
```

and the value of each element of player would be copied into the corresponding element of LeftFielder.

Although we have certainly not covered all there is in dealing with arrays, we will present one complete example for your review—a program which asks the user to name hurricanes (see Listing 4.3). A number of comments have been placed in the text. See if you can follow the step-by-step logic for yourself.

```
MODULE NamesForHurricanes;

FROM InOut IMPORT WriteString,WriteLn,Write,ReadString;

TYPE STRING=ARRAY[1..80] OF CHAR; (* declared our own type STRING *)
     Hurricane=ARRAY['A'..'Z'] OF STRING;
VAR Names:Hurricane; (* in effect, Names is a 2-dim. array *)

  PROCEDURE LoadArray;
  VAR ch:CHAR;

    PROCEDURE ReadName(a:CHAR); (* how is "a" passed?*)
    BEGIN
      WriteString('Enter name starting with '' ');
      Write(a);
      WriteString('", followed by a <cr>: ');
```

```
          ReadString(Names[a] ); (* can use ReadString with our type STRING *)
     END ReadName;

VAR FirstTime:BOOLEAN;

BEGIN (* LoadArray *)
     ch:="@"; (* initialize "ch" to value just preceeding "A" in ASCII code *)
     FirstTime:=TRUE;
     REPEAT
        ch:=CHR(ORD(ch)+1); (*calculates next "ch" value *)
        ReadName(ch);
        IF FirstTime THEN (* want to write message below just one time *)
           WriteString('(to end early, type "*" & <cr>)');
           WriteLn;
           Write(CHR(31)); (* control character to move cursor up one row *)
           FirstTime:=FALSE;
        END;
        IF (Names[ch] [1] ="*") OR (ch="Z") THEN
           Write(CHR(29)); (* control char to clear from cursor to end of line *)
           WriteLn;
           Write(CHR(31));
        END;
        Write(CHR(31));
        Write(CHR(29));
        WriteLn;
        Write(CHR(31));
     UNTIL (Names[ch] [1] ="*") OR (ch="Z");
END LoadArray;

PROCEDURE ReadArray;

     PROCEDURE TimeDelay;
     VAR i,j:CARDINAL;
     BEGIN
        j:=0;
        FOR i:=1 TO 200 DO INC(j);END;
     END TimeDelay;

VAR ch:CHAR;

BEGIN (* ReadArray *)
     ch:="@";
     WriteString('The names for hurricanes are:');
     WriteLn;WriteLn;
     REPEAT
        ch:=CHR(ORD(ch)+1);
        WriteString(Names[ch]);
        WriteLn;
        TimeDelay;
```

```
        UNTIL (Names[ch] [1] ="*") OR (ch="Z");
      END ReadArray;
   BEGIN (* main body *)
     LoadArray;
     ReadArray;
   END NamesForHurricanes.
```

LISTING 4.3

4.5 Sets

When we work with arrays we usually just work with individual elements in the arrays. We load them up—we read them out. We do not work with an entire array as a single unit—with one exception. We can assign one array variable the value of another array variable in one simple statement, for example, a:=b, where a and b are array variables.

To see if a particular element is in an array, we have to write code that checks each element of the array (we would use a repetition construct to perform the job). The structured data type, *set,* is a collection of elements just as is an array. But unlike an array, we always work with a set as a single unit.

If you recall, when we discussed the elementary data types, we avoided any development of the data type BITSET. Now is the time for its consideration along with Modula-2's capability to have virtually any type of set declared by a programmer by using an appropriate type declaration.

The elements associated with the predefined BITSET type are a set of integer values. (The maximum number of elements in a set value depends on the Modula-2 implementation being used but commonly may be limited to the word length of the computer.) Constants of type BITSET would be any set of elements selected from the integer subrange values of the Modula-2 implementation being used.

Variables of type BITSET are declared as follows:

```
VAR set1:BITSET;
```

As an example of a variable value, let us assign a few values to BITSET variables, s1, s2, s3, and s4.

```
s1:=BITSET{2,4,5,8};
s2:=BITSET{0,2,5..15};
s3:={2,4,5,8};
s4:={};
```

Note that the TYPE name precedes the set of integers which are placed within the brackets. As you can see, the word BITSET need not be used in assigning a set to a variable. But the choice of whether to prefix the set constant with the type of set can only be made for type BITSET. All other SET types must have the type identifier present. The last example, the assignment to s4, is the way the "empty set" is assigned to a variable.

Declarations of any other type of set must be made explicitly by the programmer. For example, consider that we want to declare a set type which consists of the uppercase alphabetic characters. Then we could declare,

TYPE SetOfLetters=SET OF ["A".."Z"] ;

If a variable, LetterSet, is declared, then we could write the following statement in our program:

LetterSet:=SetOfLetters {'A'..'D','F','W'} ;

Keep two ideas in mind when dealing with sets. Sets can only have constants as elements and these constants must be of an enumeration type (all predefined ordinal types and programmer-defined types) or a subrange type.

Table 4.1 Set operations

Operator	Name	Example	Description (a,b are sets, i is a constant)
+	union	a + b	Union of a & b consists of those elements that belong to a, b, or both
–	difference	a – b	Difference of a and b consists of those elements that belong to a but not to b
*	intersection	a * b	Intersection of a and b consists of those elements that belong to both a and b
/	symmetric difference	a/b	Symmetric difference of a and b consists of those elements either in a or in b but not in both (exclusive-OR)
=	equality	a = b	TRUE if a and b have the same elements
<>,(#)	inequality	a # b	TRUE if a and b do not have the same elements
<=	inclusion	a <= b	TRUE if a is a subset of b (every element of a is also an element of b)
IN	membership	i IN a	TRUE if i is an element of a

Two standard procedures are available for use with any set type. They are INCL and EXCL. A brief description of them can be found in Table 3.1 of Chapter 3. Also associated with sets are eight set operations, a description of which can be found in Table 4.1.

There are two short examples dealing with sets which we will now present. The first, Listing 4.4, is an extension of Listing 2.2, a program which counts upper and lowercase Es in user-entered text. The second of our examples, Listing 4.5, ties in with the programmer-defined data type DaysOfWeek which we used in the program of Listing 4.1.

```
MODULE VowelCounter;

FROM InOut IMPORT Read,WriteString,WriteLn,WriteCard;

TYPE VowelSet=SET OF CHAR;
VAR ch:CHAR;
    VowelCount:CARDINAL;

BEGIN
  VowelCount:=0;
  WriteString('Enter some text, ending with an "*":');
  WriteLn;WriteLn;
  REPEAT
    Read(ch);
    ch:=CAP(ch);
    IF ch IN VowelSet{'A','E','I','O','U'}THEN INC(VowelCount);END;
  UNTIL ch='*';
  WriteLn;WriteLn;
  WriteString('The number of vowels in the text is: ');
  WriteCard(VowelCount,2);
END VowelCounter.
```

LISTING 4.4

```
MODULE WorkingWeek;

FROM InOut IMPORT WriteString,WriteLn,Read;

TYPE DaysOfWeek=(Mon,Tue,Wed,Thu,Fri,Sat,Sun);
     WorkDays=SET OF DaysOfWeek;
VAR Days:WorkDays;
    d:DaysOfWeek;
    ch:CHAR;
BEGIN
  Days:=WorkDays{};
  WriteString('Indicate the days worked by typing "x",');WriteLn;
  WriteString('(use space bar if day not worked).');WriteLn;
  WriteLn;
```

```
WriteString(' Mon Tue Wed Thu Fri Sat Sun');WriteLn;
FOR d:=Mon TO Sun DO
    WriteString('   ');
    Read(ch);
    ch:=CAP(ch);
    IF ch='X' THEN INCL(Days,d);END;
END;
WriteLn;WriteLn;WriteLn;
WriteString('The days worked are:');WriteLn;
FOR d:=Mon TO Sun DO
    IF d IN Days THEN
      CASE d OF
        Mon:WriteString(' Monday');|
        Tue :WriteString(' Tuesday');|
        Wed:WriteString(' Wednesday');|
        Thu :WriteString(' Thursday');|
        Fri :WriteString(' Friday');|
        Sat :WriteString(' Saturday');|
        Sun :WriteString(' Sunday');
      END;
      WriteLn;
    END;
  END;
END WorkingWeek.
```

LISTING 4.5

4.6 Records

A *record* structure is similar to an array structure except for the fact that, unlike an array, the elements within a record hold variable values which need not be of the same data type. Furthermore, those variables can be of either a simple or structured data type. Elements of a record are also referred to as fields of that record.

To declare a record type, we should use a TYPE followed by a VAR declaration. An example of a record declaration is

```
TYPE Inventory=RECORD
                PartName:String20;
                PartNumber:String8;
                Price:REAL;
                Quantity:CARDINAL;
                Destination:(inhouse,foreign,domestic);
              END;
VAR item:Inventory;
```

where the data types String20 and String8 must have been declared previously as arrays of 20 and 8 characters, respectively. Of course, we could have used the shorthand method and simply declared

```
VAR item:RECORD
            PartName:String20;
            PartNumber:String8;
            Price:REAL;
            Quantity:CARDINAL;
            Destination:(inhouse,foreign,domestic);
        END;
```

Note the use of the reserved word RECORD along with END, both of which serve as brackets within which the field definitions for the record are stated.

To access a particular field of a record, we write the name of the record variable followed by a period, then followed by the field identifier. For example, consider our previously defined record type, namely, Inventory. To access the name of an item, we would write

```
item.PartName
```

To access the destination of the item, we would write

```
item.Destination
```

Assignment of a value to a record element can be accomplished through an assignment statement or from the keyboard. Using an assignment statement we might code:

```
item.PartName:='square pegs';
item.Destination:=domestic;
```

or from the keyboard in response to the prompt shown:

```
WriteString("Enter price of item: ");
ReadReal(item.Price);
```

At times it may be desirable to display an entire record or a portion of a record on the screen. This task can be accomplished by using appropriate I/O routines as we have so often done before. In a program which makes use of our sample record, we might write

```
WriteString('Name:            ');
WriteString(item.PartName);
WriteLn;
WriteString('Quantity:      ');
WriteCard(item.Quantity,5);
WriteLn;
WriteString('Destination: ');
CASE item.Destination OF
    inhouse:WriteString('inhouse');|
    foreign:WriteString('foreign');|
    domestic:WriteString('domestic');
END;
```

The screen output after execution of the above code might be

```
Name:        square pegs
Quantity:      350
Destination:  domestic
```

It is quite bothersome to have to repeat a record identifier each time we wish to reference the record's elements, as we did in the preceding code segment. We can eliminate this by using the WITH statement. The general form of the WITH statement is

```
WITH <record identifier> DO
    <statements; some involving field identifiers alone>
END;
```

As an example, we will rewrite the screen output code developed above, this time using a WITH statement.

```
WITH item DO
    WriteString('Name:            ');
    WriteString(PartName);
    WriteLn;
    WriteString('Quantity:     ');
    WriteCard(Quantity,5);
    WriteLn;
    WriteString('Destination: ');
    CASE Destination OF
        inhouse:WriteString('inhouse');|
```

```
          foreign:WriteString('foreign');|
          domestic:WriteString('domestic');
     END;
END;
```

A complete program which uses a RECORD type might be helpful at this time. Consider the task of developing a program which keeps a record for a runner whose distance is the mile. The record should consist of the miler's name, the total number of miles run, and the time in minutes and seconds of the runner's best mile. The program of Listing 4.6 does the job. The "main program" should be self-explanatory as should be the procedures that are invoked.

```
MODULE MilerData;

FROM InOut IMPORT Write,WriteString,WriteLn,WriteCard,
                  ReadString,ReadCard,Read;

TYPE String20=ARRAY[1..20] OF CHAR;
     Runner=RECORD
                 Name:String20;
                 TotalRuns:CARDINAL;
                 min,sec:CARDINAL;
            END;
VAR miler:Runner;
    i:CARDINAL;
    ch:CHAR;

  PROCEDURE InitRecord;
  BEGIN
     WITH miler DO
        min:=100;
        sec:=0;
        TotalRuns:=0;
     END;
     Write(CHR(12));WriteLn;
     WriteString('Enter name of miler: ');
     ReadString(miler.Name);WriteLn;
     WriteLn;
  END InitRecord;

  PROCEDURE EnterDataAndCalculate;
  VAR m,s:CARDINAL;
  BEGIN
     Write(CHR(12));WriteLn;
     INC(miler.TotalRuns);
     WriteString(miler.Name);WriteLn;
     WriteString('What was your time?');WriteLn;
```

```
    WriteString('min.: ');
    ReadCard(m);WriteLn;
    WriteString('sec.: ');
    ReadCard(s);WriteLn;
    WITH miler DO
      IF 60*m+s < 60*min+sec THEN
        min:=m;
        sec:=s;
      END;
    END;
  END EnterDataAndCalculate;

  PROCEDURE OutputInfo;
  BEGIN
    WITH miler DO
      WriteString('Best mile:');
      WriteCard(min,3);
      WriteString(' min.');
      WriteCard(sec,5);
      WriteString(' sec.');WriteLn;
      WriteString('Number of runs:');
      WriteCard(TotalRuns,3);
    END;
  END OutputInfo;

BEGIN (* main program *)
  InitRecord;
  REPEAT
    EnterDataAndCalculate;
    OutputInfo;
    FOR i:=1 TO 10 DO WriteLn;END;
    WriteString('Enter another mile? (Y/N):');
    Read(ch);
  UNTIL CAP(ch)="N";
END MilerData.
```

LISTING 4.6

The results of the program of Listing 4.6 may be a bit disappointing in that each time the program is executed, the total runs and best mile are initialized anew. No continuous record is kept unless the MilerData program remains active (that is, execution is never terminated). The use of a permanent storage device—an external file—should be incorporated into the program. Files will be a topic in a future chapter, so we will leave a discussion of them for later.

A few things bear mentioning about the subject of records. It is more likely for such a programming task, as described for our single runner, to be more useful if the solution would accomodate several runners at the same time. We can extend out solution (MODULE MilerData) to do the job by declaring an array of records as follows:

miler:ARRAY[1..NumOfMilers] OF Runner;

where Runner is the record type from Listing 4.6 and NumOfMilers is a constant appropriately declared. Now we have a data type that will accomodate any number of runners our computer's memory can handle.

Such an array of records has been incorporated into Listing 4.7, a program that emulates the processes of MODULE MilerData but, in this case, for more than one runner. Note the importation of the object CompareStr from library module Strings. CompareStr is a function procedure that can be used to compare names and thus help us to find the miler's record that is to be updated (see PROCEDURE FindMilerDesired).

The remainder of Listing 4.7 should be self-explanatory.

```
MODULE MilersData;

FROM InOut IMPORT Write,WriteString,WriteLn,WriteCard,
                  ReadString,ReadCard,Read;
FROM Strings IMPORT CompareStr;

TYPE String20=ARRAY[1..20] OF CHAR;
     Runner=RECORD
                 Name:String20;
                 TotalRuns:CARDINAL;
                 min,sec:CARDINAL;
            END;
CONST NumOfMilers=4; (* <—change this value for
                            different no. of milers *)
VAR miler:ARRAY[1..NumOfMilers] OF Runner;
    mName:String20;
    i,j:CARDINAL;
    ch:CHAR;

    PROCEDURE InitRecords;
    VAR i:CARDINAL;
    BEGIN
      FOR i:=1 TO NumOfMilers DO
          WITH miler[i] DO
             min:=100;
             sec:=0;
```

```
            TotalRuns:=0;
        END;
    END;
    Write(CHR(12));WriteLn;
    WriteString('Enter names of ');
    WriteCard(NumOfMilers,0);
    WriteString(' milers: ');
    WriteLn;WriteLn;
    FOR i:=1 TO NumOfMilers DO
        WriteString('Miler #');WriteCard(i,0);WriteString(': ');
        ReadString(miler[i].Name);
    END;
END InitRecords;

PROCEDURE FindMilerDesired;
VAR i:CARDINAL;
    found:BOOLEAN;
BEGIN
    Write(CHR(12));WriteLn;
    WriteString('Which miler do you want?');WriteLn;
    WriteLn;
    FOR i:=1 TO NumOfMilers DO
        WriteString(miler[i].Name);WriteLn;
    END;
    WriteLn;
    ReadString(mName);
    j:=0;
    found:=FALSE;
    REPEAT
        INC(j);
        IF CompareStr(mName,miler[j].Name)=0 THEN found:=TRUE;END;
    UNTIL found OR (j=NumOfMilers);
    IF NOT found THEN HALT;END;
END FindMilerDesired;

PROCEDURE EnterDataAndCalculate;
VAR m,s:CARDINAL;
BEGIN
    INC(miler[j].TotalRuns);
    WriteLn;
    WriteString(miler[j].Name);
    WriteString("'s time is?");WriteLn;
    WriteString('min: ');
    ReadCard(m);WriteLn;
    WriteString('sec.: ');
    ReadCard(s);WriteLn;
    WITH miler[j] DO
        IF 60*m+s < 60*min+sec THEN
```

```
          min:=m;
          sec:=s;
        END;
      END;
    END EnterDataAndCalculate;

    PROCEDURE OutputInfo;
    BEGIN
      WITH miler[j]  DO
        WriteString('Best mile:');
        WriteCard(min,3);
        WriteString(' min.');
        WriteCard(sec,5);
        WriteString(' sec.');WriteLn;
        WriteString('Number of runs:');
        WriteCard(TotalRuns,3);
      END;
    END OutputInfo;

  BEGIN (* main program *)
    InitRecords;
    REPEAT
      FindMilerDesired;
      EnterDataAndCalculate;
      OutputInfo;
      FOR i:=1 TO 5 DO WriteLn;END;
      WriteString('Enter another mile? (Y/N): ');
      Read(ch);
    UNTIL CAP(ch)="N";
  END MilersData.
```

LISTING 4.7

4.7 Records with Variant Parts

There are times when it is advantageous to have a record structure
where some of the fields may vary depending on some criterion. For
example, suppose we wish to set up one array of records for not just
milers but long distance runners as well. Within the one array of records
we would have two different types of records. For the milers, we could
use the same "Runner" record used in our previous examples of
records; that is, it would include a name field, along with fields for
the total number of runs, and the number of minutes and seconds for
the miler's fastest mile.

For the long distance runners, we would also include a name field.
But that might be the only common field between the two types of

records. For the long distance runners we may not be interested in the total number of runs but, rather, the runner's total mileage. Furthermore, we may not be interested in keeping track of the runner's shortest time, but may be interested in the runner's longest distance run in an outing. Thus we would like to replace the total runs, minutes, and seconds fields with simply a field each for total miles run and longest run.

Modula-2 can accommodate such variations within the record structure by use of what is called a *record variant*.

As an example of the syntax for a record which includes a variant part, we will rewrite the "Runner" record type found in the programs of Listings 4.6 and 4.7, by making the following set of declarations:

```
TYPE String20=ARRAY[1..20] OF CHAR;
     RunnerType=(mile,long);
     Runner=RECORD
               Name:String20;
               CASE Distance:RunnerType OF
                  mile:TotalRuns:CARDINAL;
                       min,sec:CARDINAL;|
                  long:TotalMiles,LongestRun:REAL;
               END; (*case*)
            END; (*record*)
```

Above, we have defined a RunnerType, and the record structure contains a field (Distance) of that type. If the value of the Distance field is set to "mile" for a particular runner, then the variant fields TotalRuns, min, and sec are valid, whereas if Distance is set to "long" then the variant fields TotalMiles and LongestRun are valid. The CASE statement within the record structure details the variant part of the record. Note that the CASE statement structure for variant parts has a syntax similar to the executable CASE statement that we discussed back in Chapter 2. It includes an END and the same use of the vertical bar character.

Variant parts of records can appear anywhere in a record structure and there can be more than one such variant part per record.

In Listing 4.8, we have employed this new variant record structure and, in effect, have rewritten MODULE MilersData (Listing 4.7) so that it could accomodate both milers and long distance runners. Note that whenever we access the variant part of the record, a CASE statement is appropriately used. This is the preferred technique for access of variant record parts.

The details of the program of Listing 4.8 should be self-explanatory in light of the program of Listing 4.7.

```
MODULE RunnersData;

FROM InOut IMPORT Write,WriteString,WriteCard,WriteLn,
                  ReadString,ReadCard,Read;
FROM RealInOut IMPORT ReadReal,WriteReal;
FROM Strings IMPORT CompareStr;

TYPE String20=ARRAY[1..20] OF CHAR;
     RunnerType=(mile,long);
     Runner=RECORD
                Name:String20;
                CASE Distance:RunnerType OF
                   mile:TotalRuns:CARDINAL;
                        min,sec:CARDINAL;|
                   long:TotalMiles,LongestRun:REAL;
                END;
            END;

CONST NumOfRunners=4;

VAR jogger:ARRAY[1..NumOfRunners] OF Runner;
    jName:String20;
    i,j:CARDINAL;
    ch:CHAR;

    PROCEDURE InitRecords;
    VAR i:CARDINAL;
    BEGIN
       Write(14C);(*14C is octal equivalent of 12:Write(14C) clears the screen*)
       WriteLn;
       WriteString('Enter names of ');
       WriteCard(NumOfRunners,0);
       WriteString(' runners along with');WriteLn;
       WriteString('whether they are milers or long');WriteLn;
       WriteString('distance runners:');WriteLn;
       FOR i:=1 TO NumOfRunners DO
          WITH jogger[i] DO
             WriteLn;
             WriteString('Runner #');WriteCard(i,0);WriteString(': ');
             ReadString(Name);
             WriteString('is a:');WriteLn;
             WriteString('(1) miler or (2) long distance runner? ');
             Read(ch);
             CASE ch OF
                '1':Distance:=mile;
                    min:=100;
```

```
                    sec:=0;
                    TotalRuns:=0;|
            '2':Distance:=long;
                 TotalMiles:=0.0;
                 LongestRun:=0.0;
         ELSE
            WriteLn;WriteLn;
            WriteString('Error detected');
            HALT;
         END;
      END;
      WriteLn;
   END;
END InitRecords;

PROCEDURE FindRunnerDesired;
VAR i:CARDINAL;
    found:BOOLEAN;
BEGIN
   Write(14C);WriteLn;
   WriteString('Which runner do you want?');WriteLn;
   WriteLn;
   FOR i:=1 TO NumOfRunners DO
      WriteString(jogger[i].Name);WriteLn;
   END;
   WriteLn;
   ReadString(jName);
   j:=0;
   found:=FALSE;
   REPEAT
      INC(j);
      IF CompareStr(jName,jogger[j].Name)=0 THEN found:=TRUE;END;
   UNTIL found OR (j=NumOfRunners);
   IF NOT found THEN HALT;END;
END FindRunnerDesired;

PROCEDURE EnterDataAndCalculate;
VAR m,s:CARDINAL;
    run:REAL;
BEGIN
   WriteLn;
   WriteString(jogger[j].Name);
   CASE jogger[j].Distance OF
      mile:WriteString(" 's time is?");WriteLn;
           WriteString('min.:');
           ReadCard(m);WriteLn;
           WriteString('sec.:');
           ReadCard(s);WriteLn;
```

```
                    WITH jogger[j] DO
                        IF 60*m+s<60*min+sec THEN
                            min:=m;
                            sec :=s;
                        END;
                        INC(TotalRuns);
                    END;|
                long:WriteString(" 's length of run is?");WriteLn;
                    ReadReal(run);WriteLn;
                    WITH jogger[j] DO
                        IF run>LongestRun THEN LongestRun:=run;END;
                        TotalMiles:=TotalMiles+run;
                    END;
            END;
        END EnterDataAndCalculate;

        PROCEDURE OutputInfo;
        BEGIN
            WITH jogger[j] DO
                CASE Distance OF
                    mile:WriteString('Best mile:');
                        WriteCard(min,3);
                        WriteString(' min.');
                        WriteCard(sec,5);
                        WriteString(' sec.');WriteLn;
                        WriteString('Number of runs:');
                        WriteCard(TotalRuns,3);|
                    long:WriteString('Longest run:');
                        WriteReal(LongestRun,12);WriteLn;
                        WriteString('Total miles:');
                        WriteReal(TotalMiles,12);
                END;
            END;
        END OutputInfo;

    BEGIN (*main body*)
        InitRecords;
        REPEAT
            FindRunnerDesired;
            EnterDataAndCalculate;
            OutputInfo;
            FOR i:=1 TO 5 DO WriteLn;END;
            WriteString('Enter another run? (Y/N): ');
            Read(ch);
        UNTIL CAP(ch)='N';
    END RunnersData.
```

LISTING 4.8

4.8 More on Assignment Compatibility

Since we have covered the topics of enumerated types, subranges, and structured data types, we can continue our discussion of assignment compatibility begun in section 1.4. You may recall that the variable, value, or expression on the right side of the assignment operator must be "data type" compatible with the variable on the left side. Such a Modula-2 specification guarantees that no inadvertent type transfers will take place (see section 1.4).

For two data types to be assignment compatible, one of the following conditions must hold true:

a) The two data types are the same; for example, both are type INTEGER

b) The two data types have been defined as equivalent; for example, one is of type CARDINAL and the other is declared as follows:

   TYPE AnotherCard=CARDINAL;

c) One data type is a subrange of the other; for example, we may declare

   TYPE SubCard=[1 .. 10];

   Then SubCard is assignment compatible with type CARDINAL

d) The two data types are both subranges of the same base type; for example, we may declare,

   TYPE IntType1=[-100 .. 50];
        IntType2=[-50 .. 50];

e) One data type is type INTEGER and the other is type CARDINAL

If any of the conditions c) through e) hold true, then it should be clearly understood by the programmer that extra care must be taken in the coding of assignment statements since run-time errors may occur due to the possibility that the value on the right side of the assignment operator does not fall within the range of the variable on the left side.

4.9 Fixed Address Variables

At times it is desirable to have control as to exactly where in the RAM memory a particular variable is located. For example, in some computer systems (referred to as memory-mapped I/O systems), data to be transmitted to an output device—such as the CRT screen, a printer, or a controller for hydraulic equipment—is sent to particular RAM locations which, although they appear as any other memory locations as far as the CPU is concerned, are actually directly connected to the output device in question.

If, for example, a particular computer system has memory location— BF68H (hexadecimal)—as the address associated with an output device, and you wish to have an integer variable n directly address that output device, then the following declaration could be made:

    VAR n[0BF68H] :INTEGER;

The number in brackets must be of type CARDINAL and can be written in either decimal, octal, or hexadecimal form. (If written in hexadecimal form, and the number begins with a number from the set A through F, it must be preceded by a zero as written in the above example.)

Since RAM memory locations are system-dependent, we can only offer you a sample program which is system-dependent. Listing 4.9 is a short program written specifically for an Apple II computer which, indeed, has a memory-mapped I/O system. The CRT screen of an Apple II computer, when used for text (as opposed to graphics), stores the text screen characters in RAM locations 1024 to 3071 (decimal).

Thus, in the program of Listing 4.9, we have declared two variables, one of type INTEGER and the other of type CHAR, and assigned those two variables to, in effect, particular screen locations by assigning them to memory locations 1500 and 1520 (decimal), respectively.

Upon executing the program, if in response to the prompt line the integer value 2500 is typed, a pair of characters will appear towards the bottom of the screen at the locations corresponding to RAM locations 1500 and 1501. The pair of characters will be a D (in normal video—that is, the character in screen color on a black background), followed by an I, (in inverse video—the character in black with the screen color for background). A pair of characters is written to the screen due to the fact that an integer variable occupies two bytes of memory.

Why are the characters D and I printed on the screen? Do they correspond to the integer value 2500? The answer is yes, but to understand it, you must look up the ASCII Screen Character Set found in the documentation provided with the Apple II computer. This documentation will reveal that a normal video D is equivalent to 196 being placed in the first memory location of the pair, whereas as inverse video, I is equivalent to 9 being placed in the second memory location of the pair. Furthermore, the first memory location represents the lower order byte of the integer number and the second memory location represents the higher order byte.

Thus, in binary notation, we have,

```
inverse I —> 9    normal D —> 196
0 0 0 0 1 0 0 1    1 1 0 0 0 1 0 0
```

Now view the above 16 bits as a 16-bit integer value and you will find that you have the value 2500 (decimal).

Next in the program, the variable ch is assigned the character whose ordinal value is 101C (octal). This causes a flashing A to be written to the CRT screen.

```
MODULE FixedMemoryAddressTest;

FROM InOut IMPORT WriteString,WriteLn,WriteInt,ReadInt,Write;

VAR N[1500] :INTEGER;(*or could be [2734B] in octal or [5DCH] in hex*)
    ch[2760B] :CHAR;(*or could be [1520] in decimal or [5F0H] in hex*)
BEGIN
   WriteLn;
   WriteString('Enter a number to be sent to screen');WriteLn;
   WriteString('location 1500 decimal:');WriteLn;
   WriteLn;
   ReadInt(N);
   WriteLn;WriteLn;
   WriteString('The character, A, will be sent to screen');WriteLn;
   WriteString('location 1520 decimal.');WriteLn;
   WriteLn;
   ch:=101C;
   Write(ch);
   WriteInt(N,10);
END FixedMemoryAddressTest.
```

LISTING 4.9

5

The Module Concept

Recall that in the introduction to Chapter 3 we turned our attention to the procedure concept and how it allows us to create an independent programming unit, the procedure, along with the idea of block structure. A programming language which takes advantage of such a structure can certainly be a powerful programming tool for accomplishing many jobs, both large and small.

Pascal is such a language. But, after some experience with a block structured language such as Pascal, one can only find that for large programming projects block structure still leaves something to be desired.

In this chapter, after a little groundwork is laid, the module concept will be introduced and, in part, investigated. Beyond this rather short beginning, our study of modules will continue in Chapter 6 where we will complete our formal study of the module concept by introducing the idea of separate compilation. After that, the remaining chapters in this book will be dedicated to the use of system-supplied modules, which will help us develop some rather sophisticated programming ideas.

5.1 Some Word Definitions and their Relation to Block Structure

At this time it would be advantageous for us to make an attempt to clearly define some terms since they will be used as we lead into a discussion of the module structure available to us in Modula-2.

As we stated in Section 3.2, a *block* consists of the declarations and statements following a procedure or program heading. But now, since we are about to introduce an entity called a module, and since a program itself is a module, we would do better to restate the definition of a block as consisting of the declarations and statements following a procedure or module heading. As noted in Chapter 3, a block may have other blocks nested within.

81

Although we have used the term *object* already in this book, we will formally state that an object may be a data type, a variable, a procedure or any of a number of other entities that have their own independent identity within a program.

The *scope* of an object is defined as the range of blocks over which the object is known, that is, the portion of the program where the compiler will recognize the object's identifier. This scope extends from the block in which the object is declared on down through all the nested blocks within. (An exception occurs when a local object is declared with the same identifier within a nested block.)

An object's *visibility* extends over its scope. That is, the object can be seen and employed anywhere within its scope—from the block in which it is declared down through all nested blocks. The object is not visible outside its block.

An object's *existence* depends on whether program execution is within the object's scope or not. If execution is occuring within an object's block, then the object exists; if not, then the object no longer exists.

These ideas about *scope, visibility,* and *existence* are the cornerstones of what is referred to as *block structure*.

In summary, block structure controls an object's scope and visibility—which is desirable. It also controls an object's existence—which is sometimes desirable. But block structure binds an object's existence to its visibility—which is undesirable.

So block structure has some rather important shortcomings. With it, we cannot separate an object's visibility from its existence. Furthermore, a procedure can access virtually every object outside of its scope, even objects it should have no chance of controlling. What is needed is to have available to the programmer a structure which allows for totally separate control of existence and visibility when desired. The Modula-2 solution is the *module!*

5.2 Types of Modules

There are four different types of modules available for our use in Modula-2. The first of these, which we have been working with all along, is called the *program module.* Next, we have two module types that always come to us in pairs—the *definition module* and the *implementation module.* This pair of modules reside in what is called a library so, at times, they may be referred to as Library Modules. The last of our module quartet is the *local module.*

The remainder of this chapter will concentrate on local modules and will make use of program modules. Chapter 6 will concentrate on the Modula-2 library facilities for creating our own library modules— that is, the coding and use of definition and implementation modules.

5.3 Module Structure - Program and Local Modules

At the outset, we would like to state that Modula-2's module structure does not in any way diminish or negate the fine qualities of block structure. In fact, block structure, as we have described it, is kept intact within module structure. Thus, the concepts of block, scope, visibility, and existence still remain implicitly valid. What module structure does for us is to give us a way to separate visibility from existence for some objects where it may be desirable. To do this, appropriate statements must be written explicitly within the Modula-2 code. The explicit statements that must be written within the code are called *import lists* and *export lists.*

Every Modula-2 program is a program module. Program modules are the only modules that, by themselves, are executable. Each program module can have an import list, but not an export list. The import list signals to the Modula-2 library which library modules and what objects within those modules are to be made available to the program module. What actually happens is that at execution time, the imported modules' codes are attached to the program module and the objects selected for importation are made visible to the program module as we have seen in the sample programs in this book.

Local modules do not stand alone, but may be nested within a program module, within a procedure, or within any other local module. (They can also be nested within an implementation module.)

Recall that a procedure can access virtually every object outside of its scope. This is not true for a local module (or any of the other three types of modules). The only way to have access to an object outside the scope of a module is to explicitly select that object for importation. That is, that object must appear on an appropriate import list.

Again recall that no object declared within a procedure is either visible or even exists outside of that procedure's scope. This need not be true for a local module (or, as we will see, a definition module). If it is desired to allow an object to exist and be visible outside of the local module then, explicitly, it must be selected for exportation. That is, that object must appear on an appropriate export list. So, a local module can have both an import and an export list. Such a pair of lists will appear just below the local module's heading.

As an example, consider the program shown in Listing 5.1. Although it does not do anything worth doing, with it we can point out how an object is imported or exported and how that affects its existence and visibility.

```
MODULE Program;

FROM InOut IMPORT WriteCard;

    PROCEDURE Square(y:CARDINAL):CARDINAL;
    VAR result:CARDINAL;
    BEGIN
      result:=y*y;
      RETURN result;
    END Square;

    MODULE Local;

    IMPORT Square;
    EXPORT Proceed,answer;

    VAR x, answer:CARDINAL;

      PROCEDURE Calculate;
      BEGIN
        INC(x,3);
        answer:=Square(x);
      END Calculate;

      PROCEDURE Proceed;
      BEGIN
        Calculate;
      END Proceed;

    BEGIN (* Local *)
      x:=5;
    END Local;

BEGIN (* Program *)
  Proceed;
  WriteCard(answer,5);
END Program.
```

LISTING 5.1

Note that the import and export lists of the local module Local are simply formed by using the reserved words IMPORT and EXPORT, respectively. After at least one space the objects to be exported/ imported are placed in any order. The choice of writing the import list first is not optional—if there is an import list, it must precede the export list.

The program executes in this fashion:

1. Execution starts at the beginning of Program.

2. Program calls Proceed.

3. Proceed calls Calculate.

4. Calculate invokes Square, among doing other things.

5. Control is finally passed back to Program and "answer" is written out to the screen.

Now let us see what happens in detail (the numbers in parentheses refer to the numbered programming steps above):

Execution begins at the top of the body of program module Program (1). Program can call Proceed (2) because Proceed appears on the export list of local module Local which allows for the existence of Proceed outside its module. Since Local is nested inside Program, all of the objects on its export list (in this case, Proceed and answer) are automatically visible to Program as long as they appear on MODULE Local's export list.

As soon as an object from module Local is requested, the body of Local is automatically executed (as are all module bodies when an object from within is used). Thus the variable x is initialized at 5. Next, Proceed calls PROCEDURE Calculate (3), another procedure within Local. Since Calculate is outside Proceed's block, it exists and is visible to Proceed.

Calculate increments x by 3 to make it 8 and invokes PROCEDURE Square (4) which, although outside of MODULE Local, appears on its import list so it is visible everywhere inside Local. Thus the value of answer is set to 64 after the invocation of Square.

After unravelling the convoluted calls to the various procedures, control is finally passed back to the body of the program module Program. Program calls WriteCard (5) which has been appropriately imported into Program from the standard library module InOut. The object to be used as the parameter for WriteCard is answer which has been calculated and has been placed on the export list of Local. So, therefore, answer exists outside of the local module and is automatically visible in the outer module Program.

It should be noted at this time that a local module, or for that matter any type of module, may have no body. That is, there may be no code (such as x:=5, found in MODULE Local of Listing 5.1) that must be executed upon entry into the module. If this is the case, the module body takes on the form of just the END statement. For example, if in Listing 5.1 x was not to be initialized, MODULE Local's body would be the one line

```
END Local;
```

instead of the three lines

```
BEGIN (* Local *)
    x:=5;
END Local;
```

In summary:

a. To ensure the *existence* of an object *outside* of its local module, that object must appear on the module's *export list.* For example:

.

.

```
MODULE Local1;
EXPORT x,P1; (* these objects will exist outside of Local1 *)
VAR x,y,z:REAL;

    PROCEDURE P1;
        (* declarations, etc. *)
    BEGIN
        (* body of P1 *)
    END P1;

BEGIN
    (* body of Local1 *)
END Local1;
```

.

.

b. To make an object *visible inside* a module, that object must appear on the module's *import list.* For example:

.
.

```
MODULE Local2;
IMPORT x;
   (* declarations, procedures, etc. *)
BEGIN
   x:=3.87;
   (* the rest of the body of Local2 *)
END Local2;
```

.
.

c. A program module can only have an import list.

d. A local module can have both an import and an export list, with the import list appearing first.

e. A module body is automatically executed when an enclosing procedure (or program module) is invoked.

f. A module is not treated as a procedure, that is, a module is *never* invoked.

5.4 Two Local Module Examples

In Listings 5.2 and 5.3 you will find two additional examples of programs which incorporate local modules. You may wish to see if you can predict what their screen outputs will be before we begin discussing them.

```
MODULE Program1;
FROM InOut IMPORT WriteString,WriteLn;

   MODULE Local1;
   IMPORT WriteString,WriteLn;
   EXPORT P1;

      PROCEDURE P1;
      BEGIN
         WriteString('In P1');WriteLn;
      END P1;

   BEGIN(*Local1*)
      WriteString('In MODULE Local1');WriteLn;
   END Local1;
```

```
BEGIN(*Program1*)
  WriteString('In MODULE Program1');WriteLn;
  P1;
  WriteString('Back in MODULE Program1');
END Program1.
```

LISTING 5.2

As the program of Listing 5.2 begins execution, "In MODULE Local1" will be the first message to appear on the CRT screen. This reflects the fact that the code found in the body of local module Local1 will be automatically executed when its enclosing program module (Program1) is invoked.

Next, the body of Program1 itself will begin execution. Thus the next message to appear on the screen will be "In MODULE Program1".

The call to PROCEDURE P1 will be recognized because P1 has been made visible outside of local module Local1 since it appears on Local1's export list. This call to P1 will result in the message "In P1" being written to the CRT screen.

Control then returns to the main body of Program1 and the final message, "Back in MODULE Program1", will be written to the screen.

```
 1    MODULE Program2;

 2    FROM InOut IMPORT WriteString,WriteLn;

 3      PROCEDURE P0;

 4        MODULE Local2;
 5        IMPORT WriteString,WriteLn;
 6        EXPORT P1;

 7          PROCEDURE P1;
 8          BEGIN
 9            WriteString('In P1');WriteLn;
10          END P1;

11        BEGIN(*Local2*)
12            WriteString('In MODULE Local2');WriteLn;
13        END Local2;

14      BEGIN(*P0*)
15          WriteString('In P0');WriteLn;
16          P1;
17      END P0;

18    BEGIN(*Program2*)
19        WriteString('In MODULE Program2');WriteLn;
```

```
20      P0;
21      WriteString('Back in MODULE Program2');
22      END Program2.
```

LISTING 5.3

The execution of the code of Listing 5.3 occurs in the following order:

The first thing to note is that although within program module Program2 there lies a local module, it is not on the very next nesting level just below the program module. (This is different than the case we had in Listing 5.2 where the local module was indeed on the very next nesting level below the program module.) Thus, the body of local module Local2, will not be executed immediately upon execution of Program2, but rather will have to wait for its execution until its enclosing procedure PROCEDURE P0 is invoked. Therefore, the first message to appear on the CRT screen will be "In MODULE Program2".

Now, since the next code line to be executed (line 20) makes a call to PROCEDURE P0, the message "In MODULE Local2" will appear on the screen, followed by the message "In P0".

PROCEDURE P1 is next called from within P0, and thus "In P1" appears next on the screen.

The final message written to the screen will be "Back in MODULE Program2".

The main idea of this second of our two examples is that the automatic execution of the body of a local module occurs only when the enclosing procedure on the next highest block level has been called.

In studying the execution order of code, when nested local modules and procedures are involved it may be best to develop some of your own test programs on the computer with which you are working.

5.5 Qualified Export from a Local Module

The exportations made from the local modules that we have thus far discussed have been what are called "unqualified". This means that if an object from a local module's export list is to be referenced, only the object's identifier need be named. Thus, in Listing 5.3, the object P1—which is exported from MODULE Local2 (line 6)—is invoked within PROCEDURE P0 (line 16) by merely writing the identifier P1.

On occasion, within a program, there may be another object which has the same identifier (possibly an object imported from a standard library module). Under this circumstance, it would be impossible to distinguish between the two objects with the same identifiers.

To alleviate this situation, we can "qualify" the exported objects from a local module which will force us to prefix any reference to an object on the qualified list with the local module's identifier followed by a period. For example, if we wish to qualify the export of P1 from MODULE Local2 of Listing 5.3, then line 6 of the program should be replaced by the line

    EXPORT QUALIFIED P1;

This will cause the compiler not to recognize any call to P1 unless it is properly qualified. Thus line 16 of the program would have to be modified to read

    Local2.P1;

for the compiler not to flag an error.

Therefore, if an export list is qualified, then any reference to an object on that list must include the module's identifier followed by a period.

On the other hand, it should be noted that a programmer can use such a qualified reference whether exportation is qualified or not. It may be desired on occasion in order to make the program code more readable.

6

Separate Compilation

Modula-2 has the capability of partitioning a program into several separately compilable units. The fundamental unit accepted by the Modula-2 compiler is called a *compilation unit.* Compilation units come in three types, namely, program modules, definition modules, and implementation modules. Note that the smallest separately compilable unit is a module—but not all the types of modules available in Modula-2 can be separately compiled. The local module (discussed in Chapter 5) is a module that cannot be separately compiled, but rather must be enclosed within either a program module or an implementation module.

In this chapter, we will concentrate our efforts on the development of definition and implementation modules. These modules come to us in pairs—a definition module with its corresponding implementation module. At times a module pair may be referred to as a library module pair, since such a pair of modules resides in the Modula-2 Library. This chapter will conclude with a pair of small case studies which will include each of the three types of compilation units available to us in Modula-2.

Why separate compilation? It makes available to a team of programmers a software development environment much like the development environment enjoyed by teams of hardware engineers. Hardware engineering teams have for a long time been able to partition large hardware systems into virtually independent, interconnecting subsystems or modules. Each engineer in the group can work on his or her assigned subsystem independently from the other subsystem developers, as long as the subsystem interfacing information is carefully defined and kept up-to-date. Thus a subsystem engineer can go off into a corner with well-defined and understood input and output information, and develop his or her part of the overall system and be fairly confident that his or her module will fit nicely into that overall system. Furthermore, modifications in hardware that may take place after the system is complete can be made in the same modular fashion.

91

With separate compilation, software systems can be developed and modified in the same way.

6.1 The Library Module Pair

As stated previously, a library module pair consists of a definition module and its associated implementation module. The names of these modules are very descriptive of their function.

The *definition module* defines all the objects that are publicly declared within the module pair, giving information as to the type of each object and parameter lists for the objects that are procedures. It further lists those objects that are made available for importation to other modules (program or implementation modules).

On the other hand, the *implementation module* contains the actual implementations of the publicly declared objects in its corresponding definition module, as well as implementations of any other objects needed privately within the module itself.

The definition module acts as the interface between its associated implementation module and the outside Modula-2 environment. It's like a promissory note—it's a software document that lists the objects that the implementation module promises to deliver on demand.

A definition module should normally be composed prior to its associated implementation module. Once composed, the definition module can be separately compiled. (At this stage, any program module can import objects from the module pair and be compiled successfully. But, since the implementations of those objects do not exist as of yet, the program module cannot be executed.)

After composing and compiling the definition module, the implementation module should be written and compiled. Upon successfully carrying out those tasks, the library module pair is complete and ready for use, in the same way that we have been using some of the standard library modules throughout the examples in this book.

You may ask, "Why have separate definition and implementation modules? Why not have these two parts placed in just one compilation unit?" There are three basic reasons for separating a library module pair into two separately compilable units:

1. *Large software system designs* utilize many programmers. Major subsystems can be identified and parceled out to pro-

grammers who can design interfaces (definition modules) which can then be used by others to test some aspects of the inter-subsystem communications even before the corresponding implementation modules are completed.

2. *Replacement implementations* can be developed and installed without the need for recompiling part or all of the software system anew.

3. Two library modules can *mutually import objects* from each other's definition module into their respective implementation modules.

6.2 Definition Modules

The general form of a definition module is:

```
DEFINITION MODULE Sample;
    < IMPORT lists, if any >
    < EXPORT QUALIFIED list >
    < CONST, TYPE, VAR declarations, if any >
    < PROCEDURE headings, if any >
END Sample.
```

The reserved word DEFINITION is used to signal to the compiler that a definition module is to be compiled. Sample, of course, is a programmer-selected identifier.

A definition module may import objects from other library modules. After any import list appears, a list of those objects available to the outside Modula-2 environment is written as an export list. Note should be made of the fact that an export list associated with a definition module must include the reserved word QUALIFIED. Thus, we have an EXPORT QUALIFIED list associated with each definition module. After the export list, all public declarations and procedure headings are written. Finally, the definition module is completed with an appropriate END statement. A definition module does not contain a module body.

What is meant by a qualified export list and why must it be employed? The word QUALIFIED requires that all references to the exported objects from the definition module in question must be preceded by the module's identifier followed by a period, in much the same way that a field of a record is qualified by the identifier of the record of which it is a part.

For example, if a definition module named Structures exports an object named LIST, then to reference that object, Structures.LIST, is written. The qualifying of each object from a definition module is required since it is not known beforehand into what programs the object may be imported.

What if this qualification was not required and the object LIST was to be imported into a program which already has used the identifier LIST for another object? Since the same identifier cannot be used for two different objects, the use of the qualifier Structures avoids the ensuing identifier clash.

You may feel that the above discussion contradicts what we have been doing thus far when importing objects from library modules (such as WriteString and WriteLn from library module InOut). Since we were assured that there would be no identifier clash in the programs we were composing, we were able to do a blanket qualification within our program modules by the use of the reserved word FROM in our import lists, and were able to name the specific objects to be imported. Therefore, for the example stated earlier, if we write the import list as follows:

FROM Structures IMPORT LIST;

then we need not prefix any reference to the object LIST with Structures within the program.

Listing 6.1a shows an example of a definition module. The objects defined within which appear on the module's export list, if imported into a program would allow the programmer to declare a variable of type BINARY, call up a procedure to write out a value of type BINARY, and to invoke a function procedure that converts a cardinal number between 0 and 255 into its binary equivalent number.

```
DEFINITION MODULE BinaryStuff;

EXPORT QUALIFIED BINARY,WriteBinary,DecimalToBinary;

TYPE BINARY=ARRAY[0..7] OF BOOLEAN;

    PROCEDURE WriteBinary(b:BINARY);

    PROCEDURE DecimalToBinary(x:CARDINAL):BINARY;

END BinaryStuff.
```

LISTING 6.1a

6.3 Implementation Modules

The general form of an implementation module is:

```
IMPLEMENTATION MODULE Sample;

<IMPORT lists, if any>

    <CONST, TYPE, VAR declarations, needed for>
    <module excluding declarations listed in      >
    <corresponding Definition Module              >

    <implementations of procedures declared in    >
    <Definition Module; local declarations,        >
    <if any                                        >

BEGIN
    <module body, optional>
END Sample.
```

In this case, the reserved word IMPLEMENTATION is used to signal the compiler that an implementation module is to be compiled. Note that the same module identifier—Sample—must be used for the implementation module as for its corresponding definition module.

After the IMPORT lists, all private declarations are made. Any CONST, TYPE, or VAR declaration made publicly in the definition module should not be repeated here. On the other hand, procedure headings, complete with their parameter lists, must appear in the implementation module, along with the code that implements those procedures. Finally, the implementation module is completed with an optional module body followed by an END statement.

Listing 6.1b illustrates an example of an implementation module which corresponds to the definition module of Listing 6.1a.

```
IMPLEMENTATION MODULE BinaryStuff;

FROM InOut IMPORT Write;

    PROCEDURE WriteBinary(b:BINARY);
    VAR i:CARDINAL;
    BEGIN
      FOR i:=7 TO 0 BY -1 DO
        IF b[i] THEN
          Write('1');
        ELSE
          Write('0');
        END;
      END;
    END WriteBinary;

    PROCEDURE DecimalToBinary(x:CARDINAL):BINARY;
    VAR b:BINARY;
        i:CARDINAL;
    BEGIN
      FOR i:=0 TO 7 DO
        IF (x MOD 2)=1 THEN
          b[i]:=TRUE;
        ELSE
          b[i]:=FALSE;
        END;
        x:=x DIV 2;
      END;
      RETURN b;
    END DecimalToBinary;

END BinaryStuff.
```

LISTING 6.1b

6.4 Using the Library Module Pair

Now that we have a fully implemented library module pair, we can import some or all of its available objects into any program module (or implementation module). An example of the use of our module pair can be found in Listing 6.1c, which should be self-explanatory.

```
MODULE BinaryDriver;

FROM InOut IMPORT WriteString,WriteLn,ReadCard;
FROM BinaryStuff IMPORT BINARY,WriteBinary,DecimalToBinary;

VAR number:CARDINAL;
    b:BINARY;

BEGIN
    WriteString('Enter a cardinal number, (0..255): ');
    ReadCard(number);
    WriteLn;
    b:=DecimalToBinary(number);
    WriteString('Its binary equivalent is: ');
    WriteBinary(b);
END BinaryDriver.
```

LISTING 6.1c

6.5 The Module Interface Diagram

To visualize the interfacing between modules within a Modula-2 programming system, a module interface diagram can be drawn. Such a diagram graphically describes the interdependencies between program modules, programmer-developed library module pairs, and the library module pairs provided with the Modula-2 implementation being used.

In the diagram, circles (or rectangles) are used to represent compilation units, with both definition and implementation modules sharing one such circle. Interfacing between modules is represented by directed line segments with arrowheads indicating the importation-exportation directions for objects. Individual objects may be listed conveniently beside their respective interfacing lines. Interdependencies between system-supplied library modules provided with the Modula-2 system are not shown in the module interface diagram.

As an example, Figure 6.1 illustrates the module interface diagram for the small programming system just completed.

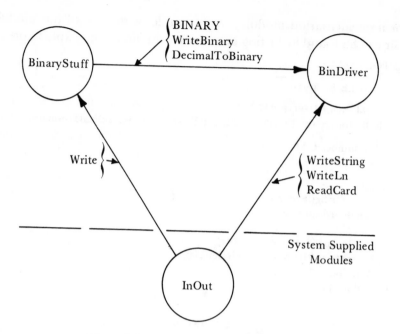

Figure 6.1. **Module interface diagram.**

6.6 Another Way to Import Objects

Thus far, all our importations into compilation units have been accomplished through the use of the coding

FROM <module identifier> IMPORT <objects>;

But there is another way to import objects into a compilation unit, as eluded to back in section 6.2. Instead of specifying the objects to be imported on the import list itself, we can merely write

IMPORT <module identifier>;

So, for example, instead of writing,

FROM InOut IMPORT WriteString,WriteLn,WriteCard;

we can simply write,

IMPORT InOut;

But there is a trade-off! When using any object from a module that has been imported by our shortcut method, the object's identifier must be qualified by prefixing each invocation of the object with the module's name. So, if we have imported InOut into a program module by writing

IMPORT InOut;

then, if we want to call the WriteString procedure, we must write

InOut.WriteString("A plague on both your houses.");

Note that a period is used to separate the module identifier from the object identifier.

After reading section 6.2, the advantage of qualifying an imported object should be obvious. It allows us to, in effect, not to be concerned over the inadvertent duplication of object names.

6.7 A Small Case Study

Consider that we wish to develop a small programming system that will give the user the capability of adding, subtracting, multiplying, and dividing any two complex numbers given in rectangular form. Furthermore, the results of the operations should also be in rectangular form.

These general complex number operations are to be made available to a simple complex arithmetic calculator program which is menu-driven, but they should also be made available for any future needs dealing with complex algebra.

With the above task in mind, it would be reasonable to develop a library module pair whose exported objects would include the four aforementioned arithmetic operations and a data type to house the real and imaginary parts of any complex number. To this end, we have developed DEFINITION MODULE ComplexOperations (see Listing 6.2a). In addition, we have included on the export list PROCEDURE Assign, along with function procedures RealPart, ImaginaryPart, and Conjugate. (The latter, although not explicitly asked for, may come in handy during some future applications, as well as the fact that it is used in the implementation of the function procedure Divide.) Assign, RealPart, and ImaginaryPart allow us to not have to access the details of the data structure used to implement the concept of a complex number. Thus, as you look over the program module CompDr (see Listing 6.2c) developed for this small case study, you will not find any reference to the inner structure of the data type Complex.

In Listing 6.2b, we have the complete IMPLEMENTATION MODULE ComplexOperations. The desired simple complex arithmetic calculator MODULE CompDr is shown in Listing 6.2c. To help envision the interdependencies established for this programming system a module interface diagram appears in Figure 6.2. The details of the code should be self-explanatory.

```
DEFINITION MODULE ComplexOperations;

EXPORT QUALIFIED Complex,Assign,RealPart,ImaginaryPart,
                 Add,Subtract,Multiply,Divide,Conjugate;

TYPE Complex=RECORD
                  real:REAL;
                  imaginary:REAL;
             END;

   PROCEDURE Assign(re,im:REAL;VAR z:Complex);

   PROCEDURE RealPart(z:Complex):REAL;

   PROCEDURE ImaginaryPart(z:Complex):REAL;

   PROCEDURE Add(z1,z2:Complex):Complex;

   PROCEDURE Subtract(z1,z2:Complex):Complex;

   PROCEDURE Multiply(z1,z2:Complex):Complex;

   PROCEDURE Divide(z1,z2:Complex):Complex;

   PROCEDURE Conjugate(z:Complex):Complex;

END ComplexOperations.
```

LISTING 6.2a

```
IMPLEMENTATION MODULE ComplexOperations;

FROM InOut IMPORT WriteString,WriteLn;

    PROCEDURE Assign(re,im:REAL;VAR z:Complex);
    BEGIN
        z.real:=re;
        z.imaginary:=im;
    END Assign;

    PROCEDURE RealPart(z:Complex):REAL;
    BEGIN
        RETURN z.real;
    END RealPart;

    PROCEDURE ImaginaryPart(z:Complex):REAL;
    BEGIN
        RETURN z.imaginary;
    END ImaginaryPart;

    PROCEDURE Add(z1,z2:Complex):Complex;
    VAR z:Complex;
    BEGIN
        z.real:=z1.real+z2.real;
        z.imaginary=z1.imaginary+z2.imaginary;
        RETURN z;
    END Add;

    PROCEDURE Subtract(z1,z2:Complex):Complex;
    VAR z:Complex;
    BEGIN
        z.real:=z1.real -z2.real;
        z.imaginary=z1.imaginary-z2.imaginary;
        RETURN z;
    END Subtract;

    PROCEDURE Multiply(z1,z2:Complex):Complex;
    VAR z:Complex;
    BEGIN
        z.real:=z1.real*z2.real -z1.imaginary*z2.imaginary;
        z.imaginary:=z1.real*z2.imaginary+z1.imaginary*z2.real;
        RETURN z;
    END Multiply;

    PROCEDURE Divide(z1,z2:Complex):Complex;
    VAR z2Conjugate,numerator,z:Complex;
        denominator:REAL;
    BEGIN
        IF (z2.real=0.0) & (z2.imaginary=0.0) THEN
        WriteLn;
        WriteString('Divide by zero error!');
```

```
        WriteLn;
        HALT;
     END;
     z2Conjugate:=Conjugate(z2);
     numerator:=Multiply(z1,z2Conjugate);
     denominator:=z2.real*z2.real+z2.imaginary*z2.imaginary;
     z.real:=numerator.real/denominator;
     z.imaginary:=numerator.imaginary/denominator;
     RETURN z;
  END Divide;

  PROCEDURE Conjugate(z:Complex):Complex;
  BEGIN
     z.imaginary:=-z.imaginary;
     RETURN z;
  END Conjugate;

END ComplexOperations.
```

LISTING 6.2b

```
MODULE CompDr;
FROM InOut IMPORT WriteLn,WriteString,Read,Write;
FROM RealInOut IMPORT ReadReal,WriteReal;
FROM Screen IMPORT ClearScreen,GotoXY;
        (* module Screen or its equivalent should be in any complete library *)
FROM ComplexOperations IMPORT Complex,Assign,RealPart,ImaginaryPart,
                                Add,Subtract,Multiply,Divide;

  PROCEDURE Stop;
  VAR z:CHAR;
  BEGIN
     GotoXY(0,22); (* GotoXY positions the cursor appropriately *)
     WriteString('Type <SP> to continue ... ');
     GotoXY(79,0);
     Read(z);
  END Stop;

  PROCEDURE Menu(VAR ch:CHAR);
  TYPE CharSet=SET OF CHAR;
  VAR Good:BOOLEAN;
  BEGIN
     ClearScreen;
     GotoXY(0,3);
     WriteString('Would you like to:');
     WriteLn;WriteLn;
     WriteString('     A(dd');WriteLn;
     WriteLn;
     WriteString('     S(ubtract');WriteLn;
```

```
    WriteLn;
    WriteString('     M(ultiply');WriteLn;
    WriteLn;
    WriteString('     D(ivide');WriteLn;
    WriteLn;
    WriteString('       two complex numbers, or');
    WriteLn;WriteLn;
    WriteString('     E(xit the program?');
    GotoXY(0,22);
    WriteString('Enter appropriate letter: ');
    REPEAT
      Read(ch);
      ch:=CAP(ch);
      IF NOT (ch IN CharSet {'A','S','M','D','E'}) THEN
        Write(CHR(8));Write(CHR(32)); (* screen formatting, see ASCII code *)
        Write(CHR(8));Write(CHR(7));
        Good:=FALSE;
      ELSE
        Good:=TRUE;
      END;
    UNTIL Good;
    IF ch='E' THEN HALT;END;
END Menu;

PROCEDURE DataEntry(ch:CHAR;VAR z1,z2:Complex);
VAR message:ARRAY[0..13] OF CHAR;
    RePart,ImPart:REAL;
BEGIN
  CASE ch OF
    'A':message:=' Addition';|
    'S':message:=' Subtraction';|
    'M':message:='Multiplication';|
    'D':message:='Division';
  END;
  ClearScreen;
  GotoXY(0,2);
  WriteString(message);
  WriteString('  of Two Complex Numbers');
  GotoXY(0,5);
  WriteString('Enter first number,(real & imag. parts)');
  WriteLn;
  WriteString('(end entry with a <space>):');
  WriteLn;WriteLn;
  ReadReal(RePart);
  WriteString('+ j( ');
  ReadReal(ImPart);
  WriteString(') ');
  Assign(RePart,ImPart,z1);
```

```
        WriteLn;WriteLn;
        WriteString('Enter second number,(in same manner):');
        WriteLn;WriteLn;
        ReadReal(RePart);
        WriteString('+ j( ');
        ReadReal(ImPart);
        WriteString(') ');
        Assign(RePart,ImPart,z2);
    END DataEntry;


    PROCEDURE Compute(ch:CHAR;z1,z2:Complex;VAR Result: Complex);
    BEGIN
        CASE ch OF
           'A':Result:=Add(z1,z2);|
           ' S':Result:=Subtract(z1,z2);|
           'M':Result:=Multiply(z1,z2);|
           'D':Result:=Divide(z1,z2);
        END;
    END Compute;


    PROCEDURE Display(Answer:Complex);
    BEGIN
        GotoXY(0,16);
        WriteString('The answer is:');WriteLn;
        WriteLn;
        WriteReal(RealPart(Answer),11);
        WriteString(' + j( ');
        WriteReal(ImaginaryPart(Answer),11);
        WriteString(' ) ');
        Stop;
    END Display;


VAR choice:CHAR;
    Z1,Z2,Result:Complex;


  BEGIN (* main body *)
    LOOP
        Menu(choice);(*loop EXIT within Menu*)
        DataEntry(choice,Z1,Z2);
        Compute(choice,Z1,Z2,Result);
        Display(Result);
    END;
  END CompDr.
```

LISTING 6.2c

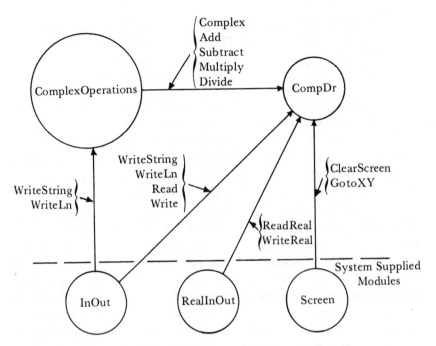

Figure 6.2 Module interface diagram for Listings 6.2a, b, & c.

6.8 A Case Study of a Limited Sort and Search Library Module

As a second small case study concerning the development of library module pairs and separate compilation, we present the following programming problem specification:

It is desired to have a library module that can search and sort any one-dimensional array of items. The module should contain the following objects:

1. An appropriate array data type to house the items.

2. A sorting routine whose input is an unsorted array and whose output is that array, sorted.

3. A routine that can search an unsorted array for the presence of a particular desired item. (Of course, such a routine can be used to search a sorted array as well, but it would not take advantage of the fact that the items in the array are sorted.)

4. A routine that can search a sorted array for the presence of a particular desired item. (This search routine should take advantage of the fact that the array is sorted and therefore be quite a bit faster than the unsorted array search routine.)

The specifications are a little ambitious for us at this point in our study of Modula-2. So, we will have to settle for a somewhat more modest and more limited sort and search library module pair.

We will design the library module so that the only array of items that can be used in conjunction with it is an array of integers. Furthermore, the maximum number of integers that will be able to be searched and/or sorted will be 1,000, although the sorting and searching routines will be able to handle smaller arrays by use of a passed parameter indicating the number of integers in the array that are to be operated on.

Thus our library module will only be usable with arrays of 1,000 or less integer values. In Chapter 8, we will learn how to write routines which can serve one-dimensional arrays of any size as well as learn how to begin to develop *generic* routines—that is, routines which can be used with virtually any data type. At that time you might try your hand at redesigning the library module pair that we will present here, giving it a more "generic" flavor.

For now, we will briefly discuss the limited programming task that we are capable of taking on at this time. The library module pair which solves our programming problem has been named LimitedSortAndSearch and appears as Listings 6.3a and 6.3b.

A glance at the definition module (Listing 6.3a) reveals that a data type consisting of 1,001 integer elements has been declared and placed on the module's export list. Why 1,001 elements rather than 1,000? The answer lies in the fact that one of our search routines will need one additional element beyond the maximum number that our integer array can accommodate (see PROCEDURE SearchSequentially in Listing 6.3b).

The three operations developed for use with the integer array data type are exported as SortArray, SearchSequentially, and SearchSortedArray.

PROCEDURE SortArray has two parameters—an integer array (Numbers) to be sorted along with the number of items (n) that actually hold valid data to be sorted. Note that the integer array variable is passed by reference, as would be expected since, after the array has been sorted, it must be passed back to the calling part of whatever program module may be making use of SortArray.

The two search routines found in DEFINITION MODULE Limited-SortAndSearch have identical parameter lists. Any appropriate integer array, along with the number of valid elements within that array and the desired integer value being searched for, are passed by value to the search routine. Returned are two parameter values—one to indicate whether the desired integer value has been found within the array and the other to indicate the array index value where the first occurence of the desired value has been found. (If the desired value is not found, the index value is set to zero.)

```
DEFINITION MODULE LimitedSortAndSearch;

EXPORT QUALIFIED IntArray,SortArray,SearchSequentially,SearchSortedArray;

TYPE IntArray=ARRAY[1..1001] OF INTEGER;

  PROCEDURE SortArray(VAR Numbers:IntArray;n:CARDINAL);

  PROCEDURE SearchSequentially(Numbers:IntArray;n:CARDINAL;
                              DesiredValue:INTEGER;
                              VAR found:BOOLEAN;
                              VAR Index:CARDINAL);

  PROCEDURE SearchSortedArray(Numbers:IntArray;n:CARDINAL;
                              DesiredValue:INTEGER;
                              VAR found:BOOLEAN;
                              VAR Index:CARDINAL);
END LimitedSortAndSearch.
```

LISTING 6.3a

The implementation of the above-mentioned operations on integer arrays can be found, of course, in the library module's implementation module (Listing 6.3b).

The algorithm used for sorting is the well-known "bubble sort". If you are not familiar with it you may wish to trace it through using a small sample integer array.

PROCEDURE SearchSequentially performs a search through an integer array in a linear fashion. That is, the search begins at the first element of the array. If that element is not the desired value, the search moves on to the next element. Each succeeding element is checked to see if it matches the desired value. This sequential search continues until a match is found. Note that a match will always be found because even if the desired value is not in the original array, it has been added as a sentinel value to the end of the array. (That is why provision has been made for one extra element in our exported data type.) Once found, the element's index value is appropriately set.

PROCEDURE SearchSortedArray performs a search on a sorted array. The algorithm used to do the job is commonly referred to as a binary search algorithm. It starts by dividing the array into approximately two halves and determines within which half the desired integer value might be (based on the fact that the array has been sorted). The half within which the number would definitely not be found is then disregarded as further processing takes place. Repeatedly, the remaining portion of the array is halved with one of the halves being disregarded. This process continues until either the desired value is found or the remaining portion of the array is reduced to effectively no elements.

```
IMPLEMENTATION MODULE LimitedSortAndSearch;

   PROCEDURE SortArray(VAR Numbers:IntArray;n:CARDINAL);
   (* a bubble sort agorithm *)
   VAR i,Temp:INTEGER;
        NoExchanges:BOOLEAN;
   BEGIN
      REPEAT
        NoExchanges:=TRUE;
        FOR i:=1 TO n-1 DO
           IF Numbers[i] > Numbers[i+1] THEN
              Temp:=Numbers[i] ;
              Numbers[i] :=Numbers[i+1] ;
              Numbers[i+1] :=Temp;
              NoExchanges:=FALSE;
           END;
        END;
      UNTIL NoExchanges;
   END SortArray;

   PROCEDURE SearchSequentially(Numbers:IntArray;n:CARDINAL;
                                DesiredValue:INTEGER;
                                VAR found:BOOLEAN;
                                VAR Index:CARDINAL);
   (* a sequential search algorithm *)
   VAR i:CARDINAL;
   BEGIN
      Numbers[n+1] :=DesiredValue; (*install sentinel*)
      i:=1;
      WHILE Numbers[i] #DesiredValue DO INC(i);END;
      IF i<=n THEN
        found:=TRUE;
```

```
        Index:=i;
     ELSE
        found:=FALSE;
        Index:=0;
     END;
  END SearchSequentially;

  PROCEDURE SearchSortedArray(Numbers:IntArray;n:CARDINAL;
                              DesiredValue:INTEGER;
                              VAR found:BOOLEAN;
                              VAR Index:CARDINAL);
  (* a binary search algorithm *)
  VAR low,middle,high:CARDINAL;
  BEGIN
     low:=1;
     high:=n;
     REPEAT
        middle:=(low+high) DIV 2;
        IF DesiredValue<Numbers[middle] THEN
           high:=middle-1;
        ELSIF DesiredValue>Numbers[middle] THEN
           low:=middle+1;
        END;
     UNTIL (DesiredValue=Numbers[middle]) OR (low>high);
     IF low<=high THEN
        found:=TRUE;
        Index:=middle;
     ELSE
        found:=FALSE;
        Index:=0;
     END;
  END SearchSortedArray;

END LimitedSortAndSearch.
```

LISTING 6.3b

In Listing 6.4 we present a driver program, MODULE SortAnd-
SearchDriver, to test out the facilities offered by MODULE Limited-
SortAndSearch. To test LimitedSortAndSearch, an appropriate integer array must be generated. This has been accomplished through
the repeated use of a pseudo-random number generator written and
placed within local module RandomNumbers. That module generates
(based on a REAL seed value) a random number whose value is greater
or equal to zero but less than one.

The only object exported from MODULE RandomNumbers is the
function procedure Random. Thus, Random is made available to the

rest of the program and is, in fact, called in the program's main body. Each time Random is invoked, the value of seed is changed. Note that each new value of seed remains in existence even though control of execution is passed out of seed's local module and on to the main body of SortAndSearchDriver.

Therein lies an application of one of the powers of the module concept as discussed in Chapter 5. Although we do not want the variable seed to be visible in the program's main body and other subroutines (where it could be incorrectly accessed and modified), we do want it to retain its existence even when execution control is outside RandomNumbers. By declaring seed at the global level of the local module, we have accomplished the desired separation of visibility from existence.

Within the main body of SortAndSearchDriver, the value returned by Random (a value from zero to just short of one) is converted to an appropriate integer value between 0 and 32766 with the help of the built-in function procedure TRUNC.

Note that a display routine has been coded so that we can view the results of any tests performed on SortArray, SearchSequentially, and SearchSortedArray.

```
MODULE SortAndSearchDriver;

FROM InOut IMPORT WriteString,WriteLn,WriteInt,WriteCard,Write,
                  ReadInt,ReadCard,Read;
FROM RealInOut IMPORT ReadReal;
FROM LimitedSortAndSearch IMPORT IntArray,SortArray,
                  SearchSequentially,SearchSortedArray;

    MODULE RandomNumbers;

    IMPORT WriteString,WriteLn,ReadReal;
    EXPORT Random;

    VAR seed:REAL;

        PROCEDURE Random():REAL;
        BEGIN
           seed:=seed*27.1828+31.2345;
           seed:=seed-FLOAT(TRUNC(seed));
           RETURN seed;
        END Random;

    BEGIN (* RandomNumbers *)
        WriteString('Enter seed value, (ex. 1.2): ');
        ReadReal(seed);
        WriteLn;
```

```
END RandomNumbers;

PROCEDURE Stop;
VAR z:CHAR;
BEGIN
   WriteLn;
   WriteString('Type any key to continue...');
   Read(z);
   Write(14C); (* clears screen *)
END Stop;

PROCEDURE DisplayArray(Nums:IntArray;N:CARDINAL);
VAR i:CARDINAL;
BEGIN
   WriteLn;
   WriteString('The numbers are:');
   WriteLn;
   FOR i:=1 TO N DO
     WriteInt(Nums[i],5);
     WriteLn;
   END;
END DisplayArray;

VAR Nums:IntArray;
    N,i,index:CARDINAL;
    num,DesiredValue:INTEGER;
    found:BOOLEAN;
    z:CHAR;

BEGIN (* main body *)
   WriteString('Enter number of elements in array:');
   ReadCard(N);
   WriteLn;
   FOR i:=1 TO N DO
     num:=TRUNC(32767.0*Random());
     Nums[i]:=num;
   END;
   DisplayArray(Nums,N);
   Stop;
   WriteString('Enter desired value:');
   ReadInt(DesiredValue);
   WriteLn;WriteLn;
   WriteString('Type any key to begin Search......');
   Read(z);
   SearchSequentially(Nums,N,DesiredValue,found,index);
   WriteLn;
   IF found THEN
     WriteInt(DesiredValue,7);
     WriteString(' has been found as element # ');
     WriteCard(index,1);
```

```
        WriteLn;WriteLn;
      ELSE
        WriteInt(DesiredValue,7);
        WriteString(' is not on the list');
        WriteLn;WriteLn;
      END;
      Stop;
      WriteLn;
      WriteString('Type any key to begin Sorting ......');
      Read(z);
      SortArray(Nums,N);
      DisplayArray(Nums,N);
      Stop;
      WriteLn;
      WriteString('Type any key to begin Search ......');(* for same DesiredValue *)
      Read(z);
      SearchSortedArray(Nums,N,DesiredValue,found,index);
      WriteLn;
      IF found THEN
        WriteInt(DesiredValue,7);
        WriteString(' has been found as element # ');
        WriteCard(index,1);
        WriteLn;WriteLn;
      ELSE
        WriteInt(DesiredValue,7);
        WriteString(' is not on the list');
        WriteLn;WriteLn;
      END;
    END SortAndSearchDriver.
```

LISTING 6.4

You might type the library module presented in this section into your computer and test out its facilities. Upon typing it in, the various parts of the system must be compiled in a particular order. First the definition module must be compiled, followed by either its corresponding implementation module or some program module which imports its facilities (either SortAndSearchDriver or one that you may compose yourself). Only after all three parts of this software project are compiled can the program module be executed.

If you do type LimitedSortAndSearch into your computer along with an appropriate driver program, you will find that if a rather sizable array is to be sorted, it will take quite a bit of time. The bubble sort routine used in PROCEDURE SortArray really turns out to be a rather poor choice of algorithms.

A significantly faster algorithm (although far from the fastest) is shown as Listing 6.5. We bring this to your attention so that you may substitute this new implementation of SortArray for the earlier one. The process is simple! Just substitute the code of Listing 6.5 for the original PROCEDURE SortArray in IMPLEMENTATION MODULE LimitedSortAndSearch. Next, recompile IMPLEMENTATION MODULE LimitedSortAndSearch. No further recompilation is necessary. Neither DEFINITION MODULE LimitedSortAndSearch or any driver program module you may be using need be recompiled. That is the power of separate compilation.

Now you should be able to execute your test program and note the faster speed with which a sizable integer array is sorted with our new SortArray algorithm.

```
PROCEDURE SortArray(VAR Numbers:IntArray;n:CARDINAL);
(* a selection sort algorithm *)
VAR i,Temp,StartIndex,index,small:INTEGER;
BEGIN
    FOR StartIndex:=1 TO n-1 DO
        small:=Numbers[StartIndex] ;
        index:=StartIndex;
        FOR i:=StartIndex+1 TO n DO
            IF Numbers[i] <small THEN
                small:=Numbers[i] ;
                index:=i;
            END;
        END;
        Temp:=Numbers[index] ;
        Numbers[index] :=Numbers[StartIndex] ;
        Numbers[StartIndex] :=Temp;
    END;
END SortArray;
```

LISTING 6.5

7

Library Modules–Part I

In this chapter, consideration will be given to a number of the library modules which in some form or other will be contained within the Modula-2 "standard" library. Because of the fact that the Modula-2 language and its accompanying "standard" library has not yet been standardized, it is not possible to present to you a fixed set of library modules for discussion. In light of this fact, we will present a set of modules whose tasks are expected to be available with any Modula-2 implementation in a form which in terms of function closely resembles the modules as offered here. As we venture forth we will point out some known differences between the modules discussed here and other implementations.

The "standard" modules under consideration in this chapter are InOut, RealInOut, SYSTEM, and Files. Although the ensuing discussion will not be exhaustive, it is included so that you may develop enough understanding of the functionality of many of the importable objects from each library module whether they correspond directly to the Modula-2 implementation with which you are working or not. It is hoped that throughout this development you will refer to your particular Modula-2 implementation's documentation.

Sample test programs will be included in most sections, although they may not necessarily make use of all the objects available in the module under consideration.

7.1 MODULE InOut

MODULE InOut gives us the capability to read and write to the default input and output devices which are usually a keyboard and monitor screen (the console), respectively. The data types that can be read and written are CHAR, arrays of CHARs (i.e. strings of characters), INTEGER, and CARDINAL. Additionally, some implementations of InOut handle data of type REAL. The InOut described here does not.

115

Data of type REAL will be dealt with through MODULE RealInOut, which is the subject of the next section.

The procedures for reading constants of the data types handled by InOut are Read, ReadString, ReadInt, and ReadCard, while the procedures for writing constants of those data types are Write, WriteString, WriteInt, and WriteCard. In addition, there is a WriteLn procedure which writes a carriage return and line feed to the output device. Also, cardinal numbers can be written to the output device as octal (base 8) or hexadecimal (base 16) numbers by using WriteOct or WriteHex procedures, respectively.

Listing 7.1, InOut's definition module, shows the number and type of parameters for each of the aforementioned procedures, among others. The cardinal number, n, found as a parameter in many of the write operations, should be set to the number of columns desired for writing out the numerical value.

It is possible to redirect the input and output to other than the default devices by using the procedures OpenInput and OpenOutput. The single parameter needed for these procedures should indicate the disk files (or other devices, such as a printer) that are to be opened. The default devices are automatically closed when OpenInput and OpenOutput are invoked.

```
DEFINITION MODULE InOut;

EXPORT QUALIFIED
                    EOL,Done,termCH,
                    OpenInput,OpenOutput,CloseInput,CloseOutput,
                    Read,ReadString,ReadInt,ReadCard,
                    Write,WriteLn,WriteString,WriteInt,WriteCard,
                    WriteOct,WriteHex;

CONST EOL=15C; (* system dependent *)

VAR Done:BOOLEAN;
    termCH:CHAR;

PROCEDURE OpenInput   (defext:ARRAY OF CHAR);
PROCEDURE OpenOutput (defext:ARRAY OF CHAR);
PROCEDURE CloseInput;
PROCEDURE CloseOutput;
PROCEDURE Read        (VAR ch:CHAR);
PROCEDURE ReadString  (VAR s:ARRAY OF CHAR);
PROCEDURE ReadInt     (VAR x:INTEGER);
PROCEDURE ReadCard    (VAR x:CARDINAL);
PROCEDURE Write       (ch:CHAR);
```

```
PROCEDURE WriteLn;
PROCEDURE WriteString  (s:ARRAY OF CHAR);
PROCEDURE WriteInt     (x:INTEGER;n:CARDINAL);
PROCEDURE WriteCard    (x,n:CARDINAL);
PROCEDURE WriteOct     (x,n:CARDINAL);
PROCEDURE WriteHex     (x,n:CARDINAL);

END InOut.
```

LISTING 7.1

Upon closing any new file or device used for input or output, control returns to the default devices (keyboard and screen). Closing is performed by the procedures CloseInput and CloseOutput.

Two variables and a constant are also available for use upon importation from InOut. The Boolean variable Done is assigned a value after every read operation and every opening or closing of a redirected input or output file. Done is set to TRUE if the operation is successful, or FALSE if not. The CHAR variable termCH is set to whatever character is used to terminate a read operation (e.g. a carriage return, $<cr>$). The constant EOL (whose value is system-dependent) is set to the End-Of-Line character and can be used to sense when an *end of line* has occurred.

There are more details concerning some of the importable objects in MODULE InOut. You should consult your particular Modula-2 User's Manual to become familiar with them.

A sample program which makes use of many of the objects within InOut can be found as Listing 7.2. The output from a typical execution of the program is included.

```
MODULE TestInOut;

FROM InOut IMPORT EOL,Done,
                  OpenOutput,CloseOutput,OpenInput,CloseInput,
                  Write,WriteLn,WriteString,WriteCard,WriteOct,WriteHex,
                  ReadCard,Read;

VAR HardCopy:BOOLEAN;
    PROCEDURE ErrorHandler;
    BEGIN
      IF NOT Done THEN
        WriteString('File error!');
        HALT;
      END;
    END ErrorHandler;
```

```
PROCEDURE FirstTest;
VAR num:CARDINAL;
BEGIN
   WriteLn;WriteLn;
   WriteString('Enter any cardinal number: ');WriteLn;
   ReadCard(num);
   IF HardCopy THEN
      WriteCard(num,5);
      WriteLn;
   END;
   WriteCard(num,10);WriteLn;
   WriteOct(num,10);WriteLn;
   WriteHex(num,10);WriteLn;
   WriteLn;
END FirstTest;

PROCEDURE SecondTest;
VAR ch:CHAR;
BEGIN
   WriteString('Enter string of characters, then <cr>:');WriteLn;
   REPEAT
      Read(ch);
       IF HardCopy THEN Write(ch);END;
   UNTIL ch=EOL;
   WriteLn;WriteLn;
END SecondTest;

BEGIN
   HardCopy:=FALSE;
   FirstTest;
   SecondTest;
   OpenOutput(' #6:'); (* PRINTER: *)
   ErrorHandler;
   HardCopy:=TRUE;
   FirstTest;
   SecondTest;
   CloseOutput;
   ErrorHandler;
   WriteString('A successful transfer');
   WriteLn;WriteLn;
   OpenInput(' #5:TESTINOUT.TEXT');
   ErrorHandler;
   SecondTest;
   CloseInput;
   ErrorHandler;
   WriteString('Another successful transfer');
END TestInOut.
```

Screen output:

Enter any cardinal number:
1984
     1984
   003700
    07C0

Enter string of characters, then $<$cr$>$:
Modula-2

printer output:

Output file? #6:   Enter any cardinal number:
250   250
goodbye   250
A successful transfer   000372

Input file? #5:TESTINOUT.TEXT   00FA
Enter string of characters, then $<$cr$>$:
MODULE TestInOut;   Enter string of characters, then $<$cr$>$:
goodbye

Another successful transfer

LISTING 7.2

The program performs a pair of tests dealing with data input and output from the default files (the keyboard and screen, respectively) and redirection of the input and output.

The Boolean variable HardCopy is used to write entered values to the printer when the output has been redirected to it.

The first test prompts the user for a cardinal number. If the response (as indicated in the "screen output") is 1984, then that value is written to the output device, initially the CRT screen, in bases 10, 8, and 16, as shown. The second test prompts for a string which is read from the keyboard character by character until the end-of-line character (carriage return) is sensed.

Next, the output is redirected to a printer. (All redirections automatically place a prompt, either "Output file?" or "Input file?" on the output device. A response of " #6:" or "PRINTER:" (for a p-system based Modula-2) makes the printer the new output device.) If the opening of the printer was unsuccessful, the program would be terminated after display of an error message through the invocation of an error handler. This not being the case in our test run, the two tests are rerun, this time with the prompts and output directed to the printer. Since input still comes from the keyboard, it, as usual, is automatically echoed to the screen (thus the "250" and "goodbye" appear as screen output).

Closing the output redirects output to the screen. After error checking and a message, the input is redirected to a file on a diskette mounted as volume # 5:. (The file happens to be the text of this program that is being executed.) A line of text is copied from the file and written to the screen, after which the input device is closed (activating the default input device, the keyboard, again). Finally, a message is written to the screen and the program terminates.

7.2 MODULE RealInOut

Type REAL values can be read and written to the input and output devices, respectively, through the importation of MODULE RealInOut. Listing 7.3, which is a listing of DEFINITION MODULE RealInOut, indicates the objects that are available to the programmer. (Again, this depends on the Modula-2 implementation with which you are working. Some implementations may incorporate the reading and writing of data type REAL within MODULE InOut.)

```
DEFINITION MODULE RealInOut;

EXPORT QUALIFIED
                Done,
                ReadReal,
                WriteReal,WriteRealOct;

VAR Done:BOOLEAN;

PROCEDURE ReadReal      (VAR x:REAL);
PROCEDURE WriteReal     (x:REAL;n:CARDINAL);
PROCEDURE WriteRealOct(x:REAL);

END RealInOut.
```

LISTING 7.3

Reading from the keyboard is accomplished through the invocation of the ReadReal procedure while writing to the screen can be accomplished through the use of the WriteReal procedure. Note that WriteReal has a second parameter of type CARDINAL associated with it for setting the number of columns desired for writing out the REAL value, which is consistent with the "Write" procedures in MODULE InOut.

Redirection of ReadReal and WriteReal to other than the default devices can be done by invoking OpenInput and OpenOutput from MODULE InOut, while returning to the default devices can be accomplished through the CloseInput and CloseOutput procedures of MODULE InOut.

PROCEDURE WriteRealOct displays, in octal notation, the bit pattern of a real number as it is stored internally in a particular computer. For example, if the real number –5.28000E+01 is stored in a variable named realnum, then execution of the instruction WriteRealOct(realnum) would result in the following screen output (for the computer used to verify most of the programs of this book):

031463 141123

which represents the following 32 bits stored in memory:

0011001100110011 1100001001010011.

The Boolean variable Done is set after each invocation of ReadReal and operates just as MODULE InOut's object Done operates. It should be noted, though, that RealInOut's Done is a separate variable from InOut's Done.

Listing 7.4 contains an example of the use of the objects found in MODULE RealInOut. The screen output from a typical execution of the program is shown. Note that if an illegal string is entered as a real number (for example, 4,076.9), it will be flagged by the Boolean variable Done.

```
MODULE TestRealInOut;

FROM RealInOut IMPORT Done,ReadReal,WriteReal,WriteRealOct;
FROM InOut IMPORT WriteString,WriteLn;
CONST SENTINEL=999.9;
VAR RealNum:REAL;

BEGIN
   REPEAT
      WriteLn;WriteLn;
      WriteString("Enter any REAL number,");WriteLn;
      WriteString("(Enter 999.9 to end): ");
      ReadReal(RealNum);
      IF NOT Done THEN
         WriteLn;
```

```
        WriteString("INPUT ERROR!");
        HALT;
      END;
      WriteLn;
      WriteString("The number entered is:");
      WriteLn;
      WriteString("in base 10, (decimal): ");
      WriteReal(RealNum,10);WriteLn;
      WriteLn;
      WriteString("This number's internal format in octal");WriteLn;
      WriteString("notation is: ");
      WriteRealOct(RealNum);
    UNTIL RealNum=SENTINEL;
END TestRealInOut.
```

Screen output:

Enter any REAL number,
(Enter 999.9 to end): 5.0

The number entered is:
in base 10, (decimal): 5.00000E+00

This number's internal format in octal
notation is: 000000 040240

Enter any REAL number,
(Enter 999.9 to end): -52.8

The number entered is:
in base 10, (decimal): -5.28000E+01

This number's internal format in octal
notation is: 031463 141123

Enter any REAL number,
(Enter 999.9 to end): 4,076.9

INPUT ERROR!

LISTING 7.4

At times it may be desirable to import function procedure Done from InOut and function procedure Done from RealInOut. If each Done is placed (in the usual manner) on the respective imports lists, the compiler will be quick to flag an error, indicating that an identifier has been used twice for two different objects. We can resolve such a problem by using the importation technique shown in the program of Listing 7.5. (This is an application of our discussion in the latter part of section 6.2 and section 6.6.)

Here we see that specific objects have been imported from InOut, namely WriteString, WriteLn, ReadInt, and WriteInt. In addition, all other objects available from InOut have been imported through the "IMPORT InOut" statement. But use of any of those additional objects (which includes Done) can only be accomplished by using the qualifier InOut. Thus, to use Done from InOut, we must write In-Out.Done which, indeed, in the program will distinguish it from the use of the object Done which has been imported explicitly from RealInOut.

```
MODULE TwoDones;

FROM RealInOut IMPORT Done,ReadReal,WriteReal;
FROM InOut IMPORT WriteString,WriteLn,ReadInt,WriteInt;
IMPORT InOut; (* used for importation of Done *)

VAR IntNum:INTEGER;
    RealNum:REAL;

BEGIN
    WriteLn;WriteLn;
    WriteString("Enter any INTEGER number: ");
    ReadInt(IntNum);
    IF NOT InOut.Done THEN
      WriteLn;
      WriteString("INTEGER INPUT ERROR!");
      HALT;
    END;
    WriteLn;
    WriteString("Enter any REAL number: ");
    ReadReal(RealNum);
    IF NOT Done THEN
      WriteLn;
      WriteString("REAL INPUT ERROR!");
      HALT;
    END;
    WriteLn;WriteLn;
    WriteString("The INTEGER number entered is: ");
    WriteInt(IntNum,5);WriteLn;
    WriteLn;
    WriteString("The REAL number entered is: ");
    WriteReal(RealNum,10);
  END TwoDones.
```

LISTING 7.5

7.3 MODULE SYSTEM

Some "standard" modules that are provided with the Modula-2 system are not to be found in the library but rather reside in the compiler. MODULE SYSTEM is such a "standard" module.

Nonetheless, an import list for a compiler-based module is written in the text of a program in the same manner that any other import list is written, so to the programmer there appears to be no apparent difference between a library module and a module which lies within the compiler.

At this time, we would like to describe just five of the many importable objects found in MODULE SYSTEM, namely, WORD, ADDRESS, ADR, SIZE, and TSIZE. The first two of these objects are imported into the library module Files, which is to be the subject of the next section. ADR will be used in one of the sample programs developed for making use of some of the facilities available in MODULE Files. (In a later chapter we will make use of both SIZE and TSIZE.) Both WORD and ADDRESS are data types, while ADR, SIZE and TSIZE are function procedures.

Data type WORD gives us the capability to access an individual memory storage unit, regardless of the data type stored there. Type WORD can be used in the parameter lists of procedures. If this is done, then the actual parameter values passed to the procedure may be of any type that uses one memory storage unit, namely types CARDINAL, INTEGER, BITSET, and pointers (we will study pointer types in Chapter 9). If the procedure's parameter list includes the data type, ARRAY OF WORD, then the actual parameter values may be of any type (the concept of this data type is a subject discussed fully in Chapter 8, and goes under the name of open array parameters). Beyond the use of type WORD in parameter lists, the only operation permissible with type WORD is assignment.

Function procedure SIZE returns the number of storage units assigned to the parameter passed to it. (Storage units may be measured in bytes or words, depending on the Modula-2 implementation being used.) TSIZE is quite an interesting function procedure. Its single parameter is not the usual variable, but rather a data type. Thus we may code TSIZE(INTEGER). The execution of such an instruction would yield the number of units of memory (bytes or words) that are occupied by variables of data type INTEGER on the system being queried. Both SIZE and TSIZE find great application when it is desirable to do what may be referred to as transportable *low level* programming.

As an example of the use of type WORD as both a parameter and in assignement statements, we could write a procedure to exchange the values associated with two different data types such as CARDINAL and INTEGER, as shown in Listing 7.6.

The program of Listing 7.6 accepts two values from the keyboard, the first a CARDINAL and the second an INTEGER. The two numbers are exchanged in PROCEDURE Exchange, passed back to the main program, and outputted to the screen. The test run shown indicates that the two numbers, 66 and –67, upon being exchanged are written to the screen as 65469 and 66. This is indeed as it should be! Why? (Hint: Negative numbers are stored in memory in 2's complement form.)

```
MODULE TestWORD;

FROM InOut IMPORT WriteString,WriteLn,WriteCard,WriteInt,ReadCard,ReadInt;

FROM SYSTEM IMPORT WORD;

    PROCEDURE Exchange(VAR w1,w2:WORD);
    VAR temp:WORD;
    BEGIN
        temp:=w1;
        w1:=w2;
        w2:=temp;
    END Exchange;

VAR CardNum:CARDINAL;
    IntNum:INTEGER;
BEGIN
    WriteString('Enter a cardinal number: ');
    ReadCard(CardNum);
    WriteLn;
    WriteString('Enter an integer number: ');
    ReadInt(IntNum);
    WriteLn;WriteLn;
    WriteString('The numbers will now be exchanged ... ');
    Exchange(CardNum,IntNum);
    WriteLn;WriteLn;
    WriteString('The cardinal number is:');
    WriteCard(CardNum,10);
    WriteLn;
    WriteString('The integer number is: ');
    WriteInt(IntNum,10);
END TestWORD.
```

Screen output:

Enter a cardinal number: 66

Enter an integer number: -67

The numbers will now be exchanged...

The cardinal number is: 65469
The integer number is: 66

LISTING 7.6

Data type ADDRESS is compatible with type CARDINAL and pointer types. All arithmetic operations available to type CARDINAL are also available to ADDRESS variables. Type ADDRESS will be used in the next section and in the program of Listing 7.10.

ADR is a function procedure with one parameter which can be a variable of any type. It returns the starting memory address of the variable that is its parameter value. This memory address is of type ADDRESS. A use of the ADR function procedure will be found in the same example in which ADDRESS can be found (see Listing 7.10).

There are other objects that can be imported from MODULE SYSTEM but they will not be described here. As some of them are needed in the remainder of this book, those objects will be considered.

7.4 MODULE Files

No predefined data type dealing with data files exists in the formal definition of Modula-2. Data file creations and manipulations are made available to the programmer through the use of the "standard" library module Files. Some Modula-2 implementations may use a different identifier for the library module that implements a file structure. The implementation considered here as MODULE Files is that developed by Volition Systems.

A *data file* may be viewed as a sequence of bytes (characters) along with a *current position* within the file (the next byte to be accessed) and an *end of file position* (the position just past the last byte of the file). Files can be accessed either sequentially or randomly. Access to a data file can be accomplished on either a byte-by-byte or a record-by-record basis.

To establish a file structure within a program, objects from MODULE Files must be imported into the program. A brief description and use of each importable object from MODULE Files will be developed in this section. During this development, you should use the listing of DEFINITION MODULE Files (Listing 7.7) as a reference. After the module's description is completed, a small programming system employing a number of the available objects from MODULE Files along with an additional example (which appears in Section 7.5) will conclude our discussion of data files.

To communicate with an externally stored data file (for example, a data file stored on a floppy diskette), the data type FILE is imported into a program. This importation allows us to declare variables of type FILE. For example, the following declaration may be made,

    VAR f:FILE;

With this declaration in place, an existing file (for example, named '#5:CustomerFile') may be opened by invoking the function procedure

    Open(f,'#5:CustomerFile')

where #5: indicates the volume number in p-system environments.

It should be noted that other implementations may offer the equivalent of Open as a regular procedure rather than as a function procedure. This will also be true for the procedures Create, Close, Release, Delete, and Rename, which will be described in this section.

Of course, a function procedure returns a value to the calling part of the program. The value returned in the case of Open is of type FileState, an enumerated data type whose constants (along with their meanings), are:

FileOK	performed file operation successfully
NameError	specified file name not found
UseError	invalid file operation
StatusError	tried to access a closed file
DeviceError	detected error in device being accessed
EndError	file position beyond end of file

FileState (or any of its individual constants) should be imported into the program, along with FILE.

Suppose that the file named CustomerFile is on a diskette that has been placed in the disk drive accessed as volume #5 of a computer system. This file can be opened and connected to a FILE variable, f, by writing the following code which includes some rudimentary error detection and handling:

```
IF Open(f, '#5:CustomerFile') # FileOK THEN
   WriteString('File Error');
   HALT;
END;
```

The status of a file can be queried by the use of function procedure FileStatus which will return to the calling part of the program a value of type FileState.

More sophisticated file error handling code can be developed by importing data type FileHandler (which is a procedure type as described in Chapter 8) along with procedure SetFileHandler.

Each of the objects, Create, Close, Release, Delete, and Rename, are function procedures and return a value of type FileState, just as does Open. The processing that these function procedures (including Open) perform will be illustrated by the following examples (assume that the variables f and g have been declared as type FILE):

Open(f,'#5:CustomerFile')
> —opens an already existing external file (on volume (drive) #5) whose name is CustomerFile, and connects it to FILE variable, f

Create (g,'#4:PartsList')
> —creates a new external file (on volume (drive) #4) whose name is PartsList and connects it to FILE variable g

Close(f)
> —closes (and preserves) the external file that has been connected to FILE variable f (#5:CustomerFile from our example)

Release(g)
> —disconnects the external file from FILE variable g and deletes it from the external device (in our example, #4:PartsList no longer exists)

Rename('#5:CustomerFile','#5:CustFile')

> —changes the name of an existing external file; the external
> file being renamed must be closed; if the file's new name
> is identical to the name of another file on the same volume,
> that other file will be deleted

Delete('#5:CustFile')

> —removes the named existing external file; the named ex-
> ternal file must be closed

Each of these six file operations will return a value of type FileState.
If they return FileOK, then that means the file operation called for
has been executed successfully.

```
DEFINITION MODULE Files;

FROM SYSTEM IMPORT WORD,ADDRESS;

EXPORT QUALIFIED
                FILE,EOF,
                FileState,FileStatus,SetFileHandler,
                Open,Create,Close,Release,Delete,Rename,
                FilePos,GetPos,GetEOF,SetPos,SetEOF,CalcPos,
                Read,ReadRec,ReadBytes,Write,WriteRec,WriteBytes;

TYPE FILE;                      (* opaque type, see Chapter 9 *)
PROCEDURE EOF(f:FILE):BOOLEAN;

TYPE FileState=(FileOK,NameError,UseError,StatusError,DeviceError,EndError);
                (* any of the constants of FileState can be imported *)
                (* into any programmer-developed module *)

PROCEDURE FileStatus(f:FILE):FileState;

TYPE FileHandler=PROCEDURE(FileState);
PROCEDURE SetFileHandler(f:FILE;handler:FileHandler);

PROCEDURE Open     (VAR f:FILE;name:ARRAY OF CHAR):FileState;
PROCEDURE Create   (VAR f:FILE;name:ARRAY OF CHAR):FileState;
PROCEDURE Close    (VAR f:FILE):FileState;
PROCEDURE Release  (VAR f:FILE):FileState;
PROCEDURE Delete   (name:ARRAY OF CHAR):FileState;
PROCEDURE Rename   (old,new:ARRAY OF CHAR):FileState;

TYPE FilePos;
PROCEDURE GetPos   (f:FILE;VAR pos:FilePos);
PROCEDURE GetEOF   (f:FILE;VAR pos:FilePos);
PROCEDURE SetPos   (f:FILE;pos:FilePos);
PROCEDURE SetEOF   (f:FILE;pos:FilePos);
PROCEDURE CalcPos  (recnum,recsize:CARDINAL;VAR pos:FilePos);
```

```
PROCEDURE Read        (f:FILE;VAR ch:CHAR);
PROCEDURE ReadRec     (f:FILE;VAR rec:ARRAY OF WORD);
PROCEDURE ReadBytes   (f:FILE;buf:ADDRESS;nbytes:CARDINAL)
                       :CARDINAL;
PROCEDURE Write       (f:FILE;ch:CHAR);
PROCEDURE WriteRec    (f:FILE;VAR rec:ARRAY OF WORD);
PROCEDURE WriteBytes  (f:FILE;buf:ADDRESS;nbytes:CARDINAL)
                       :CARDINAL;

END Files.
```

LISTING 7.7

Function procedure EOF has the job of noting whether the end of a file has been reached or not. EOF has a single parameter, a variable of type FILE, and returns a BOOLEAN value after each file reading or writing operation; TRUE if the end-of-file position has been reached or the previous operation was unsuccessful, FALSE otherwise.

Next we turn our attention to reading from and writing to files. In MODULE Files, each of these two fundamental input/output operations has three procedures dedicated to performing the tasks of reading and writing.

If a file is to be structured as a file of records, then the ReadRec and WriteRec procedures are employed. ReadRec has two parameters, the file variable and a record identifier into which the record read will be placed. ReadRec reads a complete record from the file. If a ReadRec operation is attempted at the end-of-file position, then EOF is set to TRUE and FileStatus is set to EndError. The WriteRec procedure also has two parameters (file and record variables) and writes a complete record to the file. Both ReadRec and WriteRec are capable of dealing with records of virtually any size and which are composed of fields of any data types. This is accomplished with the use of Modula-2's "generic" data type ARRAY OF WORD (see Section 7.3 for a short discussion of type WORD and Chapter 8 for a discussion of open array parameters). Type WORD must be imported into library module Files from MODULE SYSTEM, as can be seen in the import list of MODULE Files (see Listing 7.7).

The Read and Write procedures allow for reading and writing of characters to a file, one character at a time. Each procedure has a pair of parameters, a file identifier followed by a CHAR variable. If Read is invoked at the end of the end-of-file position, then EOF is set to TRUE; otherwise it is set to FALSE.

ReadBytes and WriteBytes are both function procedures which return the number of bytes actually read from or written to a file. Each procedure has three parameters, a file identifier, the address in memory storage of a variable into which or from which the bytes will be read or written, and the number of bytes to be read or written. The address parameter is of type ADDRESS (see the discussion of ADDRESS in Section 7.3). Type ADDRESS is imported into MODULE Files from MODULE SYSTEM as seen on the import list of MODULE Files (see Listing 7.7). EOF is set to TRUE when invoking ReadBytes if the actual number of bytes read is less than the number of bytes specified in the parameter list. FileStatus is set to DeviceError when invoking WriteBytes if the number of bytes actually written to the file is less than the amount specified in WriteByte's parameter list.

Use of the reading and writing procedures of MODULE Files alone allows us to perform only sequential file access operations. For example, if we read a record within a file by using the ReadRec procedure, then the current position within the file is automatically moved to the beginning of the next record. Of course, there are numerous occasions when random access to a file element is desired. Random access of files can be accomplished by making use of a set of file positioning objects found in MODULE Files along with the appropriate reading and writing procedures. These objects consist of five procedures plus a data type.

Variables of the file positioning data type, whose type identifier is FilePos, can store values which can be used to indicate the position within the file of both the current file position and the end-of-file position.

The GetPos procedure has two parameters—a file identifier and a variable of type FilePos. Invoking GetPos will place into the FilePos variable, the value of the current file position. In this way, we can note where the position of a particular file element (such as a record) is. In a similar manner, the GetEOF procedure, whose two parameters are for a file identifier and a variable of type FilePos, when invoked places into the FilePos variable the end-of-file position value.

Once we have recorded the position of a particular file element in a FilePos variable, we can later access that file element by invoking the SetPos procedure. SetPos also has two parameters, a file identifier and a variable of type FilePos. After invoking SetPos, which sets the file position to the beginning of the desired file element, that particular file element can be read or written over. Attempting to set the file position past the end-of-file will cause FileStatus to return an EndError.

The end-of-file position can be set by use of the SetEOF procedure which has the same parameter list as does SetPos. SetEOF sets the end-of-file position to the value specified in the FilePos variable. Attempting to set the end-of-file position in front of the current file position or beyond the current end-of-file position will cause FileStatus to return an EndError.

The final file position procedure available in MODULE Files is CalcPos. It calculates the absolute file position of a record (file element) based on the first two values entered for its three parameters, namely the record number (the first record of a file is numbered 0) and the number of storage units per record (usually a storage unit is a byte). The third parameter passes back to the calling part of the program the desired file position (in a variable of type FilePos).

Having completed the above short descriptions of each of the objects available from MODULE Files, it would be fitting to next develop a number of examples which make use of the bulk of these objects so that your understanding of the file facilities of Modula-2 may be enhanced. With that in mind, three complete programs will be the subjects of the next section in which we will discuss some of the code of each sample program.

7.5 Examples Using MODULE Files

In Chapter 4, section 4.6, after the development of an example dealing with records and runners, it was stated that, "The use of a permanent storage device—an external file—should be incorporated into the program." Having studied MODULE Files, we are now in a position to do just that. We will create a "file of runners" programming system modelled after the example of Listing 4.6 (MODULE MilerData).

The programming system includes two program modules. The first, MODULE GenerateFileOfMilers (see Listing 7.8), as its name implies, generates the file which will hold the records associated with the milers. In addition, each record is initialized with the names of the milers and all these initialized records are displayed on the CRT screen for visual verification. The second program module, MODULE DriveFileOf-Milers (see Listing 7.9), allows us to update the record of a particular miler, review a particular miler's record, and display all records on the CRT screen. Standard library module importations needed for each program module are illustrated in the system's module interface diagram, Figure 7.1. A rather detailed description of the operation of the programming system follows.

In program module GenerateFileOfMilers, a record variable, miler, of type Runner (see Listing 7.8) is declared and initialized, except for its Name field, in the InitRecord procedure in the same manner as was done in our earlier "miler" programs back in Chapter 4.

Next, PROCEDURE EnterNamesAndFile is called. In this procedure, the file, f, is created and placed on device #5 under the name of MFILE. Since the object Create returns a value of type FileState, that enumerated type has been imported from Files along with the other

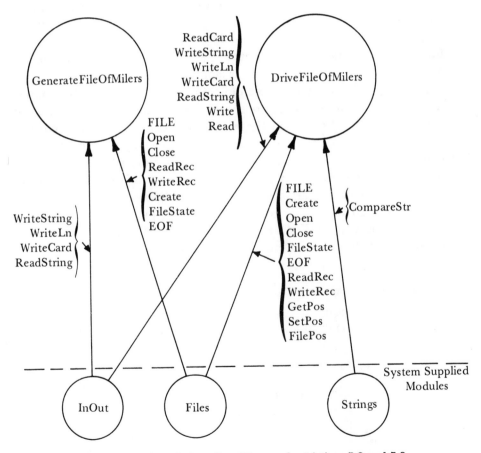

Figure 7.1. Module Interface Diagram for Listings 7.8 and 7.9.

objects listed in the Files import list. Thus, FileOK being one of the possible constants of type FileState, does not have to be explicitly imported into the program but is known to the program by virtue of the FileState importation.

If any problem arises causing the creation of the file not to occur, action is taken by the invocation of the IOError procedure which indicates to the user that a problem has occured and halts execution of the program. (Much more sophisticated error handling could certainly be built into the program by using the error handling capabilities as outlined in the previous section.)

If the file, f, is successfully set up, then the process of having the user enter the names of the milers commences. Regardless of how each name is entered, it is passed to the function procedure Capitalize which returns the name—all in uppercase letters—to the Name field of the record miler. After each such name is processed, the completely initialized record is written to the file through the WriteRec procedure. Initialization of file elements continues until a sentinel name is typed, namely the "*", after which file f is closed.

PROCEDURE ReviewCompleteFile outputs to the screen the complete file just entered in an appropriately formatted manner. Upon opening the file, the current file position is set to the initial record. The ReadRec procedure reads the record element into the record variable miler and moves the current file position to the beginning of the second record element of f. As long as the ReadRec procedure does not set the EOF variable to TRUE, record elements are read from the file, placed in the record variable, and outputted to the screen. Upon sensing that EOF is TRUE, the process discontinues and file f is closed, ending the GenerateFileOfMilers program.

```
MODULE GenerateFileOfMilers;

FROM InOut IMPORT WriteString,WriteLn,WriteCard,ReadString;
FROM Files IMPORT ReadRec,WriteRec,FILE,Create,Open,Close,FileState,EOF;

TYPE String20=ARRAY[1..20] OF CHAR;
     Runner=RECORD
                 Name:String20;
                 TotalRuns:CARDINAL;
                 min,sec:CARDINAL;
            END;
VAR f:FILE;
    miler:Runner;
```

```
PROCEDURE InitRecord;
BEGIN
   WITH miler DO
      min:=100;
      sec:=0;
      TotalRuns:=0;
   END;
END InitRecord;

PROCEDURE IOError;
BEGIN
   WriteString('I/O Error');
   HALT;
END IOError;

PROCEDURE Capitalize(name:String20):String20;
VAR CapName:String20;
    i:CARDINAL;
BEGIN
   FOR i:=1 TO 20 DO CapName[i] :=CAP(name[i] );END;
   RETURN CapName;
END Capitalize;

PROCEDURE EnterNamesAndFile;
VAR k:CARDINAL;
    name:String20;
BEGIN
   k:=0;
   IF Create(f,'#5:MFILE') #FileOK THEN IOError;END;
   WriteString('Enter names of runners,');WriteLn;
   WriteString('(type "*" as name, to end list).');WriteLn;
   REPEAT
      INC(k);
      WriteString('Name #');
      WriteCard(k,2);
      WriteString(': ');
      ReadString(name);
      miler.Name:=Capitalize(name);
      IF name[1] #'*' THEN WriteRec(f,miler);END;
   UNTIL name[1]='*';
   IF Close(f) #FileOK THEN IOError;END;
END EnterNamesAndFile;

PROCEDURE ReviewCompleteFile;
BEGIN
   IF Open(f,'#5:MFILE') #FileOK THEN IOError;END;
   WriteLn;
   WriteString('This is what is in the file:');
   ReadRec(f,miler);
```

```
        WHILE NOT EOF(f) DO
          WriteLn;
          WITH miler DO
             WriteString(Name);WriteLn;
             WriteString(' Best mile: ');
             WriteCard(min,3);
             WriteString(' min.');
             WriteCard(sec,5);
             WriteString(' sec. ');
             WriteString('Number of runs:');
             WriteCard(TotalRuns,3);
          END;
          ReadRec(f,miler);
        END;
        IF Close(f) #FileOK THEN IOError;END;
      END ReviewCompleteFile;

BEGIN
  InitRecord;
  EnterNamesAndFile;
  ReviewCompleteFile;
END GenerateFileOfMilers.
```

LISTING 7.8

MODULE DriveFileOfMilers commences with a menu (see PRO-
CEDURE Menu of Listing 7.9) which gives the user the choice of
either entering a new "run" for a miler, viewing the record of a particular miler, seeing all the records, or exiting the program. The user
response is entered into a simple character entry protection scheme,
the "REPEAT-UNTIL good" construct.

If all the records are to be viewed, file f is opened and each file
record element, in turn, is placed into the record variable miler and
formatted out to the screen in a sequential manner as was done in
MODULE GenerateFileOfMilers.

On the other hand, if viewing or updating of a particular miler's
record is desired, then, after entry of the desired miler's name and its
conversion to all uppercase letters, a simple sequential search through
file f is made. The Name field of each record element is compared to
the desired name through the importation of the procedure Compare-
Str from library module Strings (see Chapter 11). As each record element is encountered its starting file position is preserved in the FilePos
variable pos by invoking the GetPos procedure. If the desired name is
found, the associated record is displayed on the screen (ViewRec). If

the record is to be updated, PROCEDURE UpdateRec is called and information is typed in at the keyboard by the user. When the record variable miler is complete, random access to the appropriate file element is accomplished by setting the current file position to the value previously stored in the variable pos by using the SetPos procedure. Finally, the WriteRec procedure writes the new record to the file.

After each execution of a choice from the menu is performed, control is passed back to the menu again until the choice is made to exit the program.

```
MODULE DriveFileOfMilers;

FROM InOut IMPORT WriteString,WriteLn,WriteCard,ReadString,
                  Write,Read,ReadCard;
FROM Files IMPORT ReadRec,WriteRec,FILE,Create,Open,Close,
                  FileState,EOF,GetPos,SetPos,FilePos;
FROM Strings IMPORT CompareStr;

TYPE String20=ARRAY[1..20] OF CHAR;
     Runner=RECORD
                  Name:String20;
                  TotalRuns:CARDINAL;
                  min,sec:CARDINAL;
            END;
VAR f:FILE;
    miler:Runner;
    z:CHAR;
    EndProgram:BOOLEAN;

  PROCEDURE IOError;
  BEGIN
    WriteString('I/O Error');
    HALT;
  END IOError;

  PROCEDURE ViewRec;
  BEGIN
    WriteLn;
    WITH miler DO
      WriteString(Name);WriteLn;
      WriteString(' Best mile: ');
      WriteCard(min,3);
      WriteString(' min.');
      WriteCard(sec,5);
      WriteString(' sec. ');
      WriteString('Number of runs:');
      WriteCard(TotalRuns,3);
    END;
```

```
END ViewRec;

PROCEDURE FindAndSeeRec(update:BOOLEAN);

    PROCEDURE Capitalize(name:String20):String20;
    VAR CapName:String20;
        i:CARDINAL;
    BEGIN
      FOR i:=1 TO 20 DO CapName[i] :=CAP(name[i]);END;
      RETURN CapName;
    END Capitalize;

    PROCEDURE UpdateRec(pos:FilePos);
    VAR m,s:CARDINAL;
    BEGIN
      WriteLn;WriteLn;
      WITH miler DO
        WriteString('Update ');
        WriteString(Name);
        WriteString(" 's record:");
        WriteLn;WriteLn;
        INC(TotalRuns);
        WriteString('What was ');
        WriteString(Name);
        WriteString(" 's time?");WriteLn;
        WriteString('min.: ');
        ReadCard(m);WriteLn;
        IF m=0 THEN m:=100;END; (* protect vs. user entering <cr> only *)
        WriteString('sec.: ');
        ReadCard(s);WriteLn;
        IF 60*m+s < 60*min+sec THEN
          min:=m;
          sec:=s;
        END;
      END;
      SetPos(f,pos);
      WriteRec(f,miler);
    END UpdateRec;

VAR MilerName:String20;
    found:BOOLEAN;
    pos:FilePos;

BEGIN (* FindAndSeeRec *)
    Write(14C);
    WriteLn;
    WriteString('Enter name of runner: ');
    ReadString(MilerName);
    Write(14C);
    WriteLn;
```

```
   WriteString('Searching for ');
   WriteString(MilerName);
   MilerName:=Capitalize(MilerName);
   WriteString(" 's record...");WriteLn;
   IF Open(f,' #5:MFILE') # FileOK THEN IOError;END;
   GetPos(f,pos);
   ReadRec(f,miler);
   found:=FALSE;
   WHILE NOT (EOF(f) OR found) DO
       IF CompareStr(MilerName,miler.Name)=0 THEN
          found:=TRUE;
          ViewRec;
          IF update THEN UpdateRec(pos);END;
       ELSE
          GetPos(f,pos);
          ReadRec(f,miler);
       END;
   END;
   IF Close(f) # FileOK THEN IOError;END;
   IF NOT found THEN
      WriteLn;
      WriteString(MilerName);
      WriteString(" 's record not in this file.");
   END;
   WriteLn;WriteLn;
   WriteString('Type any key for menu...');
   Read(z);
END FindAndSeeRec;

PROCEDURE ReviewAll;
BEGIN
   Write(14C);
   WriteLn;
   IF Open(f,' #5:MFILE') # FileOK THEN IOError;END;
   WriteString('Review of records of all runners:');
   ReadRec(f,miler);
   WHILE NOT EOF(f) DO
       ViewRec;
       ReadRec(f,miler);
   END;
   IF Close(f) # FileOK THEN IOError;END;
   WriteLn;WriteLn;
   WriteString('Type any key for menu...');
   Read(z);
END ReviewAll;

PROCEDURE Menu;
TYPE CharSet=SET OF CHAR;
```

```
    VAR ch:CHAR;
        good,update:BOOLEAN;
    BEGIN
      Write(14C); (* clear screen *)
      WriteLn;
      WriteString('Do you want to...');WriteLn;
      WriteLn;
      WriteString('1 —> Enter a new run for a miler');WriteLn;
      WriteString('2 —> See the record of a miler');WriteLn;
      WriteString('3 —> Review all records');WriteLn;
      WriteString('       or...');WriteLn;
      WriteString('4 —> Exit the program?');WriteLn;
      WriteLn;
      WriteString('Enter appropriate number: ');
      REPEAT
        Read(ch);
        IF ch IN CharSet{'1'..'4'} THEN
          good:=TRUE;
        ELSE
          good:=FALSE;
          Write(10C); (* back space *)
          Write(07C); (* ring bell *)
        END;
      UNTIL good;
      CASE ch OF
        '1':update:=TRUE;
           FindAndSeeRec(update); |
        '2':update:=FALSE;
           FindAndSeeRec(update); |
        '3':ReviewAll; |
        '4':EndProgram:=TRUE;
      END;
    END Menu;

BEGIN (* DriveFileOfMilers *)
  EndProgram:=FALSE;
  REPEAT
    Menu;
  UNTIL EndProgram;
END DriveFileOfMilers.
```

LISTING 7.9

MODULE TestSomeObjects (see Listing 7.10) is a program created merely to indicate the way some of the thus-far unillustrated objects from Files and SYSTEM can be used. Typical screen output is included with the listing. Note that appropriate creation, opening, and closing of file f is executed throughout the program.

Since two different Reads and Writes are used in the program, the same technique for importation of the identical identifier names as used in MODULE TwoDones (Listing 7.5) has been employed in TestSomeObjects.

The program has the user enter a string of characters directly into file f in PROCEDURE EnterTextAndFile. Next, in PROCEDURE ReviewCompleteFile, the entered text is copied from file f to the screen. The next procedure to be called, ReadAndWriteBytes, uses the ADDRESS data type and ADR function procedure from SYSTEM in conjunction with the ReadBytes and WriteBytes function procedures from Files to perform data manipulation.

After an array, buf, is initialized with blanks, buf's starting address in memory is stored in ADDRESS variable, addr, by invoking the ADR procedure. Next, 30 characters are read from f starting at the current file position (which happens to be the first character in the file, in this case), and are copied into the memory area beginning at the address stored in addr. Thus the ReadBytes statement has allowed for the direct transfer from file to memory area, on the byte level, regardless of how the file data is structured.

After echoing the contents of buf to the screen, an additional 10 characters are read from f and copied to the screen starting at the current position of the file. The array, buf, is next loaded with a portion of the ASCII code starting with "A". The WriteBytes procedure is used to write into f, 15 characters of the buf array starting with its eleventh element (namely "K" through "Y"). Finally, the complete file contents is once again written to the screen.

```
MODULE TestSomeObjects;

FROM InOut IMPORT WriteString,WriteLn,ReadString;
IMPORT InOut;
FROM Files IMPORT FILE,Create,Open,Close,FileState,EOF,
                  ReadBytes,WriteBytes,Read,Write;
FROM SYSTEM IMPORT ADDRESS,ADR;

TYPE Buffer=ARRAY[1..30] OF CHAR;
VAR f:FILE;
    buf:Buffer;
    ch:CHAR;
```

```
PROCEDURE IOError;
BEGIN
   WriteString('I/O Error');
   HALT;
END IOError;

PROCEDURE EnterTextAndFile;
BEGIN
   IF Create(f,' #5:TESTFILE') # FileOK THEN IOError;END;
   WriteString('Enter text of 50 characters or more:');WriteLn;
   WriteString('(to end type "*")');WriteLn;
   WriteLn;
   InOut.Read(ch);
   WHILE ch #'*' DO
      Write(f,ch);
      InOut.Read(ch);
   END;
   IF Close(f) # FileOK THEN IOError;END;
END EnterTextAndFile;

PROCEDURE ReviewCompleteFile;
BEGIN
   IF Open(f,' #5:TESTFILE') # FileOK THEN IOError;END;
   WriteLn;WriteLn;
   WriteString('This is what is in the file:');WriteLn;
   Read(f,ch);
   WHILE NOT EOF(f) DO
      InOut.Write(ch);
      Read(f,ch);
   END;
   IF Close(f) # FileOK THEN IOError;END;
END ReviewCompleteFile;

PROCEDURE ReadAndWriteBytes;
VAR I,nBytes:CARDINAL;
       addr:ADDRESS;
BEGIN
   IF Open(f,' #5:TESTFILE') # FileOK THEN IOError;END;
   WriteLn;WriteLn;
   FOR I:=1 TO 30 DO buf[I]:=' ';END;
   addr:=ADR(buf);
   nBytes:=ReadBytes(f,addr,30);
   WriteLn;WriteLn;
   FOR I:=1 TO 30 DO InOut.Write(buf[I]);END;
   WriteLn;WriteLn;
   FOR I:=1 TO 10 DO
      Read(f,ch);
      InOut.Write(ch);
   END;
```

```
    WriteLn;WriteLn;
    ch:='A';
    FOR I:=1 TO 30 DO
        buf[I]:=ch;
        INC(ch);
    END;
        nBytes:=WriteBytes(f,ADR(buf)+10,15);
        IF Close(f) # FileOK THEN IOError;END;
    END ReadAndWriteBytes;

BEGIN (* TestSomeObjects *)
    EnterTextAndFile;
    ReviewCompleteFile;
    ReadAndWriteBytes;
    ReviewCompleteFile;
END TestSomeObjects.
```

Screen output:

Enter text of 50 characters or more:
(to end type "*")

Whose woods these are I think I know.
His house is in the village though;*

This is what is in the file:
Whose woods these are I think I know.
His house is in the village though;

Whose woods these are I think

I know.
Hi

This is what is in the file:
Whose woods these are I think I know.
HiKLMNOPQRSTUVWXYhe village though;

LISTING 7.10

7.6 MODULE Hierarchy

Now that we have had a little experience with some of the "standard" library modules, the time is ripe for saying a few words about the inter-relationships between modules within the library.

For example, although the definition module does not show it, MODULE RealInOut makes use of objects found in MODULE InOut. That is, the implementation module of RealInOut imports some objects from MODULE InOut. Thus, if you are importing RealInOut in one of your programs, it in turn is importing InOut (among other modules), and therefore InOut must be available for such importation—it must be part of the on-line programming environment.

The interrelationship between RealInOut and InOut is only one among many. In fact, we can begin to set up a partial list of "standard" library module dependencies indicating the hierarchical structure of the library as follows:

RealInOut → imports objects from → InOut, Reals

InOut   → imports objects from → Conversions, Texts

Files   → imports objects from → Storage, Program

Many of the imported modules named above have not been discussed, but the point is that the three modules cited above—which we have dealt with at length thus far in this chapter—do not stand alone but are dependent on other modules.

For example, a partial trace of the dependencies associated with the "standard" library modules (as found in the Modula-2 system by Volition Systems) is pictured in Figure 7.2. Below the modules shown in that figure lie the machine-dependent modules written for the particular hardware implementation with which you are working. (For your system, see if you can set up a library module interrelationship diagram.)

Next we will pose a few questions about library module use. Consider library module Terminal which we have not discussed but will do so at length in Chapter 10. Two of the importable objects from Terminal are WriteString and WriteLn which are used exactly as described for the objects of the same names found in MODULE InOut. So the questions arise: If the only objects to be used are WriteString and WriteLn, should MODULE InOut or MODULE Terminal be imported? Does one of those modules have an advantage over the other? Is there a trade-off in using one or the other?

The simple pair of test programs shown in Listings 7.11a and 7.11b should provide some answers to these questions. The two short programs are identical except for the library modules from which they import the procedures WriteString and WriteLn. In MODULE Import-Test1, they are imported from InOut, while in MODULE Import-Test2 they are imported from Terminal. Otherwise the programs are identical.

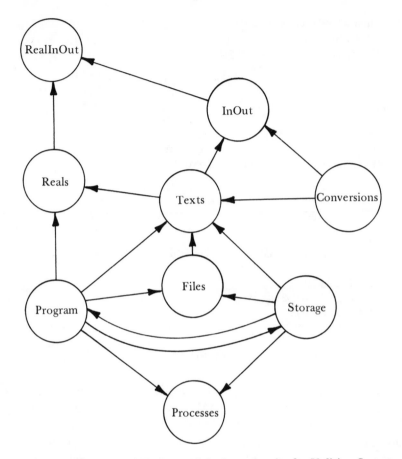

Figure 7.2. Partial trace of library module dependencies for Volition Systems Modula-2.

```
MODULE ImportTest1;

FROM Standards IMPORT MemAvail;
FROM InOut IMPORT WriteString,WriteLn;
FROM Conversions IMPORT CardToStr;

VAR x:CARDINAL;
    str:ARRAY[0..9] OF CHAR;
    dummy:BOOLEAN;

BEGIN
  WriteString('The RAM memory available is:');
  WriteLn;
  x:=MemAvail( );
```

```
        dummy:=CardToStr(x,str);
      WriteString(str);
   END ImportTest1.
```

LISTING 7.11a

```
MODULE ImportTest2;

FROM Standards IMPORT MemAvail;
FROM Terminal IMPORT WriteString,WriteLn;
FROM Conversions IMPORT CardToStr;

VAR x:CARDINAL;
      str:ARRAY[0..9] OF CHAR;
      dummy:BOOLEAN;

BEGIN
   WriteString('The RAM memory available is:');
   WriteLn;
   x:=MemAvail();
   dummy:=CardToStr(x,str);
   WriteString(str);
END ImportTest2.
```

LISTING 7.11b

The purpose of the pair of programs is to determine and write out to the screen the amount of RAM memory available for use at a particular point during the execution of the programs. In this way, we can get an idea as to how much RAM memory is actually used to import the two objects WriteString and WriteLn. To facilitate this, a function procedure MemAvail, imported from a system-dependent library module called Standards (derived from the Apple (UCSD) Pascal system), is employed. In addition, the function procedure Card-ToStr is imported from another, yet-to-be discussed library module Conversions so that the value returned by MemAvail can be displayed on the screen.

After executing each program, the free memory turns out to be 12,819 words for ImportTest1 and 15,092 words for ImportTest2. We can see that it would be more efficient in terms of available memory space if we use Terminal to import WriteString and WriteLn. However, there is a trade-off! Flexibility of use is given up. If InOut is used, then the input and output can be redirected to other than the keyboard and screen as we saw in Section 7.1. This cannot be done if MODULE Terminal is used. Furthermore, we had to resort to importation of CardToStr from Conversions to be able to write out a cardinal number when using MODULE Terminal. Of course this would not normally be the case when using MODULE InOut.

So it all depends on the application as to which library modules should be used. A good knowledge of module capabilities and dependencies are indeed valuable assets for the Modula-2 programmer.

8

Open Array Parameters and Procedure Types

The two topics to be discussed in this chapter, namely open array parameters and procedure types, will be discussed separately at first and then joined together in a small case study. As the chapter progresses, we will work towards producing "generic" routines—that is, routines that perform operations on a wide range of different data types. In the small case study at the end of the chapter we will develop a rather limited pair of generic routines for sorting and displaying.

An open array parameter is designed to be used as a formal procedure parameter. It permits us to pass one-dimensional arrays of differing length to the same destination procedure, thus allowing us to create more generalized procedures in Modula-2 when desired.

Through the use of procedure types, we can pass procedures as parameters to other procedures, although there are some limitations on the type of procedures that can be passed.

8.1 Open Array Parameters

In this section we will study *open array parameters* which we saw in Chapter 7 when we discussed library module Files. Beyond that, as we stated above, our study will lead us in the direction of writing generic procedures in Modula-2—procedures that will perform tasks on a broad class of data regardless of the types of the data involved.

Suppose it is desirable to create a table of squares and cubes of the elements which are loaded into two separate arrays of integers. Furthermore, suppose that the first of the two arrays has seven elements while the second array has 11. The first and second arrays' elements are to be loaded with consecutive integer values starting with 1 and 11, respectively.

Listing 8.1 illustrates a solution to this programming problem using the Modula-2 facilities that we have thus far discussed. A quick review of the listing reveals that the code is rather repetitive. Note that procedures LoadArray1 and LoadArray2 are almost identical, just as are procedures ProduceAndWriteTable1 and ProduceAndWriteTable2. In fact, the only differences between the corresponding pairs of procedures are the bounds employed for the indices of the arrays that are serviced by the procedures. Otherwise, the pairs of procedures are identical line for line.

This necessity of repeating virtually identical code can be relieved by employing open array parameters as formal procedure parameters instead of the bounded array parameters. For example, instead of declaring the bounded array IntArray1 (which is the identifier for ARRAY[1..7] OF INTEGER), in the formal parameter list of PROCEDURE ProduceAndWriteTable1 we can declare simply a:ARRAY OF INTEGER in the heading.

Note that the index bounds of the array (as well as the index data type) have been omitted (left "open") from the declaration. This is what is meant by an open array parameter. An open array is compatible with all one-dimensional arrays of the same base type (in our example, type INTEGER).

When an actual array is passed to a procedure employing an open array parameter, the array elements are mapped into the index range from 0 to N-1, where N is the number of actual elements in the array. This is so regardless of the actual array's index type or its bounds.

The upper bound of an open array parameter can be found by applying Modula-2's standard function HIGH(a) (see Table 3.1) where a is the one-dimensional array passed.

An open array can itself be passed as an actual parameter to another procedure having an appropriate open array parameter but it cannot be assigned directly to another array. We can only access an open array element by element.

```
MODULE WithoutOpenArrays;

FROM InOut IMPORT WriteLn,WriteString,WriteInt;

TYPE IntArray1=ARRAY[1..7] OF INTEGER;
     IntArray2=ARRAY[1..11] OF INTEGER;

VAR a1:IntArray1;
    a2:IntArray2;

    PROCEDURE LoadArray1(VAR a:IntArray1;num:INTEGER);
    VAR I:CARDINAL;
    BEGIN
```

```
    FOR I:=1 TO 7 DO
       a[I] :=num;
       INC(num);
    END;
END LoadArray1;

PROCEDURE LoadArray2(VAR a:IntArray2;num:INTEGER);
VAR I:CARDINAL;
BEGIN
    FOR I:=1 TO 11 DO
       a[I] :=num;
       INC(num);
    END;
END LoadArray2;

PROCEDURE ProduceAndWriteTable1(a:IntArray1);
VAR I:CARDINAL;
       num,numSquared,numCubed:INTEGER;
BEGIN
    FOR I:=1 TO 7 DO
       num:=a[I] ;
       numSquared:=num*num;
       numCubed:=numSquared*num;
       WriteInt(num,5);
       WriteInt(numSquared,10);
       WriteInt(numCubed,15);
       WriteLn;
    END;
END ProduceAndWriteTable1;

PROCEDURE ProduceAndWriteTable2(a:IntArray2);
VAR I:CARDINAL;
       num,numSquared,numCubed:INTEGER;
BEGIN
    FOR I:=1 TO 11 DO
       num:=a[I] ;
       numSquared:=num*num;
       numCubed:=numSquared*num;
       WriteInt(num,5);
       WriteInt(numSquared,10);
       WriteInt(numCubed,15);
       WriteLn;
    END;
END ProduceAndWriteTable2;

BEGIN
    LoadArray1(a1,1);
    LoadArray2(a2,11);
    WriteString('   Squares and Cubes');
```

```
    WriteLn;
    WriteString(' Number  Squared   Cubed');
    WriteLn;
    ProduceAndWriteTable1(a1);
    ProduceAndWriteTable2(a2);
END WithoutOpenArrays.
```

LISTING 8.1

An application of open array parameters to the programming problem at hand yields the result shown in Listing 8.2. Notice that the program code is shortened considerably, since we have been able to eliminate the redundancy of writing separate procedures for each array to be loaded and manipulated. Note that the indices used for the FOR-DO loops now must go from 0 to HIGH(a), as discussed above.

Of course, the identical screen output is produced from each solution to our programming problem, but using open array parameters has reduced the size of both the program text (source code) and its executable code (object code), as well as producing a more readable and therefore more easily modifiable program. This last statement holds true since it has been shown that program size affects a program's readability and the amount of time it takes to debug and/or modify that program.

```
MODULE WithOpenArrays;

FROM InOut IMPORT WriteLn,WriteString,WriteInt;

TYPE IntArray1=ARRAY[1..7] OF INTEGER;
     IntArray2=ARRAY[1..11] OF INTEGER;

VAR a1:IntArray1;
    a2:IntArray2;

    PROCEDURE LoadArray(VAR a:ARRAY OF INTEGER;num:INTEGER);
    VAR I:CARDINAL;
    BEGIN
      FOR I:=0 TO HIGH(a) DO
        a[I]:=num;
        INC(num);
      END;
    END LoadArray;

    PROCEDURE ProduceAndWriteTable(a:ARRAY OF INTEGER);
    VAR I:CARDINAL;
        num,numSquared,numCubed:INTEGER;
```

```
    BEGIN
      FOR I:=0 TO HIGH(a) DO
        num:=a[I] ;
        numSquared:=num*num;
        numCubed:=numSquared*num;
        WriteInt(num,5);
        WriteInt(numSquared,10);
        WriteInt(numCubed,15);
        WriteLn;
      END;
    END ProduceAndWriteTable;
BEGIN
    LoadArray(a1,1);
    LoadArray(a2,11);
    WriteString('   Squares and Cubes');
    WriteLn;
    WriteString(' Number  Squared    Cubed');
    WriteLn;
    ProduceAndWriteTable(a1);
    ProduceAndWriteTable(a2);
END WithOpenArrays.
```

LISTING 8.2

As a second example of the use and power of open array parameters, let us consider the task of catenating (or concatenating) two arrays of the same base type. For example, if we have two integer arrays of 7 and 11 elements, respectively, the catenation routine that we will write will produce, as its output, one 18-element array containing the 7 elements of the first array followed by the 11 elements of the second array.

Our second series of illustrative programs starts with Listing 8.3 where three character arrays are initialized, followed by the catenation of the first with the second, the result of which is placed into the third array. Finally, the catenated third array is displayed on the computer screen.

The three arrays that are declared hold elements of type CHAR, while the index types are all different, namely types CARDINAL, INTEGER, and CHAR.

After the arrays are initialized, PROCEDURE CatenateCharArrays is invoked. The actual arrays a, b, and c are passed to CatenateChar-Arrays where the formal parameter list includes two pass-by-value open arrays of CHAR and one pass-by-reference open array of CHAR. Within the procedure itself, the arrays are handled as if their indices were all of type CARDINAL. The procedure loads array z with the elements from arrays x and y and then passes the result back to array c.

Note that by using open array parameters, CatenateCharArrays makes no demands on the size of the arrays passed, nor the index type used for those arrays, except for the fact that the two arrays to be catenated must fit into the third array. Thus, the third array passed must have a number of elements which, at least, is equal to the sum of the number of elements found in the first two arrays.

Next, note that PROCEDURE DisplayCharArray can be used as a generalized CHAR array display routine since it also employs an open array parameter.

Now that we have been successful in creating more generalized routines by employing open array parameters, where the index size is virtually unbounded and its data type can be any legal data type for array indices, can we develop even more generalized routines by eliminating the need to explicitly declare the data type of the array elements themselves—the base type?

The answer to this question is in the affirmative. By using an ARRAY OF WORD as an open array parameter, we can develop even more generalized routines. In fact, open array parameters employing type WORD allow any variable to be interpreted as a sequence of computer words. If you recall (see section 7.3), type WORD gives us the capability to access an individual memory storage unit regardless of the data type stored there. For example, in Listing 8.3, we could change the heading of CatenateCharArrays to read

```
PROCEDURE CatenateCharArrays(x,y:ARRAY OF WORD;
                             VAR z:ARRAY OF WORD);
```

and the procedure would yield the same results.

The advantage of doing this is that the routine can now be used to catenate arrays of any objects whether they are characters, integers, real numbers, or complicated record structures. Why? Because with this new parameter list, data is viewed, not as type CHAR or type REAL, etc., but as just so many words in memory—that is, it is viewed as type WORD. After the catenation process is performed and array z is passed back to the calling part of the program, the data is once again viewed as its original data type.

Thus, instead of calling our catenation routine CatenateCharArrays, we might as well call it just CatenateArrays since we can now pass any type arrays to it.

In Listing 8.4, we have rewritten our catenation procedure as outlined above and placed it in a test program where it is called on to perform the catenation of arrays of type INTEGER, REAL, CHAR, String20, and Grade (where String20 and Grade are defined within the program).

With PROCEDURE CatenateArrays in place we indeed have a generic catenation procedure. Other routines to perform specific tasks can be constructed generically, although they may not be as simply developed as was PROCEDURE CatenateArrays.

Generic procedures are just the type of objects that can be thought of as reusable code and stored in the Modula-2 library. Such tasks as searching and sorting arrays and files would make good subjects for generic procedures. The development of a library of generic routines would go a long way toward the establishment of an inventory of off-the-shelf software components for programmers and software engineers, in the same manner as the IC (integrated circuits) components industry has established for electronic hardware engineers.

```
MODULE CatenateTest1;

FROM InOut IMPORT Write;

    PROCEDURE CatenateCharArrays(x,y:ARRAY OF CHAR;
                                 VAR z:ARRAY OF CHAR);

    VAR I,Hx,Hy:CARDINAL;
    BEGIN
        Hx:=HIGH(x);
        FOR I:=0 TO Hx DO
            z[I] :=x[I] ;
        END;
        Hy:=HIGH(y);
        FOR I:=0 TO Hy DO
            z[Hx+1+I] :=y[I] ;
        END;
    END CatenateCharArrays;

VAR a:ARRAY[1..10] OF CHAR;
    b:ARRAY[-1..3] OF CHAR;
    c:ARRAY['a'..'o'] OF CHAR;
```

```
      PROCEDURE InitCharArrays;
      VAR I:CARDINAL;
          J:INTEGER;
          ch,C:CHAR;
      BEGIN
        ch:='A';
        FOR I:=1 TO 10 DO
          a[I]:=ch;
          INC(ch);
        END;
        FOR J:=-1 TO 3 DO
          b[J]:=ch;
          INC(ch);
        END;
        FOR C:='a' TO 'o' DO
          c[C]:='&';
        END;
      END InitCharArrays;

      PROCEDURE DisplayCharArray(x:ARRAY OF CHAR);
                                VAR I:CARDINAL;
      BEGIN
        FOR I:=0 TO HIGH(x) DO
          Write(x[I]);
        END;
      END DisplayCharArray;

  BEGIN
    InitCharArrays;
    CatenateCharArrays(a,b,c);
    DisplayCharArray(c);
  END CatenateTest1.
```

LISTING 8.3

```
. MODULE CatenateTest2;

FROM SYSTEM IMPORT WORD;
FROM InOut IMPORT WriteInt,WriteLn,WriteString,WriteCard,
                  ReadString,ReadCard;
FROM RealInOut IMPORT WriteReal;

    PROCEDURE CatenateArrays(x,y:ARRAY OF WORD;
                             VAR z:ARRAY OF WORD)
    VAR I,Hx,Hy:CARDINAL;
    BEGIN
      Hx:=HIGH(x);
      FOR I:=0 TO Hx DO
        z[I]:=x[I];
      END;
```

```
        Hy:=HIGH(y);
        FOR I:=0 TO Hy DO
            z[Hx+1+I] :=y[I] ;
        END;
    END CatenateArrays;
VAR aInt:ARRAY[1..10] OF INTEGER;
    bInt:ARRAY[1..5] OF INTEGER;
    cInt:ARRAY[1..15] OF INTEGER;

    PROCEDURE LoadIntegerArrays( );
    VAR num:INTEGER;
        I:CARDINAL;
    BEGIN
        num:=0;
        FOR I:=1 TO 10 DO
            aInt[I] :=num;
            INC(num);
        END;
        FOR I:=1 TO 5 DO
            bInt[I] :=num;
            INC(num);
        END;
        FOR I:=1 TO 15 DO
            cInt[I] :=99;
        END;
    END LoadIntegerArrays;

    PROCEDURE DisplayIntegerArray(x:ARRAY OF INTEGER);
    VAR I:CARDINAL;
    BEGIN
        FOR I:=0 TO HIGH(x) DO
            WriteInt(x[I],10);
            WriteLn;
        END;
    END DisplayIntegerArray;

VAR aReal:ARRAY[1..10] OF REAL;
    bReal:ARRAY[1..5] OF REAL;
    cReal:ARRAY[1..15] OF REAL;

    PROCEDURE LoadRealArrays( );
    VAR num:REAL;
        I:CARDINAL;
    BEGIN
        num:=0.0;
        FOR I:=1 TO 10 DO
            aReal[I] :=num;
            num:=num+1.0;
        END;
```

```
        FOR I:=1 TO 5 DO
          bReal[I] :=num;
          num:=num+1.0;
        END;
        FOR I:=1 TO 15 DO
          cReal[I] :=99.0;
        END;
      END LoadRealArrays;

    PROCEDURE DisplayRealArray(x:ARRAY OF REAL);
    VAR I:CARDINAL;
    BEGIN
      FOR I:=0 TO HIGH(x) DO
        WriteReal(x[I],15);
        WriteLn;
      END;
    END DisplayRealArray;

  TYPE String20=ARRAY[0..19] OF CHAR;

  VAR aStr:ARRAY[1..4] OF String20;
      bStr:ARRAY[1..3] OF String20;
      cStr:ARRAY[1..7] OF String20;

    PROCEDURE LoadStringArrays( );
    VAR I:CARDINAL;
    BEGIN
      FOR I:=1 TO 4 DO
        WriteString('Enter string: ');
        ReadString(aStr[I]);
      END;
      FOR I:=1 TO 3 DO
        WriteString('Enter string: ');
        ReadString(bStr[I]);
      END;
    END LoadStringArrays;

    PROCEDURE DisplayStringArray(x:ARRAY OF String20);
    VAR I:CARDINAL;
    BEGIN
      FOR I:=0 TO HIGH(x) DO
        WriteString(x[I]);
        WriteLn;
      END;
    END DisplayStringArray;

  TYPE Grade=RECORD
                name:String20;
                mark:[0..100];
             END;
```

```
VAR aStudent:ARRAY[3..4] OF Grade;
    bStudent:ARRAY[-1..1] OF Grade;
    cStudent:ARRAY[1..5] OF Grade;

  PROCEDURE LoadGradeArrays();
  VAR I:INTEGER;
      score:CARDINAL;
  BEGIN
    FOR I:=3 TO 4 DO
       WriteString('Enter name: ');
       ReadString(aStudent[I].name);WriteLn;
       WriteString('Enter numeric grade: ');
       ReadCard(score);WriteLn;
       aStudent[I].mark:=score;
    END;
    FOR I:=-1 TO 1 DO
       WriteString('Enter name: ');
       ReadString(bStudent[I].name);WriteLn;
       WriteString('Enter numeric grade: ');
       ReadCard(score);WriteLn;
       bStudent[I].mark:=score;
    END;
  END LoadGradeArrays;

  PROCEDURE DisplayGradeArray(x:ARRAY OF Grade);
  VAR I:CARDINAL;
  BEGIN
    FOR I:=0 TO HIGH(x) DO
       WriteString(x[I].name);
       WriteCard(x[I].mark,10);
       WriteLn;
    END;
  END DisplayGradeArray;

BEGIN
  LoadIntegerArrays();
  CatenateArrays(aInt,bInt,cInt);
  DisplayIntegerArray(cInt);
  WriteLn;WriteLn;
  LoadRealArrays();
  CatenateArrays(aReal,bReal,cReal);
  DisplayRealArray(cReal);
  WriteLn;WriteLn;
  LoadStringArrays();
  CatenateArrays(aStr,bStr,cStr);
  DisplayStringArray(cStr);
  WriteLn;WriteLn;
  LoadGradeArrays();
```

```
        CatenateArrays(aStudent,bStudent,cStudent);
        DisplayGradeArray(cStudent);
    END CatenateTest2.
```

LISTING 8.4

8.2 PROCEDURE TYPES

In addition to the various data types we have thus far discussed, Modula-2 makes available to the programmer what are called *procedure types.* Thus, variables of type PROCEDURE can be declared within a program. A variable of this type holds information about the location in memory of the procedure to which it, in effect, is pointing to.

Once a procedure variable has been appropriately declared, it can have other procedures that fit the format of the procedure type declaration assigned to it. After that assignment has been made, the procedure variable can be invoked. Thus, the two legal operations that can be performed on procedure variables are assignment and invocation.

As an example, consider the following procedure type declaration,

```
TYPE ProcType=PROCEDURE(CARDINAL,CARDINAL);
```

Note the usual use of the reserved word TYPE followed by a type identifier. The type, which in this case is a regular procedure (as opposed to a function procedure), has two pass-by-value parameters, each of type CARDINAL.

Next, we can declare a variable of type ProcType, if we wish, by simply writing

```
VAR P:ProcType;
```

after which P can be assigned an appropriate procedure through a statement such as

```
P:=WriteCard;
```

(assuming WriteCard has been imported into the program from library module InOut).

In making the assignment to P, a procedure whose parameter list matches the procedure type declaration in number, order, and type of parameters must be selected. Furthermore, only the procedure's identifier is used in the assignment statement.

Now that P has been assigned a value, it can be called just as any other procedure would be with the invocation

P(num,10);

where num is a variable of type CARDINAL. The result of such a call would be equivalent to an invocation of WriteCard(num,10) which results in the writing of the value of num in 10 columns to the output device.

A procedure type declaration, in essence, creates a template for a procedure. Any procedure that fits the template, whether it be developed by that programmer or selected from the library, can be assigned to a variable of that procedure type.

In Listing 8.5, we have a short example of the use of the procedure type discussed above. The program makes use of the fact that the three objects WriteCard, WriteOct, and WriteHex from MODULE InOut fit the same procedure type template that has been declared at the top of the program. With this in mind, PROCEDURE WriteArray has been coded. It accepts two parameters—an array of cardinal numbers and a procedure of type ProcType. The WriteArray procedure can thus be used to write out to the screen the cardinal array passed to it either in base 10, base 8, or base 16 form. A sample screen output is shown along with the program in Listing 8.5.

```
MODULE ProcedureTypeUse;

FROM InOut IMPORT WriteCard,WriteOct,WriteHex,WriteString,WriteLn,
      ReadCard;

TYPE ProcType=PROCEDURE(CARDINAL,CARDINAL);
     CardArray=ARRAY[1..5] OF CARDINAL;

VAR CardNums:CardArray;

    PROCEDURE LoadArray(VAR a:ARRAY OF CARDINAL);
    VAR i:CARDINAL;
    BEGIN
      FOR i:=0 TO HIGH(a) DO
        ReadCard(a[i]);
      END;
    END LoadArray;
```

```
    PROCEDURE WriteArray(a:ARRAY OF CARDINAL;P:ProcType);
    VAR i:CARDINAL;
    BEGIN
      FOR i:=0 TO HIGH(a) DO
        P(a[i],8);
      END;
    END WriteArray;

BEGIN
  WriteString('Load a cardinal array:');WriteLn;
  LoadArray(CardNums);
  WriteLn;WriteLn;
  WriteString('The array values in decimal:');WriteLn;
  WriteArray(CardNums,WriteCard);
  WriteLn;WriteLn;
  WriteString('The array values in octal:');WriteLn;
  WriteArray(CardNums,WriteOct);
  WriteLn;WriteLn;
  WriteString('The array values in hexadecimal:');WriteLn;
  WriteArray(CardNums,WriteHex);
END ProcedureTypeUse.
```

Screen output:

Load a cardinal array:
1234 56789 987 54 14

The array values in decimal:
 1234 56789 987 54 14

The array values in octal:
 002322 156725 001733 000066 000016

The array values in hexadecimal:
 04D2 DDD5 03DB 0036 000E

LISTING 8.5

Procedure types can be declared as regular procedures, as we have already seen, or as function procedures. The general formats for these two procedure types are respectively

```
TYPE ProcType=PROCEDURE(<data type>,<data type>,...<data type>);
TYPE FuncType=PROCEDURE(<data type>,...<data type>):<data type>;
```

Each data type on the formal parameter lists of these procedure type declarations can be either a pass-by-value or pass-by-reference parameter, with the usual VAR (followed by a space) indicating a pass-by-reference parameter.

A procedure type declaration for a parameterless procedure need not be declared since it has been predefined in Modula-2. The type identifier for such a procedure type is PROC. Thus, just as we can declare variables of type INTEGER, we can declare parameterless procedure variables of type PROC. For example, we might declare,

VAR P,Q:PROC;

where P and Q are programmer selected identifiers.

Standard procedures cannot be directly assigned to a procedure variable, but such an assignment can take place indirectly through the use of a "dummy" procedure. Consider, for example, that we wish to assign the standard procedure INC(x,n) (see Table 3.1) to a procedure variable. We would place it within a dummy procedure as shown in the program of Listing 8.6.

Note that when assigning the procedure variable P, a particular procedure, that assignment does not invoke that procedure. Rather, the statement P(x,3) is the call to the assigned procedure.

```
MODULE IncTest;

FROM InOut IMPORT Write;

    PROCEDURE IncChar(VAR ch:CHAR;n:CARDINAL);
    BEGIN
       INC(ch,n);
    END IncChar;

VAR P:PROCEDURE(VAR CHAR,CARDINAL);
    x:CHAR;

BEGIN
    x:="A";
    Write(x);
    P:=IncChar;
    P(x,3);
    Write(x);
END IncTest.
```

LISTING 8.6

When dealing with parameterless function procedures, whether declaring them as a procedure type, writing their procedure headings, or invoking them, an empty parameter list must be included. An example each of a type declaration, a heading, and an invocation of parameterless function procedures are:

```
TYPE ParameterlessFunc=PROCEDURE():CARDINAL;
PROCEDURE F1():CARDINAL;
y:=F1();
```

where y is of type CARDINAL.

Furthermore, although not required by Modula-2, you may find it worthwhile to include an empty parameter list with the invocation and within the heading of a regular parameterless procedure for consistency. That is, all of your procedure calls and headings would have a parameter list whether empty or not. Note that we have done exactly that in Listing 8.4.

8.3 A Small Case Study Using Open Array Parameters and Procedure Types

In this section we will develop a library module that will perform the jobs of sorting and displaying any length arrays whose base type occupies one word of memory. Types INTEGER and CARDINAL fit into this category along with arrays of two characters defined by String2=ARRAY[0..1] OF CHAR. A test program will also be developed to test the library module facilities.

Listing 8.7a is the definition module of the library module One-WordArrays. The module uses data type WORD, so it must be imported from MODULE SYSTEM. OneWordArrays exports the array sorting procedure SortArray and the array displaying procedure DisplayArray. Along with each of these procedures, an enumerated data type is also exported. The library module user must pass up to DisplayArray not only the array to be written to the CRT screen, but also the type of data that is to be displayed. This is accomplished through the use of the enumerated type ObjectType from which the user can select from the three values card, int, and str2 which, in effect, passes to DisplayArray the data type being written. The last parameter passed to DisplayArray, n, indicates the number of columns in which the data will be displayed.

Coupled with SortArray is the enumerated type LessThanType. During the sorting routine, comparisons between two array element values must be made. Passing a value from the list of constants of Less-

ThanType to SortArray allows it to select the proper comparison code, whether the data be numeric or alphabetic.

In Listing 8.7b, the implementation module for OneWordArrays is detailed. The implementation of the algorithm used for sorting goes under the name of a selection sort and can be described as follows.

Consider that the array to be sorted is in main memory. The first element value in the array is assigned to a variable (in our example, named small), and a sequential search through the remainder of the array is begun in which each succeeding array element value is compared to small. If the array element value is less than small, then small is reassigned this new smaller value and its index value within the array is noted. Upon completion of the search, the array element residing at the index value associated with small is exchanged with the first element of the array. In this way, the new first element in the array is indeed the smallest value among all the array elements.

This process of assigning an initial value to small, searching and exchanging, continues—this next time—starting with the second array element being initially assigned to small. Each search and exchange pass through the array reduces by one the remaining portion of the array yet to be sorted. Thus, the total number of passes made are one less than the number of elements in the array being sorted.

IMPLEMENTATION MODULE OneWordArrays makes use of a pair of procedure types (FuncType and ProcType) and a WORD-to-String2 conversion routine, along with three comparison functions and three display procedures (one each for the three data types that can be used with the library module). A detailed analysis of the implementations of these objects is left for the reader.

WordArrayTest (Listing 8.7c) tests the use of the newly-coded library module. Note that a selection of the three arrays, with arbitrary index types and lengths, are loaded and employed in the test. The module interface diagram, depicting the various imports and exports for this small case study, is shown in Figure 8.1.

```
DEFINITION MODULE OneWordArrays;

FROM SYSTEM IMPORT WORD;

EXPORT QUALIFIED SortArray,LessThanType,
                 DisplayArray,ObjectType,
                 String2;
TYPE String2=ARRAY[0..1] OF CHAR;
     LessThanType=(cardLessThan,intLessThan,str2LessThan);
     ObjectType=(card,int,str2);
```

```
PROCEDURE SortArray(VAR x:ARRAY OF WORD;LT:LessThanType);
PROCEDURE DisplayArray(x:ARRAY OF WORD;O:ObjectType ;n:CARDINAL);
END OneWordArrays.
```

LISTING 8.7a

```
IMPLEMENTATION MODULE OneWordArrays;

FROM SYSTEM IMPORT WORD;
FROM InOut IMPORT WriteLn,WriteString,WriteCard,WriteInt,Write;
FROM Strings IMPORT CompareStr;

TYPE FuncType=PROCEDURE(WORD,WORD):BOOLEAN;
     ProcType=PROCEDURE(WORD,CARDINAL);

  PROCEDURE WordToStr2(x:WORD;VAR s2:WORD);
  BEGIN
    s2:=x;
  END WordToStr2;

  PROCEDURE CardLessThan(x,y:WORD):BOOLEAN;
  VAR xCARD,yCARD:CARDINAL;
  BEGIN
    xCARD:=CARDINAL(x);
    yCARD:=CARDINAL(y);
    IF xCARD<yCARD THEN
      RETURN TRUE;
    ELSE
      RETURN FALSE;
    END;
  END CardLessThan;

  PROCEDURE IntLessThan(x,y:WORD):BOOLEAN;
  VAR xINT,yINT:INTEGER;
  BEGIN
    xINT:=INTEGER(x);
    yINT:=INTEGER(y);
    IF xINT<yINT THEN
      RETURN TRUE;
    ELSE
      RETURN FALSE;
    END;
  END IntLessThan;

  PROCEDURE Str2LessThan(x,y:WORD):BOOLEAN;
  VAR xStr2,yStr2:String2;
  BEGIN
    WordToStr2(x,xStr2);
    WordToStr2(y,yStr2);
```

```
    IF CompareStr(xStr2,yStr2)=-1 THEN (* if xStr2 < yStr2 then *)
      RETURN TRUE;
    ELSE
      RETURN FALSE;
    END;
END Str2LessThan;

PROCEDURE SortArray(VAR x:ARRAY OF WORD;LT:LessThanType);
        (* a selection sort *)
VAR n,StartIndex,index,i:CARDINAL;
    small,Temp:WORD;
    F:FuncType;
BEGIN
  CASE LT OF
    cardLessThan: F:=CardLessThan;|
    intLessThan:  F:=IntLessThan;|
    str2LessThan: F:=Str2LessThan;
  END;
  n:=HIGH(x);
  FOR StartIndex:=0 TO n-1 DO
    small:=x[StartIndex] ;
    index:=StartIndex;
    FOR i:=StartIndex+1 TO n DO
      IF F(x[i] ,small) THEN
        small:=x[i] ;
        index:=i;
      END;
    END;
    Temp:=x[index] ;
    x[index] :=x[StartIndex] ;
    x[StartIndex] :=Temp;
  END;
END SortArray;


PROCEDURE Card(x:WORD;columns:CARDINAL);
VAR xCARD:CARDINAL;
BEGIN
  xCARD:=CARDINAL(x);
  WriteCard(xCARD,columns);
END Card;


PROCEDURE Int(x:WORD;columns:CARDINAL);
VAR xINT:INTEGER;
BEGIN
  xINT:=INTEGER(x);
  WriteInt(xINT,columns);
END Int;
```

```
PROCEDURE Str2(x:WORD;columns:CARDINAL);
VAR xStr2:String2;
    i:CARDINAL;
BEGIN
  WordToStr2(x,xStr2);
  IF columns > 2 THEN
    FOR i:=1 TO columns-2 DO Write(' ');END;
  END;
  WriteString(xStr2);
END Str2;

PROCEDURE DisplayArray(x:ARRAY OF WORD;O:ObjectType;
                       n:CARDINAL);
VAR i:CARDINAL;
    P:ProcType;
BEGIN
  CASE O OF
    card:P:=Card; |
    int: P:=Int; |
    str2:P:=Str2;
  END;
  FOR i:=0 TO HIGH(x) DO
    P(x[i],n);
    WriteLn;
  END;
END DisplayArray;

END OneWordArrays.
```

LISTING 8.7b

```
MODULE WordArraysTest;

FROM InOut IMPORT WriteLn,WriteString,ReadCard,ReadInt,ReadString;
FROM OneWordArrays IMPORT SortArray,LessThanType,
                          DisplayArray,ObjectType,String2;

MODULE LoadArrays;

IMPORT WriteString,ReadCard,ReadInt,ReadString,String2;
EXPORT LoadCardArray,LoadIntArray,LoadStr2Array;

  PROCEDURE LoadCardArray(VAR x:ARRAY OF CARDINAL);
  VAR i:CARDINAL;
  BEGIN
    FOR i:=0 TO HIGH(x) DO
      WriteString('Enter cardinal number: ');
      ReadCard(x[i]);
    END;
  END LoadCardArray;
```

```
PROCEDURE LoadIntArray(VAR x:ARRAY OF INTEGER);
VAR i:CARDINAL;
BEGIN
  FOR i:=0 TO HIGH(x) DO
     WriteString('Enter integer number: ');
     ReadInt(x[i]);
  END;
END LoadIntArray;

PROCEDURE LoadStr2Array(VAR x:ARRAY OF String2);
VAR i:CARDINAL;
BEGIN
  FOR i:=0 TO HIGH(x) DO
     WriteString('Enter 2 characters: ');
     ReadString(x[i]);
  END;
END LoadStr2Array;

END LoadArrays;

TYPE COLOR=(black,brown,red,orange,yellow,green,blue,violet,gray,white);

VAR A:ARRAY[2..9] OF CARDINAL;
    B:ARRAY COLOR OF INTEGER;
    C:ARRAY[-1..4] OF String2;

BEGIN
  LoadCardArray(A);
  WriteLn;
  SortArray(A,cardLessThan);
  WriteLn;
  DisplayArray(A,card,10);
  WriteLn;
  LoadIntArray(B);
  WriteLn;
  SortArray(B,intLessThan);
  WriteLn;
  DisplayArray(B,int,10);
  WriteLn;
  LoadStr2Array(C);
  WriteLn;
  SortArray(C,str2LessThan);
  WriteLn;
  DisplayArray(C,str2,10);
END WordArraysTest.
```

LISTING 8.7c

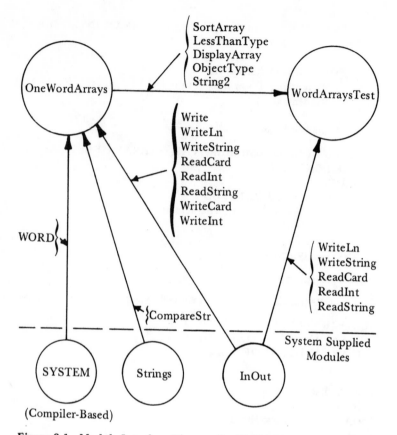

Figure 8.1. Module Interface Diagram for Listings 8.7a, 8.7b, and 8.7c.

9

Pointer and Opaque Types

Two topics will be discussed in this chapter, namely pointer types and opaque types. Why are they discussed in the same chapter? The answer is that an opaque type is generally implemented as a pointer type. What this notion means will become clear during our discussion of opaque types.

The first part of this chapter will center around the questions of what pointer types are, how they can be declared, and how they can be used, while the latter part of the chapter will be devoted to the meaning and use of opaque types.

9.1 Pointer Types

In all the programs we have presented in the text thus far, we have had to declare beforehand (before any executable code within the block under consideration is encountered) all variables through the use of TYPE and VAR declarations. If, for example, we desire to use an array of real numbers, we can describe the array structure through a TYPE declaration and establish an "array of reals" variable through a VAR declaration. The size of the array has to be predetermined regardless of the actual needs of any particular execution of the program involved. For instance, if it is desirable to temporarily store an unknown number of test grades within a program using the aforementioned array of reals, we would have to estimate the largest possible expected number of grades, maybe put in a factor of safety, and then declare that adjusted size array (even if in a particular execution of the program only a handful of grades are to be processed).

This beforehand setting of the sizes and actual number of variables needed is called *static allocation of memory* and can prove to be quite inefficient—it designates RAM memory space to variables regardless of whether that space is entirely used during any particular execution or not. Furthermore, any used but no longer needed memory space—along with the unused portion of the space—cannot be recovered for any other purpose as long as program control is within the scope of the block of code being executed.

Such a limitation can indeed hamper the efficient use of the memory store of the computer and, therefore, the size of the data and code associated with a particular program.

Modula-2 has a mechanism to remedy the situation. If we choose to use this mechanism, it will allow us to allocate memory areas for variables as they are needed during program execution. When they are no longer needed, we will be able to deallocate those memory areas, placing the disposed-of memory back on the computer's list of available memory space where it then can be used for other purposes.

Thus, using the Modula-2 mechanism for *dynamic memory allocation,* we can create (in essence, declare) RAM memory areas for new variables during program execution and dispose of those variables whenever it is expedient to do so, also during program execution. This is what is meant by dynamic memory allocation.

To set up the capability for dynamic memory allocation within a Modula-2 program, we use pointers. A *pointer* is a variable which allows us to reference a location in memory. The size and logical structure of this memory location being pointed to, along with a pointer variable identifier, must be declared in the usual manner within the declaration part of a program. A pointer variable in effect holds the RAM memory address of the first word of the memory area that it is pointing to.

For example, if we wish to set up a variable p that will point to a REAL number, then in the declaration part of the program we might write,

```
TYPE RealPtr=POINTER TO REAL;
VAR p:RealPtr;
```

Note that we have written TYPE and VAR declarations. The only thing new is the use of the sequence of reserved words—POINTER TO—which tell the compiler that we are setting up a pointer type (not a REAL type). The TYPE declaration declares a pointer type called RealPtr. This type of pointer can only be used to point to memory areas which are set up to house data objects of type REAL. The variable declaration is used to declare one variable (p) of the above pointer type; p can now be used to reference any number of memory areas of type REAL, one at a time.

Now that we have a way to reference a memory area, we can use the Modula-2 standard procedure NEW(< pointer variable >) to create a new memory area during execution. To later dispose of this memory area after it has outlived its usefulness in the program, we can invoke the standard procedure DISPOSE(< pointer variable >), making sure that the pointer variable is indeed assigned to the memory area we wish to dispose of. To use both the NEW and DISPOSE standard procedures, we must import MODULE Storage, and in particular the objects ALLOCATE and DEALLOCATE, into our program. (MODULE Storage is a standard library module provided with all Modula-2 systems; see Chapter 11.)

In summary, to use the dynamic memory allocation facilities available in Modula-2:

1. We must declare a pointer type along with pointer variables of that type.

2. We must import Storage (ALLOCATE and DEALLOCATE) into the program.

3. Now we can use NEW to set a pointer variable (the parameter of NEW) to reference a new memory area of the designated type.

4. We can use DISPOSE to release the memory area being pointed to by the pointer variable (which is the parameter of DISPOSE).

As a demonstration of the use of pointers, consider the sequence of statements in the program of Listing 9.1. Since the standard procedures NEW and DISPOSE are used in the program, the procedures ALLOCATE and DEALLOCATE have been appropriately imported into the program from MODULE Storage (see line 2 of Listing 9.1).

Lines 3 and 4 declare a pair of pointer variables which will reference INTEGER variables as the TYPE declaration indicates. It should be understood that as the program begins to execute, the pointer variables p and q do exist, but at the outset (line 5) they point to nowhere.

```
1    MODULE PointerDemo;

2    FROM Storage IMPORT ALLOCATE,DEALLOCATE;

3    TYPE IntPtr=POINTER TO INTEGER;
4    VAR p,q:IntPtr;
```

```
 5    BEGIN
 6       NEW(p);
 7       p∧:=7;
 8       q:=p;
 9       INC(p∧);
10       q:=NIL;
11       NEW(q);
12       q∧:=10;
13       DISPOSE(p);
14       NEW(p);
15       p∧:=q∧;
16       p:=q;
17    END PointerDemo.
```

LISTING 9.1

Lines 6 through 16 of the listing create, dispose of and manipulate this pair of pointer variables and the memory locations they reference. To help visualize the result of each instruction, we will make use of a simple diagram (see Figure 9.1) to depict a pointer and the variable it references. A pointer will be represented by its identifier within a circle, whereas a referenced memory area will consist of a rectangle enclosing the referenced variable's value. An arrow emanating from a pointer will be used to indicate the location that is being referenced by that pointer.

As we move through the program, line by line, both Listing 9.1 and Figure 9.2 should be referred to.

In line 6, an INTEGER variable is created and is pointed to by pointer variable p. Line 7 assigns the value 7 to that variable. This is accomplished by writing p∧:=7. The up arrow ("∧") following a pointer variable refers not to the pointer variable itself, but rather to the memory area that the named pointer is referencng. Thus, the coding p∧:=7 actually assigns the value 7 to the INTEGER variable referenced by p, at that point in the execution of the program.

In line 8, the other pointer variable q is set to reference the same INTEGER variable that p is pointing to. Next, in line 9, the variable being pointed to by p is incremented by 1. Of course, since q is pointing to the same memory area as is p, q∧ has also been incremented by 1.

In line 10, the pointer q is disassociated with the memory area it was referencing and is set to point to no memory area at all. This is accomplished by assigning q the value NIL. NIL is a standard identifier in Modula-2 and is used to actually assign a value to a pointer when that pointer is not to point to any memory area.

Figure 9.1. Standard diagram of memory location being referenced by pointer variable.

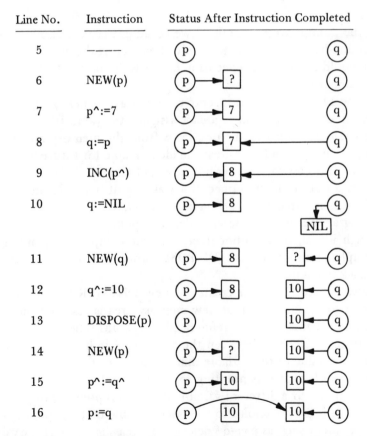

Figure 9.2. Diagram of memory locations being referenced by pointer variables during execution of Listing 9.1.

The assignment of NIL is different from the case where a pointer is undefined. (Note that as execution of our program began, both p and q were undefined.) What is the difference? It lies in our ability to sense the status of a pointer variable. There are occasions when it is desirable to check whether a pointer is referencing a memory area or not. We can perform the check if the pointer is in one of two states— either pointing to a memory area, or its value is NIL. The following code segment will then perform the check:

```
IF p=NIL THEN
   WriteString('The pointer value is NIL');
ELSE
   WriteString('The pointer is referencing a memory area');
END;
```

If the pointer were undefined we could not use the above code to determine its status, since the result of executing the above code segment would result in the execution of the ELSE part of the IF-THEN-ELSE construct.

In line 11, the pointer q is set to reference a new memory area, after which (line 12) that memory area is assigned the value 10.

Line 13 disassociates the pointer p from the memory area it had been pointing to, and that area is made available for future use in the program, if necessary. Pointer p is now undefined.

When a pointer is undefined (such as p is, at this point in the program), it is referred to as a *dangling pointer.* Care must be taken by the programmer not to reference dangling pointers. Such a reference, although illegal, may go undetected by the compiler, depending on the implementation of the DISPOSE procedure of the particular Modula-2 being used.

Now, we see that after creating a new INTEGER variable with p pointing to it (line 14), that new memory area is assigned the same value that the memory area referenced by q holds (line 15).

Note the difference between the statements in lines 15 and 16. In line 15, the value of the variable that p is pointing to is set to the value of the variable that q is pointing to, whereas in line 16 the pointer p is set to point to a different variable than it was pointing to previous to line 16—it is set to point to the same variable that q is pointing to. So a statement such as p^:=q^ deals with a reassignment of the values of referenced variables. On the other hand, a statement such as p:=q deals with a reassignment of the pointer itself.

It should be pointed out that the statement found in line 16 makes for rather poor programming practice. Why? Because we have reassigned the pointer p to point to a different INTEGER variable from the one it had been pointing to without, beforehand, properly disposing of the original INTEGER variable referenced by p. Having done this, it has left us with no way to access the original INTEGER variable and no way to return it to the available memory store of the computer. Such a programming "mistake", although not detectable by the compiler or during execution, should be avoided.

As a second example dealing with pointers, we will involve ourselves with one of the standard "data structure" concepts studied in computer science—the stack. A stack can be thought of as an area in memory where data items (such as characters, real numbers, etc.) are kept. Items can be added to or deleted from a stack only via passage through its one access point in an orderly manner.

A stack initially containing three integer data items is depicted in Figure 9.3. Note that a stack, in concept at least, has an unlimited capacity to hold data items and has but one access point as indicated. A variable named "top" will be used to indicate which data item sits at the very top of the stack. Adding an item to a stack is traditionally referred to as *pushing* that item onto the stack, whereas deleting an item from a stack is traditionally referred to as *popping* that item off the stack. The reverse of the order in which items are pushed onto a stack is the only order in which items can be popped off the stack. Thus, a stack is commonly referred to as a last-in, first-out structure (LIFO).

Considering the stack depicted in the figure, only the item pointed to by top can be popped off the stack. To pop the item –29 off the stack, we must first pop 14 off the stack. Each time a pop operation is executed, top is readjusted to indicate the new top of the stack. Thus, as 14 is popped off the stack, top is reassigned to point to –29 and the stack appears as in Figure 9.3b. The next pop operation pops –29 off the stack and top is assigned to point to 57 as shown in Figure 9.3c. Pushing the item 106 onto the stack results in Figure 9.3d, where top has been reassigned to point to 106 as expected.

Although a stack can be implemented in a number of ways, we will concentrate on a widely-used implementation which makes use of dynamic memory allocation and pointers. Thus, the variable top will be a pointer type in the program we will be developing below.

As a new item is pushed onto our dynamically implemented stack, the pointer top is set to point to it. The new item will be accompanied

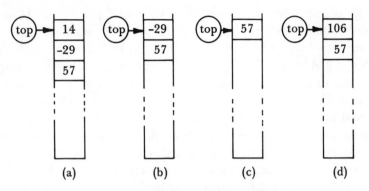

Figure 9.3. "Popping" and "Pushing" data in a stack data structure.

by a pointer that will be set to point to the item that top had been just previously pointing to, thus creating the ordering of the items in the stack. When an item is popped off the stack, top will be adjusted to point to the next item in line.

We will call this collection of an item and its associated pointer a *cell* or a *node* of the stack. Each cell of the stack can be structured as a record type, one field holding the item value and the other field holding a pointer to the next cell in the stack. In the illustrative example to follow, the "item" field will store a single character. Thus, the type declarations for implementing the character stack for our next example would be of the form

```
TYPE StackCellPtr=POINTER TO StackCell;
     StackCell=RECORD
               item:CHAR;
               next:StackCellPtr;
          END;
```

Note that there is a peculiarity associated with the above pair of type declarations. It is caused by the dilemma of needing to declare a pointer type that points to a record which has, as one of its fields, the same type pointer. If we declare the pointer type first, as illustrated above, we find ourselves referring to a data type (StackCell) before it has been defined through a type declaration. On the other hand, if we declare the record type (StackCell) first, we also find ourselves referring to a data type (StackCellPtr) before it has been properly defined. To alleviate this situation, Modula-2 compilers have been implemented to allow for this one use of an identifier (of the cell type that a pointer is to reference) without its prior type declaration. However, the cell type declaration must subsequently be forthcoming or the compiler will flag the error at an appropriate point in the compilation process.

```
MODULE StackWithPointers;

FROM Storage IMPORT ALLOCATE,DEALLOCATE;
FROM InOut IMPORT WriteString,WriteLn,Write,Read,EOL;

TYPE StackCellPtr=POINTER TO StackCell;
     StackCell=RECORD
                    item:CHAR;
                    next:StackCellPtr;
               END;

VAR top:StackCellPtr;

   PROCEDURE InitStack();
   BEGIN
      top:=NIL;
   END InitStack;

   PROCEDURE Empty():BOOLEAN;
   VAR E:BOOLEAN;
   BEGIN
      IF top=NIL THEN
        E:=TRUE;
      ELSE
        E:=FALSE;
      END;
      RETURN E;
   END Empty;

   PROCEDURE Push(x:CHAR);
   VAR Ptr:StackCellPtr;
   BEGIN
      NEW(Ptr);
      Ptr^.item:=x;
      Ptr^.next:=top;
      top:=Ptr;
   END Push;

   PROCEDURE Pop():CHAR;
   VAR x:CHAR;
        Ptr:StackCellPtr;
   BEGIN
      IF NOT Empty() THEN
        Ptr:=top;
```

```
        x:=Ptr^.item;
        top:=Ptr^.next;
        DISPOSE(Ptr);
      ELSE
        WriteString('Stack underflow');
      END;
      RETURN x;
    END Pop;

  VAR ch:CHAR;

  BEGIN
    InitStack();
    WriteString('Type in characters ending with a <cr>,');WriteLn;
    WriteString(' (they will be pushed on a stack):');WriteLn;
    Read(ch);
    WHILE ch #EOL DO
        Push(ch);
        Read(ch);
    END;
    WriteLn;
    WriteString('Now all characters will be popped off:');WriteLn;
    WHILE NOT Empty() DO
        Write(Pop());
    END;
  END StackWithPointers.
```

LISTING 9.2

A short illustrative program employing the stack data structure using a pointer type is shown in Listing 9.2. Note that appropriate importations and global declarations have been made. Once again, use will be made of a symbolic memory diagram to depict the declared pointers and record structure.

Figure 9.4a illustrates a pointer—Ptr—of type StackCellPtr pointing to a StackCell type. Since the StackCell type is a record consisting of two fields, the rectangle used to symbolize the StackCell memory space is divided into two fields—an item field and a pointer field.

If the program of Listing 9.2 is executed, and the characters 'E', 'C', 'A', 'E', and 'P' are pushed onto the stack, the symbolic memory diagram shown in Figure 9.4b is the result.

Referring to the program of Listing 9.2 after initializing the stack by setting the pointer top to NIL, characters are read and pushed onto the stack. This process is continued until the end-of-line character

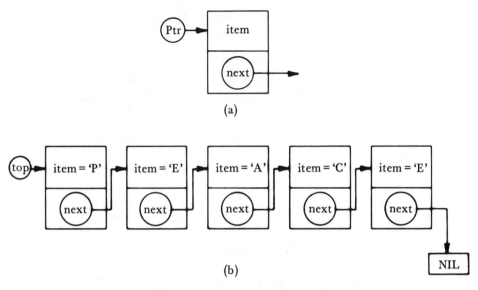

Figure 9.4. a) Stack data structure using a pointer type.
b) Symbolic memory diagram for Listing 9.2.

(EOL) is detected, after which all items on the stack are popped off—
in reverse order, of course.

It may be instructive to detail the push and pop procedures by developing a series of diagrams for each operation, as was done for the
first pointer example (Figure 9.2).

Figure 9.5 illustrates the sequence of events employed by a push
operation, and Figure 9.6 depicts the sequence of events employed
by a pop operation. Note that for the push operation, it is assumed
that the pointer top has been set to point to a StackCell memory location by a previous operation.

The push operation consists of three tasks, namely

1. Create a new memory area, (cell).

2. Assign appropriate values to each field of the cell.

3. Set the pointer top (or whatever you may call it) to point to the
   newly created cell.

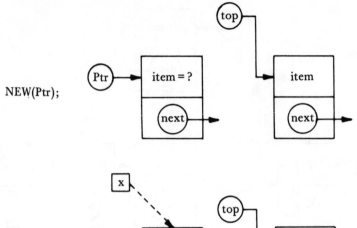

NEW(Ptr);

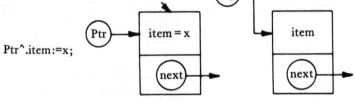

Ptr^.item:=x;

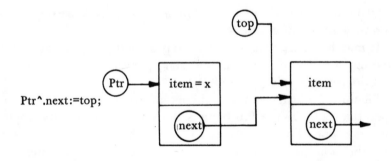

Ptr^.next:=top;

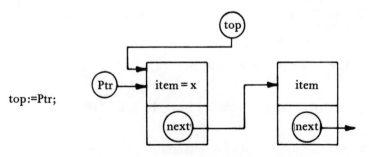

top:=Ptr;

Figure 9.5. The Push operation.

These tasks are detailed in the sequence of diagrams found in Figure 9.5, where we see that the instruction NEW(Ptr) sets up a new memory area of the type StackCell, with the pointer Ptr referencing it. This is followed by an appropriate assignment to the item field of the cell to which Ptr is pointing. Next, the pointer field (next) associated with the StackCell memory area is set up to point to the same cell that top has been referencing. The last instruction reassigns top to point to the newly-created cell which Ptr has been referencing.

To perform a pop operation, there must be at least one cell in the stack to be popped off. Thus, when a call to the function procedure Pop is made, the condition of the pointer top is checked to see if it is pointing to NIL or not. If it is not pointing to NIL, then the assumption is that top is referencing a cell. (Note that it is therefore imperative that, as a minimum, the programmer has properly initialized the stack with the invocation of InitStack at the outset of the program code.)

Now, with the condition that top is not equal to NIL, the three tasks comprising a pop operation can be executed. These three tasks are:

1. Copy the item field value of the cell being popped off the stack.

2. Reassign top to reference the next cell in the stack.

3. Deallocate the memory space that is no longer needed as a cell of the stack structure.

The instructions which implement the above tasks are detailed in the sequence of diagrams found in Figure 9.6. The implementation consists of four instructions, the first of which sets Ptr to point to the same cell that top is referencing. This is followed by copying into an appropriately typed variable—x—the value found in the item field pointed to by Ptr. Next, top is reassigned to point to the same cell that the next field pointed to by Ptr is referencing. Finally, the memory cell pointed to by Ptr is deallocated by invoking Modula-2's standard procedure DISPOSE. Of course, since the pop operation has been implemented as a function procedure, a return statement, (RETURN x), appears as the last instruction in PROCEDURE Pop.

It should be noted that the pointer type as defined in Modula-2 is a powerful tool for the efficient implementation of numerous computer science algorithms—many dealing with the subject of what are called *linked lists* and their processing.

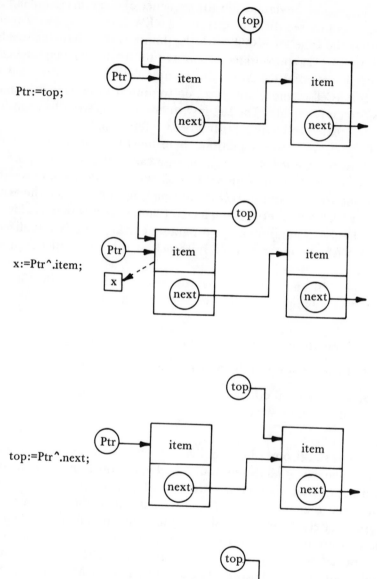

Ptr:=top;

x:=Ptr^.item;

top:=Ptr^.next;

DISPOSE(Ptr);

Figure 9.6. The Pop operation.

9.2 Opaque Types

Through the use of Modula-2 as we know it thus far, a programmer can set up abstract data structures and the pertinent operations upon those structures which closely reflect the actual problem being solved. By the judicious construction of procedures, these data abstractions can be operated upon without regard to the representational details of their implementation.

Even with these capabilities, though, there still remain two clear shortcomings which it is desirable to overcome.

To illustrate the first shortcoming, consider the case where a library module (both definition and implementation modules) has been installed on a system for the use of a team of programmers. Up to this point in our discussion of Modula-2, although the data structures and the operations defined for them can be used in the manner in which they were intended, it is still possible for a programmer to, inadvertently or otherwise, perform manipulations upon the inner structure of the declared data structures. This is caused by the fact that the representational details of these importable data structures are made "public" in a definition module and therefore are individually accessible to manipulation by the user of the module. Such manipulation may cause undetected execution errors and side effects as well as reducing both the readability and logical structure within a program.

The second shortcoming deals with the possible future modification of the implementation details of any data structure that has been made available for importation from a library module. If later, after the library module has been employed in some programming projects, the implementation of the library module is modified, and that modification includes any change in the structure of the data types available for import from the module, then that change must appear in the definition module. This will necessitate a complete recompilation of not only the implementation module, but also the definition module and, in turn, the program or library modules that make use of that modified library module. Again we are faced with an undesirable outcome—the complete recompilation of all modules of a software system that interfaces with the newly modified library module.

To overcome these shortcomings, Modula-2 has a mechanism for "hiding" the representational details of a data structure entirely within a library module's implementation module. Any such data structure that is to be hidden can be done so through the use of what are called *opaque types*. Opaque types are most often pointer types which are set to reference the data structure that is to be hidden (although it is possible to declare a subrange of a standard type as an opaque type as well).

In this section, we will concentrate our effort on declaring an opaque type which is a pointer. A series of library module implementations, dealing with stacks, will be developed and will be used to illustrate the use of information hiding and opaque types.

The concept of a stack need not be implemented by the use of pointers, as was accomplished in the last section. In the first illustration in our series of modules, we will make use of a stack implementation that employs an integer array to hold the items to be kept in the stack, and a marker to indicate which array element is currently the "top" element of the stack.

To set up such a stack structure, we can make the following declarations:

```
CONST maxstack=20;
TYPE STACK=RECORD
              item:ARRAY[1..maxstack] OF INTEGER;
              top:[0..maxstack] ;
           END;
```

where the value of the constant maxstack can be set to the anticipated maximum number of items to be stacked (along with a factor of safety).

This array stack structure can be used by ensuring that only a single element of the array is accessible at any particular moment. This can be accomplished by continuously adjusting the value of the variable top to the array index value of what is considered the "top" of the stack structure and using it exclusively as the index value when accessing the stack. Therefore, as we push and pop items on and off the stack, top is appropriately incremented or decremented so that it reflects the new position of the top of the stack.

Now let us consider the following programming task:

Integer values are to be entered from an input device and separated according to whether they are odd or even, after which the odd numbers are to be printed on the CRT screen in the reverse order of their entry, followed by a similar printout of the even numbers entered.

Program module OddAndEven, shown in Listing 9.3a, can be used to perform the above programming task. In that module, it is assumed that there exists a library module (StackOperations) from which a stack data structure named STACK can be imported along with the four operations we introduced in the program of Listing 9.2, namely Empty (which checks whether a stack is empty or not), Push (which pushes an item on a stack), Pop (which pops an item off a stack), and Initialize (which initializes a new stack to empty).

Furthermore, library module StackOperations must give us the capability of setting up a number of stacks simultaneously, as we will need two integer stacks—one for the odd integers and one for the even integers.

It should be noted that nowhere in the specification of the programming task or in the development of the program module for its solution have we had to specify the representational details of the stack data structure to be used, nor the details of how the four stack operations are to be implemented. In fact, our top-level solution has been consciously kept independent of any coding details so that we can use the program module of Listing 9.3a with any implementation of the library module, whether it be our first version or a much more efficient and sophisticated future version.

Such an approach to programming is referred to as *object-oriented design* where the design of the programming solution centers around the abstract objects stated in the specification of the programming task instead of concentrating on how we can represent those objects within the limitations of the programming language being used. Modula-2 is indeed a language where such an object-oriented approach to programming problems can be easily made.

```
MODULE OddAndEven;

FROM InOut IMPORT WriteInt,ReadInt,WriteString,WriteLn;
FROM StackOperations IMPORT STACK,Empty,Push,Pop,Initialize;

VAR OddStack,EvenStack:STACK;

    PROCEDURE LoadStacks;
    VAR n:INTEGER;
    BEGIN
        WriteString('Type any integers, (to end, type 9999):');
        WriteLn;
        ReadInt(n);
        WriteLn;
        WHILE n <> 9999 DO
            IF ODD(n) THEN
                Push(OddStack,n);
            ELSE
                Push(EvenStack,n);
```

```
            END;
            ReadInt(n);
            WriteLn;
        END;
    END LoadStacks;

    PROCEDURE DumpStacks;
    BEGIN
        WriteLn;
        WriteString('The odd integers in reverse order are:');WriteLn;
        WHILE NOT Empty(OddStack) DO
            WriteInt(Pop(OddStack),7);
            WriteLn;
        END;
        WriteLn;
        WriteString('The even integers in reverse order are:');WriteLn;
        WHILE NOT Empty(EvenStack) DO
            WriteInt(Pop(EvenStack),7);
            WriteLn;
        END;
    END DumpStacks;

BEGIN
    Initialize(OddStack);
    Initialize(EvenStack);
    LoadStacks;
    DumpStacks;
END OddAndEven.
```

LISTING 9.3a

Our first version of library module StackOperations is illustrated in Listing 9.3b, where DEFINITION MODULE StackOperations is shown. Here we see some details emerging. Note that the stack structure is implemented by using the array and marker structure previously discussed in this section. Further note that the four procedures that implement the needed stack operations include a STACK variable in their parameter lists. (Compare these procedure headings with their counterpart procedure headings found in Listing 9.2.)

In Listing 9.3c we have the implementation of the four stack operations. PROCEDURE Initialize merely sets the marker—top—of a stack variable to zero. PROCEDURE Empty tests to see if the value of top (associated with a particular stack) is zero. Such a value for top indicates that the stack is indeed empty. The push operation (see PROCEDURE Push) is implemented by first incrementing the value of top and then assigning the desired integer value to the item array element whose index value is top. Note that since the bounds of an array have to be declared beforehand, a check is made to see if the value of top is already at its maximum possible value (maxstack). If so, an error condition called a stack overflow occurs.

The pop operation is implemented, in effect, as the reverse of the push operation. An integer variable is assigned the value found in the current top element of the item array, followed by a decrement of the value of top. Pop, being a function procedure, returns the value that was copied into the integer variable. Again there may be an error condition, called a stack underflow, that occurs. We may be asking to pop a value off an empty stack. To guard against this, upon entry into PROCEDURE Pop the particular stack in question is tested as to whether it is empty or not.

Library module StackOperations, as implemented in Listing 9.3b and 9.3c, will perform their jobs and thus we have a working library module to go along with program module OddAndEven. But is it enough to just be able to "perform their jobs"? It is really not good enough if the intention is that the newly-designed library module is to be used as a general tool when dealing with stacks.

At the outset of this section, we pinpointed two shortcomings associated with the way we can, up to this point in our study of Modula-2, compose library modules. Now we can illustrate these shortcomings with the example we are presently discussing.

Note that the representational details of the data type STACK are made "public" in DEFINITION MODULE StackOperations (Listing 9.3b). This means that we could, for example, in program module OddAndEven employ the code line OddStack.top:=13 after initializing OddStack. Later, we could write OddStack.item[19] :=123. Of course, both these assignments would be deliberate and wrong, and should not be done. But there may be occasions when an inadvertent assignment may appear in a module importing StackOperations that will threaten its integrity. So, we must guard against that shortcoming of our implementation of the desired library module.

After having developed StackOperations as we have, using an array and marker for the stack implementation, consider our discovering that it would be more advantageous to implement the stack structure using pointer types as was done in the previous section. Since the representational details of the stack implementation are public, any change in that representation will also be public and will thus necessitate the recompilation of not only the definition and implementation modules of StackOperations, but also the recompilation of program module OddAndEven (and any other module that imports StackOperations).

Both shortcomings illustrated above are undesirable and can be avoided by representing the stack structure by an opaque type which allows us to keep the representational details of the stack structure "private". If we use an opaque type, we will not have to detail the structure of the stack in DEFINITION MODULE StackOperations but rather detail it only within IMPLEMENTATION MODULE Stack-Operations whose coding details are not available to the user of the library module.

```
DEFINITION MODULE StackOperations;

EXPORT QUALIFIED STACK,Initialize,Empty,Push,Pop;

CONST maxstack=20;

TYPE STACK=RECORD
                item:ARRAY[1..maxstack] OF INTEGER;
                top:[0..maxstack];
            END;

    PROCEDURE Initialize(VAR s:STACK);

    PROCEDURE Empty(s:STACK):BOOLEAN;

    PROCEDURE Push(VAR s:STACK;x:INTEGER);

    PROCEDURE Pop(VAR s:STACK):INTEGER;
END StackOperations.
```

LISTING 9.3b

```
IMPLEMENTATION MODULE StackOperations;

FROM InOut IMPORT WriteString;

    PROCEDURE Initialize(VAR s:STACK);
    BEGIN
        s.top:=0;
    END Initialize;

    PROCEDURE Empty(s:STACK):BOOLEAN;
    VAR E:BOOLEAN;
    BEGIN
        IF s.top=0 THEN
            E:=TRUE;
        ELSE
            E:=FALSE;
        END;
```

```
    RETURN E;
END Empty;

PROCEDURE Push(VAR s:STACK;x:INTEGER);
BEGIN
    IF s.top=maxstack THEN
        WriteString('Stack overflow');
    ELSE
        INC(s.top);
        s.item[s.top] :=x;
    END;
END Push;

PROCEDURE Pop(VAR s:STACK):INTEGER;
VAR x:INTEGER;
BEGIN
    IF Empty(s) THEN
        WriteString('Stack underflow');
    ELSE
        x:=s.item[s.top] ;
        DEC(s.top);
    END;
    RETURN x;
END Pop;

END StackOperations.
```

LISTING 9.3c

To insure privacy of the stack structure, we must change our view of type STACK. Instead of perceiving type STACK as a record with an array field (item) and a field which we have called a marker (top), let type STACK be a pointer type that points to the record structure just enumerated. By doing this, we can declare STACK as an opaque type by merely declaring

TYPE STACK;

with no type definition to follow in DEFINITION MODULE Stack-Operations. Listing 9.3d illustrates a newly-modified DEFINITION MODULE StackOperations.

Along with this new definition module, the full details of type STACK must be explicitly given in a type declaration in the corresponding IMPLEMENTATION MODULE StackOperations as shown in Listing 9.3e. In this new version, the variable s, which appears in each of the four stack operations' parameter lists, is a pointer type and so must be treated as such. The necessary modifications should be easily understood by making a comparison between corresponding stack operations in Listings 9.3c and 9.3e.

Now, any attempt, by a user of our modified version of library module StackOperations to access the representational details of the stack structure will fail. In fact, if the user is not privy to the source code of the implementation module, he or she will not even know how the structure of the stack has been formulated. Has it been implemented by use of an array and marker record, or has it been structured by an item and pointer record? The integrity of the implementation details has indeed been preserved by the use of an opaque type—thus eliminating the first shortcoming.

```
DEFINITION MODULE StackOperations;

EXPORT QUALIFIED STACK,Initialize,Empty,Push,Pop;

TYPE STACK;

    PROCEDURE Initialize(VAR s:STACK);

    PROCEDURE Empty(s:STACK):BOOLEAN;

    PROCEDURE Push(VAR s:STACK;x:INTEGER);

    PROCEDURE Pop(VAR s:STACK):INTEGER;

END StackOperations.
```

LISTING 9.3d

```
IMPLEMENTATION MODULE StackOperations;

FROM InOut IMPORT WriteString;
FROM Storage IMPORT ALLOCATE;

CONST maxstack=20;

TYPE STACK=POINTER TO RECORD
                        item:ARRAY[1..maxstack] OF INTEGER;
                        top:[0..maxstack] ;
                      END;

    PROCEDURE Initialize(VAR s:STACK);
    BEGIN
        NEW(s);
        s^.top:=0;
    END Initialize;
```

```
PROCEDURE Empty(s:STACK):BOOLEAN;
VAR E:BOOLEAN;
BEGIN
   IF s∧.top=0 THEN
     E:=TRUE;
   ELSE
     E:=FALSE;
   END;
   RETURN E;
END Empty;

PROCEDURE Push(VAR s:STACK;x:INTEGER);
BEGIN
   IF s∧.top=maxstack THEN
     WriteString('Stack overflow');
   ELSE
     INC(s∧.top);
     s∧.item[s .top] :=x;
   END;
END Push;

PROCEDURE Pop(VAR s:STACK):INTEGER;
VAR x:INTEGER;
BEGIN
   IF Empty(s) THEN
     WriteString('Stack underflow');
   ELSE
     x:=s∧.item[s∧.top] ;
     DEC(s∧.top);
   END;
   RETURN x;
END Pop;

END StackOperations.
```

LISTING 9.3e

Furthermore, with our new definition module in hand, we can substitute any other implementation module we wish (as long as it interfaces appropriately with the definition module) with only that new implementation needing to be recompiled. And so, the second shortcoming stated at the outset of this section is also eliminated.

A new implementation module for library module StackOperations, which employs the item and pointer record implementation of a stack, is shown in Listing 9.3f. The details of the code should be self-explanatory in light of our previous discussion of such a stack structure.

```
IMPLEMENTATION MODULE StackOperations;
FROM InOut IMPORT WriteString;
FROM Storage IMPORT ALLOCATE,DEALLOCATE;
TYPE STACK=POINTER TO RECORD
                          item:INTEGER;
                          next:STACK;
                    END;
  PROCEDURE Initialize(VAR s:STACK);
  BEGIN
    s:=NIL;
  END Initialize;

  PROCEDURE Empty(s:STACK):BOOLEAN;
  VAR E:BOOLEAN;
  BEGIN
    IF s=NIL THEN
      E:=TRUE;
    ELSE
      E:=FALSE;
    END;
    RETURN E;
  END Empty;

  PROCEDURE Push(VAR s:STACK;x:INTEGER);
  VAR Ptr:STACK;
  BEGIN
    NEW(Ptr);
    Ptr^.item:=x;
    Ptr^.next:=s;
    s:=Ptr;
  END Push;

  PROCEDURE Pop(VAR s:STACK):INTEGER;
  VAR x:INTEGER;
      Ptr:STACK;
  BEGIN
    IF Empty(s) THEN
      WriteString('Stack underflow');
    ELSE
      Ptr:=s;
      x:=Ptr^.item;
      s:=Ptr^.next;
      DISPOSE(Ptr);
    END;
    RETURN x;
  END Pop;
END StackOperations.
```

LISTING 9.3f

Library Modules–Part II

As implemented on a single processor machine (1 CPU), Modula-2 has both high- and low-level facilities to simulate the concurrent execution of two or more processes. Time-sharing (time-multiplexing) of the processor among the processes within a program can be accomplished in a controlled manner through the use of a pair of standard modules.

The high-level facilities used to simulate concurrency are encapsulated in the standard library module Processes, whereas the low-level facilities are found in the compiler-based module SYSTEM from which we have already studied a number of objects (see section 7.3).

In this chapter we will discuss the concept of coroutines which can be implemented using the SYSTEM module, and the concept of sequential processes which can be implemented using MODULE Processes. As the development of these two concepts take form, the needed objects from SYSTEM and Processes will be presented. Each concept will be illustrated with a series of programs of increasing complexity. The only difference between these two concepts is the method used for scheduling the execution of the individual processes involved in a given program.

Some of the objects from the library module Terminal will be rather important to the development of the illustrative examples, so we will begin this chapter with a short study of that module.

10.1 MODULE Terminal

Importation of library module Terminal into a program gives us the facility to read characters from the keyboard and write characters to the screen. In addition, Terminal allows us to sense whether a key has been typed at the keyboard or not. This sensing is referred to as *keyboard polling*. Such a polling capability plays a central role in a number of the programs developed in this chapter.

Listing 10.1 is the listing of DEFINITION MODULE Terminal. It explicitly shows the objects available for importation from Terminal.

```
DEFINITION MODULE Terminal;

EXPORT QUALIFIED Read,BusyRead,ReadAgain,ReadLn,
                 Write,WriteString,WriteLn;

PROCEDURE Read(VAR ch:CHAR);
PROCEDURE BusyRead(VAR ch:CHAR);
PROCEDURE ReadAgain;
PROCEDURE ReadLn(VAR s:ARRAY OF CHAR);

PROCEDURE Write(ch:CHAR);
PROCEDURE WriteString(s:ARRAY OF CHAR);
PROCEDURE WriteLn;

END Terminal.
```

LISTING 10.1

Seven procedures constitute the module. The first four listed are
for reading from the keyboard while the remaining three are for writing
to the CRT screen.

Four of the objects importable from Terminal (namely Read, Write,
WriteString, and WriteLn) function in much the same manner as their
counterparts do as found in library module InOut. The Read procedure
has one parameter of type CHAR. When invoked, it awaits a single
keystroke to be entered at the keyboard. The typed character will automatically be written to the screen (echoed). The Write procedure
displays the value of its single character parameter onto the screen.
Likewise, the WriteString procedure displays the value of its string parameter on the screen. The screen cursor can be moved to the beginning
of the next line (carriage return) by invoking the WriteLn procedure.

The ReadLn procedure may be likened to the ReadString procedure
found in module InOut. It also has one parameter—an array of characters. The procedure reads a sequence of typed characters until a
carriage return is sensed. Each character typed is echoed back to the
screen. If a backspace is typed, the most recently typed character in
the string is deleted from both the string parameter and the screen
echo. The final keystroke, the carriage return, does not become part
of the string but merely indicates the end of the entered string.

The remaining two procedures set module Terminal apart from In-
Out. PROCEDURE BusyRead does not wait for a key to be typed at
the keyboard but immediately returns whether or not a key has been
previously typed since the last read was made. If one has, that character is read from the input buffer and returned, but it is not echoed

to the screen when read. If a character has not been typed, the null character—(0C)—is returned. Thus BusyRead can be used to test if a key has been typed or not.

The ReadAgain procedure takes the last character that has been read and places it into the input buffer so that it can be read once again.

10.2 Coroutines and Completing Our View of MODULE SYSTEM

Our previous discussion of MODULE SYSTEM (see section 7.3) was not complete, as stated at that time. In this section we will complete the job, as the remaining objects available to us from SYSTEM will be used in implementing what will be referred to as *coroutines*.

Modula-2 can be used to establish coroutines which are independently executing procedures. Coroutines are created by specifying a parameterless procedure in the outermost program block for the coroutine to execute and an area in memory for the coroutine to execute in. A coroutine remains inactive until it is called by another coroutine. A basic application of the coroutine concept is found in the relationship between an executing Modula-2 program and its supporting software system (operating system). With its coroutine programming capabilities, Modula-2 can be used to write process schedulers, that is, programs that schedule how various subprograms are to run.

Coroutines are either active (executing) or inactive. Only one coroutine executes at a time. Communication between coroutines is accomplished though a coroutine call. Such a call activates the called coroutine and inactivates the calling coroutine.

Coroutine calls are different from procedure calls in that, unlike procedure calls, coroutine calls do not imply a subsequent return to the calling coroutine—they directly transfer control between the two coroutines without causing a return to the calling coroutine when the called coroutine comes to completion.

Generally, a procedure which is a coroutine takes the form of an unconditional loop (LOOP-END construct). Changing the state of the coroutine from active to inactive takes place, as stated previously, through coroutine transfer statements.

If any coroutine reaches the end of its procedure body, the enclosing program and all other coroutines within automatically terminate.

Modula-2 uses the term *process* when referring to coroutines. Thus the terms coroutine and process will be used interchangeably in what follows.

MODULE SYSTEM exports the objects needed to develop coroutines, namely PROCESS, NEWPROCESS, TRANSFER, IOTRANSFER, and LISTEN.

PROCESS is a data type through which all coroutine (process) calls are made. Thus, each coroutine in a program is referred to by a variable identifier of type PROCESS.

The creation of a new process (coroutine) is accomplished with the procedure, NEWPROCESS, whose formal procedure heading has the form

PROCEDURE NEWPROCESS(P:PROC;A:ADDRESS;N:CARDINAL;
VAR P1:PROCESS);

where P is a parameterless procedure declared at the outermost (global) level of a compilation unit. It is the procedure that the new process will execute. Note that P is of type PROC (see section 8.2).

A, denotes the starting address of the area in RAM in which the coroutine will execute, while N denotes the size of that area in storage units (of the particular machine with which you are working). A and N can be most easily developed by using MODULE SYSTEM's function procedures, ADR and SIZE (see section 7.3), with the area in question being declared as an array.

P1 is the process variable identifier assigned to the new process. Thus, any transfers involving the newly-created coroutine will make reference to the coroutine's process variable identifier—not the name of the procedure that the coroutine controls.

As a rule of thumb the process area should contain, at a minimum, 100 words of storage. If the space provided for the process is too small, a stack overflow will occur and the appropriate error message will appear on the computer screen.

A coroutine is called through the procedure TRANSFER, whose heading has the form

PROCEDURE TRANSFER(VAR OLD,NEW:PROCESS);

TRANSFER suspends execution of (inactivates) the currently executing process, assigns its state to the process variable OLD, and resumes execution of (activates) the process associated with the process variable NEW. Both OLD and NEW should, of course, have been appropriately initialized through the use of PROCEDURE NEWPROCESS.

The remaining facilities available from MODULE SYSTEM are used for real-time system applications. IOTRANSFER acts similarly to TRANSFER in that the current process is inactivated and the named process resumes its execution. In addition, the next processor interrupt transfers control back to the original, previously inactivated, process. Typically, the IOTRANSFER procedure is used to transfer control to a peripheral device connected to the computer. Upon completion of the peripheral device's operation, an interrupt is signalled to that effect and a transfer back to the original process is performed.

To distinguish one peripheral device from another, each device is assigned an interrupt vector address. Furthermore, devices may be given interrupt priorities. A low-priority device cannot interrupt higher-priority devices, although at opportune moments it may be desirable to temporarily lower the current priority of a high-priority device so that a lower-priority interrupt can occur. This can be accomplished through the use of the procedure LISTEN.

A series of three programs will now be developed to illustrate the use of some of the coroutine facilities available to us through the importation of MODULE SYSTEM.

10.3 A First Coroutine Example

An early spring Daisy may be picked from a field and, as the petals are plucked from its center, you may alternately query, "She loves me... She loves me not...". Our first coroutine example, program module Daisy shown in Listing 10.2, simulates such an activity.

In the main body, a counter, n, is initialized, two coroutines are created (the WriteLove and WriteNotLove procedures), and execution is transferred from the main body to one of the coroutines. The two newly created coroutines are parameterless procedures declared in the outermost block of the program module.

Note that the NEWPROCESS parameters have not only named the procedures that will be the coroutines, but also have set aside 200 WORD memory areas (through the ADR and SIZE invocations in conjunction with a pair of array variables) in which the coroutines are to execute. Furthermore, the newly-created coroutines will be referenced through the identifiers Love and NotLove.

Transfer of execution from the main body (whose execution is suspended upon transfer) to coroutine Love is accomplished with the TRANSFER procedure. The enclosing program module is itself a coroutine (a coroutine that is not explicitly created within our example but rather through the underlying operating system). Upon transfer to coroutine Love, the PROCESS variable identifier Main becomes associated with the main body of the program module. (This identifier now remains associated with the main body and execution control could be passed back to it through the use of Main, if desired. No such transfer takes place in Daisy, but that type of transfer will be used in the next two examples.)

Once coroutine Love takes control, we find ourselves entering a LOOP-END construct. After incrementing the counter n, the instruction Write('She loves me.') is executed. The Write instruction is found as an exported object from the local module WriteOut (which has, in turn, imported a pair of objects from library module Terminal). The Write instruction passes up the string, 'She loves me.', and it is written out to the CRT screen. Thus the first output line appears on the screen. Next, a test is performed as to whether n is equal to the NumberOf-Petals value. Since that is not the case, execution of coroutine Love is suspended at this point, and control is transferred to coroutine NotLove.

Again we find ourselves in a LOOP-END construct, and n is incremented. Next, the instruction Write('She loves me not.') is executed which invokes the Write procedure from MODULE WriteOut. Again n is tested, execution of NotLove is suspended, and control is transferred, this time back to coroutine Love. Transfer of control back means execution (of the coroutine transferred back to) is resumed at the instruction just following the point at which the coroutine (Love, in this case) was previously suspended. Coroutine Love has control of the processor as we come to the END of the LOOP-END construct and jump to the beginning of the loop. Once again n is incremented, 'She loves me.' is written to the screen, n is tested, and a transfer to NotLove takes place, with execution being resumed at the point of the previous suspension of NotLove.

Execution continues in this alternating manner, from one coroutine to the other and back again, until finally, when the value of n equals the value of NumberOfPetals, a coroutine LOOP-END construct is EXITed and execution of program module Daisy terminates in a normal fashion.

The complete screen output from Daisy is included in Listing 10.2.

```
MODULE Daisy;
```

```
FROM SYSTEM IMPORT WORD, ADR,SIZE,PROCESS,
                        NEWPROCESS,TRANSFER;
IMPORT Terminal;

  MODULE WriteOut;
  IMPORT Terminal;
  EXPORT Write;

    PROCEDURE Write(s:ARRAY OF CHAR);
    VAR i:CARDINAL;
    BEGIN
      FOR i:=0 TO HIGH(s) DO Terminal.Write(s[i]);END;
      Terminal.WriteLn;
    END Write;

  END WriteOut;

CONST NumberOfPetals=19;

VAR n:CARDINAL;
    Love,NotLove:PROCESS;

  PROCEDURE WriteLove; (* coroutine Love *)
  BEGIN
    LOOP
      INC(n);
      Write('She loves me.');
      IF n=NumberOfPetals THEN
        EXIT;
      ELSE
        TRANSFER(Love,NotLove);
      END;
    END;
  END WriteLove;

  PROCEDURE WriteNotLove; (* coroutine NotLove *)
  BEGIN
    LOOP
      INC(n);
      Write('She loves me not.');
      IF n=NumberOfPetals THEN
        EXIT;
      ELSE
        TRANSFER(NotLove,Love);
      END;
    END;
  END WriteNotLove;

VAR Main:PROCESS;
    A,B:ARRAY[1..200] OF WORD;
```

```
BEGIN
  n:=0;
  NEWPROCESS(WriteLove,ADR(A),SIZE(A),Love);
  NEWPROCESS(WriteNotLove,ADR(B),SIZE(B),NotLove);
  TRANSFER(Main,Love);
END Daisy.
```

Screen output:

She loves me.
She loves me not.
She loves me.
She loves me not.
She loves me.
She loves me not.
She loves me.
She loves me not.
She loves me.
She loves me not.
She loves me.
She loves me not.
She loves me.
She loves me not.
She loves me.
She loves me not.
She loves me.
She loves me not.
She loves me.

LISTING 10.2

10.4 A Keyboard Polling Example Using Coroutines

Our second example shown in Listing 10.3 develops a rudimentary keyboard entry routine which shares the resources of our single processor machine with another "background computing task". As long as there is no keyboard entry to be processed, the background computing task executes. If a character is entered at the keyboard, the routine for processing the keystroke performs its task. After completion of the keystroke processing, the background computing resumes.

A trace through MODULE KeyboardPolling (Listing 10.3) might be useful. At the beginning of the main body a numeric variable y is initialized and the user is prompted as to how to terminate the program. Next, a pair of coroutines are created through the use of PROCEDURE NEWPROCESS—one for performing the background computing task and the other for processing all keyboard entries. Procedure names are associated with each coroutine created along with their corresponding coroutine identifiers, and appropriately-sized memory areas are set aside in RAM for each coroutine.

Now, through the use of PROCEDURE TRANSFER, execution in the main body is suspended, the main body is associated with the PROCESS identifier Main, and processor control is transferred to coroutine Entry, our keyboard entry coroutine.

After entering a LOOP-END construct, the user is prompted with the message "Enter letter: ". Next, coroutine Entry is suspended at that point and coroutine Other, our keyboard polling and background computing coroutine, is activated. Again a LOOP-END construct is entered and immediately the BusyRead procedure (imported from MODULE Terminal) is used to detect whether a character has been entered at the keyboard or not. If a character has not been entered, then BusyRead returns the null character (0C) in the variable ch, and the variable y is incremented. (INC(y) is representative of any background computing task.)

Upon reaching the end of the LOOP-END construct in coroutine Other, execution, of course, jumps to the beginning of the loop and once again the keyboard is "polled" for an entry. As long as no entry is detected, the background computing task continues. If, on the other hand, a keystroke is detected, BusyRead returns other than the null character to ch and the THEN part of the IF construct is executed. The ReadAgain procedure (also imported from MODULE Terminal) is invoked so that the previously entered keystroke can be placed back in the input buffer in order that it can be reread at the appropriate time. Control is now transferred back to coroutine Entry and execution in it resumes from its previously suspended point. This means that the Read(ch) instruction, when executed, reads the keystroke just placed back in the input buffer. (Read(ch) is representative of any keyboard entry task.)

Processing continues in coroutine Entry where the value of ch is checked against the sentinel value "*". If the asterisk has not been entered, execution jumps to the beginning of the LOOP-END construct in Entry and the prompt "Enter letter: " is again written to the screen, after which execution is once again transferred to coroutine Other and the background processing resumes with keyboard polling for each iteration through the LOOP-END construct within Other. If an asterisk has been typed at the keyboard then the accumulated value of y is written to the screen and the LOOP-END construct of coroutine Entry is EXITed.

Instead of allowing the exiting of the loop to terminate execution of the program, we have illustrated how, even though we wish to end execution of the coroutines, we can continue processing within the program itself. This is accomplished by transferring control from Entry to Main through the use of TRANSFER(Entry,Main), found as the last instruction within coroutine Entry.

Now that we are back in the main body, additional processing can be carried out (as represented by writing to the CRT screen the message "Back in the main body").

In summary, our second coroutine example has presented us with a rudimentary technique for allowing the computer to respond to a keyboard interrupt where the keyboard entry routine can obtain the processor resources virtually immediately. This is regardless of what the background computing task may be, since in this example we have given, in effect, a higher priority to processing the keystrokes than to the incrementing of y.

```
MODULE KeyboardPolling;
FROM SYSTEM IMPORT WORD,NEWPROCESS,PROCESS,TRANSFER,
                   ADR,SIZE;
FROM Terminal IMPORT WriteString,WriteLn,BusyRead,ReadAgain,Read;
FROM InOut IMPORT WriteCard;

VAR Main,Entry,Other:PROCESS;
    y:CARDINAL;
  PROCEDURE KeyboardEntry;
  VAR ch:CHAR;
  BEGIN
    LOOP
      WriteString('Enter letter:  ');
      TRANSFER(Entry,Other);
      (* keyboard entry task *)
      Read(ch);
      WriteLn;
      IF ch='*' THEN
        WriteLn;WriteLn;
        WriteString('The accumulated value is:  ');
        WriteCard(y,5);
        EXIT;
      END;
    END;
    TRANSFER(Entry,Main);
  END KeyboardEntry;
```

```
PROCEDURE OtherJob;
VAR ch:CHAR;
BEGIN
   LOOP
      (* keyboard polling *)
      BusyRead(ch);
      IF ch #0C THEN
         ReadAgain;
         TRANSFER(Other,Entry);
      ELSE
         (* background computing task *)
         INC(y);
      END;
   END;
END OtherJob;

VAR A,B:ARRAY[1..1000] OF WORD;

BEGIN
   y:=0;
   WriteLn;
   WriteString('To end type "*":');
   WriteLn;
   NEWPROCESS(OtherJob,ADR(A),SIZE(A),Other);
   NEWPROCESS(KeyboardEntry,ADR(B),SIZE(B),Entry);
   TRANSFER(Main,Entry);
   (* additional processing after both coroutines are suspended *)
   WriteLn;
   WriteString('Back in the main body');
END KeyboardPolling.
```

Screen output:

```
To end type "*":
Enter letter: M
Enter letter: O
Enter letter: D
Enter letter: U
Enter letter: L
Enter letter: A
Enter letter: -
Enter letter: 2
Enter letter: *

The accumulated value is: 1248
Back in the main body
```

LISTING 10.3

10.5 A Small Case Study Using Coroutines

We can take the keyboard polling, coroutine concept and apply it to a more substantial program that has some practical application. Suppose that you have been developing a program to load a file of records. Each record consists of a last name field, a first name field, and a numeric data field. Each time you enter a new record it is desirable to immediately check for a duplicate last name. (For the sake of simplicity, only last names are checked in this example—not what one should obviously do—that is to check both last and first name for duplication.)

The duplication checking is accomplished with a simple search routine (a sequential search that makes a comparison between a newly entered last name and each last name field within the file of records.)

As the file increases in size, it becomes apparent that the time for making the search is beginning to take up a rather uncomfortably large segment of the data entry time, so it would be desirable to reduce this searching time.

With that scenario and the previous two examples considered in this section it should be clear that coroutines might be useful in alleviating the problem. We will develop our next illustrative example using coroutines and keyboard polling to enter data from the keyboard into a file of records and, interleaved with that data entry, conduct a search for duplicate last names. The search will immediately begin after the last name is entered and will be interrupted only when additional data for that record is actually being entered at the keyboard. In this way, the sequential search can use the time between the completion of the entry into one data field and the beginning of the entry into the next data field, thus reducing the overall time it takes to enter data and search for a duplicate.

A program which does the aforementioned pair of tasks concurrently (on a single processor using coroutines) is shown in Listing 10.4.

The main body of MODULE EnterDataAndDoSearch (lines 119–127) consists in part of a call to HeadingStuff (which is self-explanatory), the opening of our TESTFILE into which we are going to add nonduplicate records, the creation of two coroutines having adequate memory space within which to execute, and a transfer from Main (the PROCESS identifier selected for the main body) to Enter (the coroutine identifier associated with PROCEDURE EnterData). Note also that Search is the identifier used in association with PROCEDURE NameSearch.

Thus, two coroutines have been established—Enter which will perform the data entry task and Search which will perform the dual tasks of searching and keyboard polling.

The two coroutines must communicate with each other concerning two conditions, namely the question as to whether a duplicate last name has been found and the question as to whether the sequential search has been completed. This communication link is set up through the use of the two global BOOLEAN variables duplicate and finished.

Upon executing TRANSFER(Main,Enter) (line 124), control is passed to PROCEDURE EnterData (lines 35–71). Once the Boolean variable finished is initialized at TRUE, we move into the usual LOOP-END construct of a coroutine. If we are beginning to enter a new record, then execution of the THEN part of the IF-THEN construct (lines 44–50) occurs. In this portion of code the last name is entered and checked as to whether it is a sentinel (the asterisk) or not (lines 47–48). If so, the LOOP-END is exited and execution is transferred back to the main body (line 70) where TrailingStuff (line 125) is called, the file we are working with is closed, and the program terminates.

If the last name entered is not the sentinel value then it is placed in the last name field of our record structure RecStuff (line 49; see lines 10–14 for the record structure), and a prompt for the first name is written to the screen.

At this point coroutine Enter is suspended (the search has not yet begun, let alone finished), and control is passed to coroutine Search (PROCEDURE NameSearch, (lines 72–104)) so that the sequential search may commence.

```
1    MODULE EnterDataAndDoSearch;

2    FROM SYSTEM IMPORT WORD,NEWPROCESS,PROCESS,
                            TRANSFER,ADR,SIZE;
3    FROM Terminal IMPORT WriteString,WriteLn,BusyRead,ReadAgain,ReadLn;
4    FROM Conversions IMPORT StrToCard,CardToStr;
5    FROM Files IMPORT FILE,Open,Close,WriteRec,ReadRec,FileState,
6                        EOF,GetEOF,FilePos,SetPos,CalcPos;
7    FROM Strings IMPORT CompareStr;

8    TYPE String10=ARRAY[0..9] OF CHAR;
9         String16=ARRAY[0..15] OF CHAR;
10        Rec=RECORD
11              lastname:String16;
12              firstname:String10;
13              data:CARDINAL;
14            END;
```

```
15    VAR Main,Enter,Search:PROCESS;
16         A,B:ARRAY[1..1000] OF WORD;
17         F:FILE;
18         RecStuff:Rec;
19         i:CARDINAL;
20         finished,duplicate:BOOLEAN;

21      PROCEDURE HeadingStuff;
22      BEGIN
23        WriteLn;
24        WriteString('   Add new records to end of file');WriteLn;
25        WriteString('  (To end entry, type "*" as last name)');WriteLn;
26        WriteString('——————————————————————');WriteLn;
27        WriteLn;
28      END HeadingStuff;

29      PROCEDURE IOError;
30      BEGIN
31        WriteLn;
32        WriteString('I/O Error');
33        HALT;
34      END IOError;

35      PROCEDURE EnterData; (* coroutine Enter *)
36      VAR n:String16;
37           d:String10;
38           dummy:BOOLEAN;
39           pos:FilePos;
40      BEGIN
41        finished:=TRUE;
42        LOOP
43          IF finished THEN
44            WriteLn;
45            WriteString('Enter last name: ');
46            finished:=FALSE;
47            ReadLn(n);
48            IF n[0]='*' THEN EXIT;END;
49            RecStuff.lastname:=n;
50            WriteString('Enter first name: ');
51          END;
52          IF NOT finished THEN TRANSFER(Enter,Search);END;
53          IF NOT duplicate THEN
54            ReadLn(RecStuff.firstname);
55            WriteString('Enter data: ');
56          END;
57          IF NOT finished THEN TRANSFER(Enter,Search);END;
58          IF NOT duplicate THEN
59            ReadLn(d);
```

```
60              dummy:StrToCard(d,RecStuff.data);
61              WriteLn;WriteLn;
62            END;
                 (*if data entry completed first, go finish up search*)
63            IF NOT finished THEN TRANSFER(Enter,Search);END;
64            IF NOT duplicate THEN
                 (*set the "current file position" to end-of-file*)
65              GetEOF(F,pos);
66              SetPos(F,pos);
                 (*write just entered record at end-of-file*)
67              WriteRec(F,RecStuff);
68            END;
69          END;
70          TRANSFER(Enter,Main);
71        END EnterData;

72      PROCEDURE NameSearch; (* coroutine Search *)
73      VAR ch:CHAR;
74          RecStuff1:Rec;
75          pos:FilePos;
76      BEGIN
77        LOOP
             (*reset "current file position" to beginning*)
78          CalcPos(0,28,pos);
79          SetPos(F,pos);
80          duplicate:=FALSE;
81          ReadRec(F,RecStuff1);
82          WHILE NOT EOF(F) AND NOT duplicate DO
83            IF CompareStr(RecStuff.lastname,RecStuff1.lastname)=0 THEN
84              WriteLn;
85              WriteString('   Found a duplicate');WriteLn;
86              WriteString('   —record not entered into file');WriteLn;
87              duplicate:=TRUE;
88            END;
89            IF NOT duplicate THEN
90              ReadRec(F,RecStuff1);
91              BusyRead(ch);
92              IF ch #0C THEN
93                ReadAgain;
94                TRANSFER(Search,Enter);
95              END;
96            END;
97          END; (*WHILE*)
98          WriteLn;
99          WriteString('   *** Finished search ***');
100         WriteLn;
101         finished:=TRUE;
```

```
102              TRANSFER(Search,Enter);
103          END;
104      END NameSearch;

105      PROCEDURE TrailingStuff;
106      VAR d:String10;
107          dummy:BOOLEAN;
108      BEGIN
109        WriteLn;
110        WriteString('Last record processed was: ');WriteLn;
111        WriteLn;
112        WITH RecStuff DO
113          WriteString(lastname);WriteString(', ');
114          WriteString(firstname);
115          dummy:=CardToStr(data,d);WriteString('    ');
116          WriteString(d);
117        END;
118      END TrailingStuff;

119  BEGIN
120      HeadingStuff;
121      IF Open(F,'#5:TESTFILE') #FileOK THEN IOError;END;
122      NEWPROCESS(NameSearch,ADR(A),SIZE(A),Search);
123      NEWPROCESS(EnterData,ADR(B),SIZE(B),Enter);
124      TRANSFER(Main,Enter);
125      TrailingStuff;
126      IF Close(F) #FileOK THEN IOError;END;
127  END EnterDataAndDoSearch.
```

LISTING 10.4

A LOOP-END construct is entered, the current file position is set
to the beginning of TESTFILE, the Boolean variable duplicate is initialized as FALSE, and the first record is read (lines 77–81). Now the
search begins (lines 82–97). Note that the search uses CompareStr
(from library module Strings) to compare the newly-entered last name
with each lastname field in TESTFILE. When and if a duplicate is
found, appropriate messages are printed (lines 85–86,99), duplicate
and finished are assigned TRUE, and control is transferred back to
Enter.

After each comparison is made, if a duplicate is not found a new
record is read from the file (line 90) and the keyboard is polled for
an entry (line 91). If an entry has not occurred the search continues
until either a duplicate is found or the end-of-file marker is reached
(line 82). If a keyboard entry is sensed, then, through the use of the
usual code (lines 92–95), the search is suspended and coroutine Enter

is reactivated at the point of its last suspension, in this case line 53 where the first name is entered to its completion, a new prompt for data is displayed (line 55), and depending on the value of finished, control is transferred back to Search or not.

This process of passing control back and forth between the two coroutines continues until either the data entry for a new record is completed, a duplicate last name is found, or the sequential search is completed and no duplicate is found.

Note that in coroutine Enter, after each data field is completely entered, an opportunity for transfer to coroutine Search is offered (lines 52,57,63). In coroutine Search, during each iteration through the WHILE-DO construct, the keyboard is polled and a transfer can take place, if necessary (line 94). The only exception to that is the case where a duplicate is found under which condition a transfer takes place after the appropriate messages have been displayed (line 102).

Finally, if a record is completely entered and no duplicate is found, it is appended to the end of TESTFILE (lines 64–68).

We would like to conclude our view of the third coroutine example in our series of three with the following suggestions for enhancement of the program. All data entries into TESTFILE should be done using function procedure CAP (see section 3.5) so that there will be no distinction between the names Wirth, WIRTH, and wirth, etc. Of course, the checking for duplicates should be made on the concatenation of both the last and first names. Finally, after the last name is entered and the search is begun, additional time can be saved by bringing in the other data fields one character at a time—with the search continuing between character entries.

10.6 MODULE Processes

Standard library module Processes implements high-level facilities for simulating concurrency on a single processor. As mentioned at the beginning of this chapter, Processes will be associated with what we will refer to as sequential processes.

Sequential processes are implemented by the use of queues (first-in, first-out lists) which are set up by MODULE Processes. A sequential process is either active and executing or inactive and residing on a queue. Changing the state of activation of a sequential process is accomplished using what are called *signals*.

Through the use of a signal, a sequential process may be activated or it may suspend itself and be placed on the signal's queue. At some later point in time, that suspended process may be reactivated. This resumption of its execution can only occur when it has reached the front of the queue on which it has been residing.

So, unlike what happens with coroutines, a direct transfer does not occur from one sequential process to another. Rather, MODULE Processes, through signals, sets up a schedule as to which sequential process is to be activated next. Objects found in Processes allows the programmer to control the use of the scheduling of the sequential processes created within a program.

Listing 10.5 is a listing of DEFINITION MODULE Processes. The objects available for importation from Processes are SIGNAL, StartProcess, SEND, WAIT, Awaited, and Init.

```
DEFINITION MODULE Processes;

EXPORT QUALIFIED SIGNAL,StartProcess,SEND,WAIT,Awaited,Init;

TYPE SIGNAL;

PROCEDURE StartProcess(P:PROC;n:CARDINAL);
PROCEDURE SEND(VAR s:SIGNAL);
PROCEDURE WAIT(VAR s:SIGNAL);
PROCEDURE Awaited(s:SIGNAL):BOOLEAN;
PROCEDURE Init(VAR s:SIGNAL);

END Processes.
```

LISTING 10.5

A sequential process is created by invoking the StartProcess procedure. StartProcess has two parameters, the first of which identifies a parameterless procedure declared in the outermost block of the compilation unit. This named parameterless procedure is, in fact, the sequential process (just as the named parameterless procedure in MODULE SYSTEM's NEWPROCESS is a coroutine). The parameterless procedure is of the predeclared data type PROC (see section 8.2). The second parameter value passed to StartProcess indicates the amount of memory space reserved in RAM in which the sequential process will execute.

A sequential process can exist in any one of three possible states. It can be *executing,* be *ready* (by being placed on what is referred to as a ready queue), or be *suspended* (and be placed on the suspending signal's queue).

The establishment of variables of data type SIGNAL (an opaque type; see section 9.2) are the vehicles through which the state of a sequential process may be altered. Communication between processes occurs through the use of signal variables (as well as through the usual global variables). Before a signal variable can be used within a process, it must be initialized by invoking the Init procedure.

As soon as a sequential process is created through the invocation of the StartProcess procedure, it is placed on the ready queue from where it can be activated through the use of PROCEDURE WAIT.

PROCEDURE WAIT both suspends a sequential process and activates another sequential process. It suspends the presently executing process (the one in which it has been invoked) and places it on the queue of the signal named as its parameter. Thus the statement WAIT(sig) appearing in a sequential process will inactivate that process and place it on sig's queue (where, of course, sig has been a properly declared and initialized SIGNAL variable). The process is placed at the end of the signal's queue.

WAIT then selects the first process in line from the ready queue (the process that has the longest tenure on the ready queue), and that process resumes (or begins) execution.

If the WAIT procedure is called and there is no process waiting on the ready queue, a *deadlock* is caused and the enclosing program is terminated.

PROCEDURE SEND activates the first process in line on the queue of SEND's named SIGNAL parameter and places the process in which the SEND resided on the ready queue. If the SEND procedure points to an empty signal queue, then the calling process continues uninterrupted execution.

Function procedure Awaited returns a BOOLEAN value which indicates whether the named signal's queue is empty or not.

For ease of reference and to summarize the actions of the three procedures StartProcess, WAIT and SEND, we offer the following remarks:

| StartProcess | PLACES named PROCESS ON READY QUEUE | —— |

WAIT	PLACES PROCESS	SELECTS PROCESS
(if ready queue	in which it is	FROM beginning
contains at	invoked, ON	of READY QUEUE
least 1 process)	SIGNAL QUEUE	

WAIT	a processing DEADLOCK, PROGRAM TERMINATED
(if ready queue	
is empty)	

SEND	PLACES PROCESS	SELECTS PROCESS
(if signal queue	in which it is	FROM beginning
contains at	invoked, ON	of SIGNAL QUEUE
least 1 process)	READY QUEUE	

SEND	is a NULL OPERATION
(if signal queue	sending process continues to execute
is empty)	

Two illustrative examples will next be developed which should enhance your understanding of the concept of sequential processes and its implementation through the use of MODULE Processes.

10.7 Two Examples Using Sequential Processes

Our first example is a rewrite of MODULE Daisy (Listing 10.2) which was developed during our discussion of coroutines. This time, we will produce the same result using the concept of sequential processes and MODULE Processes. The rewritten program is shown in Listing 10.6.

```
MODULE Daisy;

FROM Processes IMPORT StartProcess,SIGNAL,SEND,WAIT,Init;
IMPORT Terminal;

  MODULE WriteOut;

  IMPORT Terminal;
  EXPORT Write;

    PROCEDURE Write(s:ARRAY OF CHAR);
    VAR i:CARDINAL;
    BEGIN
      FOR i:=0 TO HIGH(s) DO Terminal.Write(s[i]);END;
      Terminal.WriteLn;
    END Write;

  END WriteOut;
```

```
CONST NumberOfPetals=19;

VAR ForOther:SIGNAL;
    n:CARDINAL;

  PROCEDURE WriteLove; (* a sequential process *)
  BEGIN
    LOOP
      INC(n);
      Write('She loves me.');
      IF n=NumberOfPetals THEN
        EXIT;
      ELSE
        SEND(ForOther);
      END;
    END;
  END WriteLove;

  PROCEDURE WriteNotLove; (* a sequential process *)
  BEGIN
    WAIT(ForOther);
    LOOP
      INC(n);
      Write('She loves me not.');
      IF n=NumberOfPetals THEN
        EXIT;
      ELSE
        WAIT(ForOther);
      END;
    END;
  END WriteNotLove;

VAR forever:SIGNAL;

BEGIN
  n:=0;
  Init(ForOther);
  Init(forever);
  StartProcess(WriteNotLove,200);
  StartProcess(WriteLove,200);
  WAIT(forever);
END Daisy.
```

LISTING 10.6

Once again, in the main body a counter, n, is initialized. This is followed by the initialization of the two declared SIGNAL variables ForOther and forever. Next, two sequential processes are created (the WriteLove and WriteNotLove procedures), each being given the same size memory areas within which to execute (as were given the two co-routines of our coroutine version of MODULE Daisy).

It should be understood that at this point, the two sequential processes have been placed on the ready queue, with WriteNotLove first, followed by WriteLove.

The WAIT(forever) instruction suspends execution of the main body of the program module (which acts as a sequential process) and places it on the queue of the signal listed as the parameter of WAIT, namely the signal forever. WAIT further selects the first sequential process in line from the ready queue (WriteNotLove, in this case), and its execution begins. (Note that now WriteLove has moved to the beginning of the ready queue.)

Immediately upon beginning execution of WriteNotLove, we encounter WAIT(ForOther), which suspends further execution of WriteNotLove, places it on the ForOther signal's queue, and begins the execution of WriteLove, the first and only sequential process now found on the ready queue.

Execution of WriteLove finds us in a LOOP-END construct where the counter n is incremented and the message 'She loves me.', is written to the screen (using the same local module WriteOut Write instruction as was used in our coroutine version of Daisy).

Next, n is tested. Since it is not equal to NumberOfPetals at this time, the SEND(ForOther) instruction is executed; since the ForOther signal's queue contains one sequential process (WriteNotLove), it suspends execution of WriteLove, places it on the ready queue, and resumes the execution of WriteNotLove at the point of its previous suspension. Thus we enter the LOOP-END construct of WriteNotLove, increment n, and display on the screen 'She loves me not.'. This is followed by the usual test for n, the result of which is that the WAIT(ForOther) instruction is executed which suspends WriteNotLove, places it back on the signal queue, and execution of WriteLove is resumed. Being at the end of the LOOP-END construct in WriteLove, a jump is executed to the beginning of the loop where n is incremented, the appropriate message is displayed, n is tested, and the cycle of events continues with the suspension of WriteLove and resumption of WriteNotLove.

This alternation between sequential processes continues until finally n equals NumberOfPetals, a LOOP-END construct is EXITed, execution within a sequential process comes to an end, and the program terminates.

The screen output resulting from the execution of MODULE Daisy of Listing 10.6 is identical to that of our earlier MODULE Daisy in Listing 10.2.

So, you can see you really have a choice! You can express concurrency through the use of a low-level module (SYSTEM) using coroutines, or express it through the use of a high-level module (Processes) using sequential processes. There is a rather close relationship between the two techniques. In fact, many of the same objects from SYSTEM used to implement coroutines are imported into the implementation module of MODULE Processes.

The second sequential processes example shown in Listing 10.7 mirrors the second coroutine example that we previously developed (see Listing 10.3). Thus, a detailed, line-by-line trace through the program will be left for you to develop for yourself, although we would like to make a few comments regarding the program.

From the main body of the program, after appropriate signals are initialized and the two sequential processes are created, the main process is suspended and placed on a signal's queue. Then, after completion of the tasks of the two sequential processes, instead of terminating the program, the main process is awakened and resumes its execution.

Note that the two sequential processes do not alternate their execution but rather—as was done in their coroutine counterpart—PROCEDURE OtherJob remains active, where the variable y continues to increment and keyboard polling is done, until a keyboard interrupt is, in fact, detected. At that point, the PROCEDURE KeyboardEntry gains control of the CPU (processor) and resumes its execution. Once KeyboardEntry has performed its assigned task, PROCEDURE OtherJob resumes its incrementing and polling again.

```
MODULE KeyboardPolling;

FROM Processes IMPORT StartProcess,SIGNAL,SEND,WAIT,Init;
FROM Terminal IMPORT WriteString,WriteLn,BusyRead,ReadAgain,Read;
FROM InOut IMPORT WriteCard;

VAR main,sig:SIGNAL;
    y:CARDINAL;

    PROCEDURE KeyboardEntry;
    VAR ch:CHAR;
```

```
        BEGIN
          LOOP
             WriteString('Enter letter:  ');
             SEND(sig);
             (* keyboard entry task *)
             Read(ch);
             WriteLn;
             IF ch='*' THEN
                WriteLn;WriteLn;
                WriteString('The accumulated value is: ');
                WriteCard(y,5);
                EXIT; (* exit the LOOP-END construct *)
             END;
          END;
          SEND(main);
        END KeyboardEntry;

        PROCEDURE OtherJob;
        VAR ch:CHAR;
        BEGIN
          WAIT(sig);
          LOOP
             BusyRead(ch);
             IF ch # 0C THEN
                ReadAgain;
                WAIT(sig);
             ELSE
                (* background computing task *)
                INC(y);
             END;
          END;
        END OtherJob;
   BEGIN
      y:=0;
      WriteLn;
      WriteString('To end type "*":');
      WriteLn;
      Init(main);
      Init(sig);
      StartProcess(OtherJob,1000);
      StartProcess(KeyboardEntry,1000);
      WAIT(main);
      (* additional processing after both sequential processes are suspended *)
      WriteLn;
      WriteString('Back in the main body');
   END KeyboardPolling.
```

LISTING 10.7

This processing continues until the sentinel value "*" is sensed, at which time the main body resumes its execution, thus ending the pseudo-concurrent execution of the two sequential processes. If you think about it, a transfer to the main body, whether it be effected by a TRANSFER from SYSTEM as was the case with the coroutine version of KeyboardPolling, or a SEND from Processes, does not preclude the possibility of a reactivation of the pair of sequential processes. A simple adjustment in PROCEDURE KeyboardEntry will allow us to reactivate the sequential processes. In Listing 10.8, we have done the job.

On the other hand, if, as in MODULE Daisy, we actually completed the execution of one of the processes—actually came to the last END of one of the processes, not only would the sequential processes be terminated but the program as well.

```
MODULE KeyboardPolling1;

FROM Processes IMPORT StartProcess,SIGNAL,SEND,WAIT,Init;
FROM Terminal IMPORT WriteString,WriteLn,BusyRead,ReadAgain,Read;
FROM InOut IMPORT WriteCard;

VAR main,sig:SIGNAL;
    y:CARDINAL;

  PROCEDURE KeyboardEntry;
  VAR ch:CHAR;
  BEGIN
    LOOP
      WriteString('Enter letter: ');
      SEND(sig);
      (* keyboard entry task *)
      Read(ch);
      WriteLn;
      IF ch='*' THEN
        WriteLn;WriteLn;
        WriteString('The accumulated value is: ');
        WriteCard(y,5);
        SEND(main); (* this placement allows for reactivation of processes *)
      END;
    END;
  END KeyboardEntry;

  PROCEDURE OtherJob;
  VAR ch:CHAR;
  BEGIN
    WAIT(sig);
    LOOP
      BusyRead(ch);
```

```
            IF ch # 0C THEN
               ReadAgain;
               WAIT(sig);
            ELSE
               (* background computing task *)
               INC(y);
            END;
         END;
      END OtherJob;
   BEGIN
      y:=0;
      WriteLn;
      WriteString('To end type "*":');
      WriteLn;
      Init(main);
      Init(sig);
      StartProcess(OtherJob,1000);
      StartProcess(KeyboardEntry,1000);
      WAIT(main);
      (* additional processing after both sequential processes are suspended *)
      WriteLn;
      WriteString('Back in the main body');
      WriteLn;
      (* reactivate sequential processes *)
      WriteLn;WriteLn;
      WAIT(main);
      WriteLn;
      WriteString('Again back in the main body');
   END KeyboardPolling1.
```

LISTING 10.8

11

Library Modules–Part III

In this concluding chapter, we will bring to light additional library modules that may be provided with each Modula-2 system, in one form or other. It should be noted that the Modula-2 "standard" library has not been standardized at this writing, so we can only bring to you a sense of the type of modules that might be expected with any Modula-2 system along with some modules that might prove to be desirable assets. So as to be specific, the modules presented here are some of those supplied with the Volition Systems Modula-2 compiler.

A detailed explanation of the library modules shown in this chapter or their equivalent is left to the documentation supplied with the particular Modula-2 compiler with which you may be working. We will merely display the definition module and make a few comments regarding the module's use where it appears appropriate.

11.1 MODULE Texts

A text stream is defined as a sequence of characters structured into lines. Module Texts allows us to create such a structure and provides us with the operations to sequentially read and write data from and to text streams. Listing 11.1 is DEFINITION MODULE Texts. Some Modula-2 systems may combine their equivalent of module Files and Texts into one single library module.

```
DEFINITION MODULE Texts;

FROM Files IMPORT FILE;

EXPORT QUALIFIED TEXT,input,output,console,Connect,Disconnect,
                 EOT,EOL,TextStatus,TextState,SetTextHandler,
                 Read,ReadInt,ReadCard,ReadLn,ReadAgain,
                 Write,WriteString,WriteInt,WriteCard,WriteLn;

TYPE TEXT;                          (* Opaque text stream type *)
VAR input,output,console:TEXT;      (* Predeclared text streams *)
```

221

```
PROCEDURE EOT(t:TEXT):BOOLEAN;  (* If TRUE, end of text has been read *)
PROCEDURE EOL(t:TEXT):BOOLEAN;  (* If TRUE, end of line has been read *)

TYPE TextState=(TextOK,FormatError,FileError,ConnectError);
                              (* Error indicator type *)

PROCEDURE TextStatus(t:TEXT):TextState;
                              (* Returns whether error has occurred
                                 or not *)

TYPE TextHandler=PROCEDURE(TextState);
                              (* Error handler type *)

PROCEDURE SetTextHandler(t:TEXT ;handler:TextHandler);
                              (* Pairs off a TEXT variable with an error
                                 handling procedure *)

PROCEDURE Connect(VAR t:TEXT;f:FILE):TextState;
                              (* Connects text stream to file variable *)

PROCEDURE Disconnect(VAR t:TEXT):TextState;
                              (* Disconnects text stream from
                                 file variable *)

PROCEDURE Read        (t:TEXT;ch:CHAR);
PROCEDURE ReadInt     (t:TEXT;s:ARRAY OF CHAR);
PROCEDURE ReadCard    (t:TEXT;i:INTEGER;n:CARDINAL);
PROCEDURE ReadLn      (t:TEXT;c,n:CARDINAL);
                              (* Reads a "line" of text *)

PROCEDURE ReadAgain(t:TEXT);       (* Last character read is read again by
                                       next read operation *)

PROCEDURE Write        (t:TEXT;ch:CHAR);
PROCEDURE WriteString  (t:TEXT;s:ARRAY OF CHAR);
PROCEDURE WriteInt     (t:TEXT;i:INTEGER;n:CARDINAL);
PROCEDURE WriteCard    (t:TEXT;c,n:CARDINAL);
PROCEDURE WriteLn      (t:TEXT);

END Texts.
```

LISTING 11.1

11.2 MODULE Reals

Reals may be used in conjunction with MODULE Texts for the writing and reading of floating point numbers to and from text streams. In Listing 11.2 we have the definition module for Reals.

```
DEFINITION MODULE Reals;

FROM Texts IMPORT TEXT;

EXPORT QUALIFIED RealToStr,StrToReal,ReadReal,WriteReal;

PROCEDURE ReadReal (t:TEXT;VAR r:REAL);

PROCEDURE WriteReal (t:TEXT;r:REAL;n:CARDINAL;digits:INTEGER);

PROCEDURE RealToStr(r:REAL;digits:INTEGER;
                    VAR s:ARRAY OF CHAR):BOOLEAN;

PROCEDURE StrToReal(s:ARRAY OF CHAR;VAR r:REAL):BOOLEAN;

END Reals.
```

LISTING 11.2

11.3 MODULE Storage

MODULE Storage gives us the capability to manage the RAM memory dynamically—that is, during program execution. With the importation of ALLOCATE and DEALLOCATE from Storage, we can make use of the two built-in procedures NEW and DISPOSE as we did back in Chapter 9 when dealing with pointer types, or develop our own memory management facilities. DEFINITION MODULE Storage is shown in Listing 11.3.

```
DEFINITION MODULE Storage;

FROM SYSTEM IMPORT ADDRESS;

EXPORT QUALIFIED ALLOCATE,DEALLOCATE,Available;

PROCEDURE ALLOCATE    (VAR p:ADDRESS;size:CARDINAL);

PROCEDURE DEALLOCATE(VAR p:ADDRESS;size:CARDINAL);

PROCEDURE Available    (size:CARDINAL):BOOLEAN;

END Storage.
```

LISTING 11.3

11.4 MODULE MathLib0

MODULE MathLib0 (Listing 11.4) provides us with some basic mathematical functions. Angles associated with sin, cos, and arctan are in radian measure. Additional mathematical library modules will, no doubt, also become available.

```
DEFINITION MODULE MathLib0;

EXPORT QUALIFIED sqrt,exp,ln,sin,cos,arctan,real,entier;

PROCEDURE sqrt   (x:REAL):REAL; (* The square root of x *)
PROCEDURE exp    (x:REAL):REAL; (* The value e(=2.71828...) to
                                    the x power *)
PROCEDURE ln     (x:REAL):REAL; (* The natural logarithm, (base e),
                                    of x *)
PROCEDURE sin    (x:REAL):REAL;
PROCEDURE cos    (x:REAL):REAL;
PROCEDURE arctan (x:REAL):REAL; (* The angle whose tangent is x *)
PROCEDURE real   (x:INTEGER):REAL; (* Converts type INTEGER to
                                    type REAL *)
PROCEDURE entier (x:REAL):INTEGER; (* The largest integer that is less
                                    than or equal to x *)

END MathLib0.
```

LISTING 11.4

11.5 MODULE Decimals

MODULE Decimals (Listing 11.5) can be used for business-type computations. Along with its mathematical routines, the module provides us with both input and output numeric formatting *pictures* (which can include the dollar sign, a decimal point, and a comma as a separator.)

```
DEFINITION MODULE Decimals;

EXPORT QUALIFIED DECIMAL,DecDigits,DecPoint,DecSep,DecCur,DecStatus,
                 DecState,DecValid,StrToDec,DecToStr,NegDec,CompareDec,
                 AddDec,SubDec,MulDec,DivDec,Remainder,SetDecHandler;

CONST DecDigits=19;
      DecCur   ='$';
      DecPoint='.';
      DecSep  =',';

TYPE DECIMAL;              (* opaque type for decimal numbers of up to 19 digits *)
     DecState=(NegOvfl,Minus,Zero,Plus,PosOvfl,Invalid);
                          (* indicates sign of decimal or that error has occurred *)

VAR DecValid:BOOLEAN; (* set after every operation *)
    Remainder:CHAR;    (* remainder digit - set after execution of DivDec *)
```

```
PROCEDURE StrToDec(String:ARRAY OF CHAR;
                    Picture:ARRAY OF CHAR):DECIMAL;
PROCEDURE DecToStr(Dec:DECIMAL;Picture:ARRAY OF CHAR;
                    VAR RsltStr:ARRAY OF CHAR);
                    (* the above 2 objects convert decimals between
                       internal and external machine formats *)

TYPE DecHandler=PROCEDURE(DecState);
                    (* error handling objects *)
PROCEDURE SetDecHandler(handler:DecHandler);
PROCEDURE DecStatus(Dec:DECIMAL):DecState;

PROCEDURE CompareDec(Dec0,Dec1:DECIMAL):INTEGER;(* compares 2
                                                    decimals *)

PROCEDURE AddDec    (Dec0,Dec1:DECIMAL):DECIMAL;(* addition *)
PROCEDURE SubDec    (Dec0,Dec1:DECIMAL):DECIMAL;(* subtraction *)
PROCEDURE MulDec    (Dec0,Dec1:DECIMAL):DECIMAL;(* multiplication *)
PROCEDURE DivDec    (Dec0,Dec1:DECIMAL):DECIMAL;(* division - remainder
                                                    in Remainder *)

PROCEDURE NegDec    (Dec:DECIMAL):DECIMAL;       (* negation *)

END Decimals.
```

LISTING 11.5

11.6 MODULE Strings

Variable-length character strings can be declared, manipulated, and modified with the use of library module Strings, whose definition module is presented in Listing 11.6.

```
DEFINITION MODULE Strings;

EXPORT QUALIFIED STRING,Assign,Insert,Delete,
                  Pos,Copy,Concat,Length,CompareStr;

TYPE STRING=ARRAY[0..80] OF CHAR;

PROCEDURE Assign  (VAR source,dest:ARRAY OF CHAR);
        (* used to assign one string variable, (dest), value of another (source) *)

PROCEDURE Insert  (substr:ARRAY OF CHAR;VAR str:ARRAY OF CHAR;
                    inx:CARDINAL);
        (* insert substr into str, starting at str[inx] *)

PROCEDURE Delete  (VAR str:ARRAY OF CHAR;inx,len:CARDINAL);
        (* delete len characters from str, starting at str[inx] *)
```

PROCEDURE Pos   (substr,str:ARRAY OF CHAR):CARDINAL;
  (* returns index value of first character of first occurrence of substr in
    str; if substr not in str, returns HIGH(str)+1 *)

PROCEDURE Copy   (str:ARRAY OF CHAR;inx,len:CARDINAL;
                         VAR result:ARRAY OF CHAR);
  (* copies len characters from str, starting at str[inx] *)

PROCEDURE Concat(s1,s2:ARRAY OF CHAR;VAR result:ARRAY OF CHAR);
  (* returns concatenation of s1 and s2 *)

PROCEDURE Length (VAR str:ARRAY OF CHAR):CARDINAL;
  (* returns number of characters in str *)

PROCEDURE CompareStr(s1,s2:ARRAY OF CHAR):INTEGER;
  (* compares s1 and s2; returns –1 if s1 < s2
                          0 if s1=s2
                          1 if s1 > s2 *)

END Strings.

LISTING 11.6

11.7 MODULE Conversions

MODULE Conversions (Listing 11.7) provides us with the capability
of converting numeric quantities between different representations,
namely integer, cardinal, hexadecimal, and character string.

DEFINITION MODULE Conversions;

FROM SYSTEM IMPORT WORD;

EXPORT QUALIFIED IntToStr,StrToInt,CardToStr,StrToCard,HexToStr,StrToHex;

PROCEDURE IntToStr   (i:INTEGER;VAR s:ARRAY OF CHAR):BOOLEAN;
PROCEDURE StrToInt   (s:ARRAY OF CHAR;VAR i:INTEGER):BOOLEAN;
PROCEDURE CardToStr (c:CARDINAL;VAR s:ARRAY OF CHAR):BOOLEAN;
PROCEDURE StrToCard(s:ARRAY OF CHAR;VAR c:CARDINAL):BOOLEAN;
PROCEDURE HexToStr (w:WORD;VAR s:ARRAY OF CHAR):BOOLEAN;
PROCEDURE StrToHex (s:ARRAY OF CHAR;VAR w:WORD):BOOLEAN;

END Conversions.

LISTING 11.7

11.8 MODULE ASCII

MODULE ASCII (Listing 11.8) supplies us with convenient symbolic identifiers for all the ASCII control characters.

```
DEFINITION MODULE ASCII;

EXPORT QUALIFIED nul,soh,stx,etx,eot,enq,ack,bel,
                 bs, ht, lf, vt, ff, cr, so, si,
                 dle,dc1,dc2,dc3,dc4,nak,syn,etb,
                 can,em, sub,esc,fs, gs, rs, us,
                 del;

CONST nul=00C; soh=01C; stx=02C; etx=03C; eot=04C; enq=05C; ack=06C; bel=07C;
      bs =10C; ht =11C; lf =12C; vt =13C; ff =14C; cr =15C; so =16C; si =17C;
      dle =20C; dc1=21C; dc2=22C; dc3=23C; dc4=24C; nak=25C; syn=26C; etb=27C;
      can=30C; em =31C; sub=32C; esc =33C; fs =34C; gs =35C; rs =36C; us =37C;
      del =177C;

END ASCII.
```

LISTING 11.8

11.9 MODULE Screen

Some fundamental screen control routines are found in MODULE Screen (Listing 11.9).

```
DEFINITION MODULE Screen;

EXPORT QUALIFIED HomeCursor,ClearScreen,EraseLine,GotoXY;

PROCEDURE HomeCursor; (* moves cursor to upper left hand corner of screen *)
PROCEDURE ClearScreen;  (* clears the entire text screen; places cursor at
                           upper left hand corner of screen *)
PROCEDURE EraseLine;    (* clear from cursor position to end of present line *)
PROCEDURE GotoXY(x,y:CARDINAL); (* move cursor to screen column x,
                                   row y *)

END Screen.
```

LISTING 11.9

11.10 MODULE SystemTypes

System-dependent attributes are supplied by MODULE SystemTypes as shown in Listing 11.10.

```
DEFINITION MODULE SystemTypes;

EXPORT QUALIFIED MinInt,MaxCard,AdrsPerWord,CharsPerWord;

CONST MinInt  =-32768; (* minimum INTEGER value assumable *)
      MaxInt  = 32767; (* maximum INTEGER value assumable *)
      MaxCard= 65535; (* maximum CARDINAL value assumable *)

      AdrsPerWord  =2; (* number of addressable RAM units per memory word *)
      CharsPerWord =2; (* number of characters per memory word *)

END SystemTypes.
```

LISTING 11.10

11.11 MODULE Standards

MODULE Standards is included here since, you may recall, we made use of one of its objects (MemAvail) in section 7.6. Standards is a special module that allows you to access UCSD Pascal's low-level standard procedures if your Modula-2 is implemented on the UCSD operating system. Listing 11.11 presents the available objects with no comments.

```
DEFINITION MODULE Standards;

FROM SYSTEM IMPORT ADDRESS;

EXPORT QUALIFIED MoveLeft,MoveRight,FillChar,Scan,Time,ScanType,
                 PowerOfTen,Alloc,Mark,Release,MemAvail;

TYPE ScanType=(ScanUntil,ScanWhile);

PROCEDURE MoveLeft  (SrcAddr:ADDRESS;SrcInx:CARDINAL;
                     DestAddr:ADDRESS;DestInx:CARDINAL;
                     NBytes:CARDINAL);
PROCEDURE MoveRight(SrcAddr:ADDRESS;SrcInx:CARDINAL;
                     DestAddr:ADDRESS;DestInx:CARDINAL;
                     NBytes:CARDINAL);
PROCEDURE FillChar  (DestAddr:ADDRESS;DestInx:CARDINAL;
                     NBytes:CARDINAL;FillVal:CHAR);
PROCEDURE Scan      (NumChars:INTEGER;ForPast:ScanType;Target:CHAR;
                     Source:ADDRESS;SrcInx:CARDINAL):INTEGER;

PROCEDURE Time(VAR Hi,Lo:CARDINAL);

PROCEDURE Alloc     (VAR p:ADDRESS;words:CARDINAL);
PROCEDURE Mark      (VAR p:ADDRESS);
PROCEDURE Release   (VAR p:ADDRESS);
PROCEDURE MemAvail( ):CARDINAL;
```

PROCEDURE PowerOfTen(e:CARDINAL):REAL;

END Standards.

LISTING 11.11

11.12 MODULE Bits

MODULE Bits provides us with the capability of accessing bit and byte fields of word quantites. Bits' definition module is shown as Listing 11.12.

DEFINITION MODULE Bits;

FROM SYSTEM IMPORT WORD,ADDRESS;

EXPORT QUALIFIED LoadByte,StoreByte,LoadField,StoreField;

PROCEDURE LoadByte (base:ADDRESS;offset:CARDINAL):CARDINAL;
     (* load byte from byte address, base[offset] *)
PROCEDURE StoreByte (base:ADDRESS;offset,ValueToStore:CARDINAL);
     (* store byte at byte address, base[offset] *)

PROCEDURE LoadField(VAR w:WORD ;NumbersOfBits:CARDINAL;
               RightMostBit:CARDINAL):CARDINAL;
     (* load specified bit field from word w *)
PROCEDURE StoreField(VAR w:WORD ;NumbersOfBits:CARDINAL;
               RightMostBit:CARDINAL;ValueToStore:CARDINAL);
     (* store specified bit field into word w *)

END Bits.

LISTING 11.12

11.13 MODULE Program

MODULE Program is a Volition Systems specific library module. We include it here (Listing 11.13) since reference was made to it in section 7.6. With MODULE Program we can create a program module that allows us to execute other program modules.

DEFINITION MODULE Program;

EXPORT QUALIFIED Call,CallMode,ErrorMode,CallResult,
               Terminate,SetEnvelope,EnvMode;

```
TYPE CallResult =(NormalReturn,ProgramHalt,RangeError,SystemError,
                  FunctionError,StackOverflow,IntegerError,
                  DivideByZero,AddressError,UserHalt,CodeIOError,
                  UserIOError,InstructionError,FloatingError,
                  StringError,StorageError,VersionError,
                  MissingProgram,MissingModule,LibraryError,
                  NotMainProcess,DuplicateName);

     CallMode  =(Shared,Unshared);
     ErrorMode=(SystemTrap,CallerTrap);

PROCEDURE Terminate(exception:CallResult);

PROCEDURE Call(programName:ARRAY OF CHAR;
               calltype:CallMode;errors:ErrorMode):CallResult;

TYPE EnvMode    =(AllCalls,UnsharedCalls,FirstCall);

PROCEDURE SetEnvelope(init,term:PROC;mode:EnvMode);

END Program.
```

LISTING 11.13

Modula-2 Reserved Words and Symbols

AND	LOOP
ARRAY	MOD
BEGIN	MODULE
BY	NOT
CASE	OF
CONST	OR
DEFINITION	POINTER
DIV	PROCEDURE
DO	QUALIFIED
ELSE	RECORD
ELSIF	REPEAT
END	RETURN
EXIT	SET
EXPORT	THEN
FOR	TO
FROM	TYPE
IF	UNTIL
IMPLEMENTATION	VAR
IMPORT	WHILE
IN	WITH

+	=
−	#
*	< >
/	>
:=	> =
.	<
,	< =
;	&
:	(
..	)
'	[
"	]
|	{
^	}

Appendix B

The ASCII Character Set
(American Standard Code for Information Interchange)

Ord dec	Values oct	Char	Ord dec	Values oct	Char	Ord dec	Values oct	Char	Ord dec	Values oct	Char
0	0	nul	32	40	sp	64	100	@	96	140	'
1	1	soh	33	41	!	65	101	A	97	141	a
2	2	stx	34	42	"	66	102	B	98	142	b
3	3	etx	35	43	#	67	103	C	99	143	c
4	4	eot	36	44	$	68	104	D	100	144	d
5	5	enq	37	45	%	69	105	E	101	145	e
6	6	ack	38	46	&	70	106	F	102	146	f
7	7	bel	39	47	'	71	107	G	103	147	g
8	10	bs	40	50	(	72	110	H	104	150	h
9	11	ht	41	51	)	73	111	I	105	151	i
10	12	lf	42	52	*	74	112	J	106	152	j
11	13	vt	43	53	+	75	113	K	107	153	k
12	14	ff	44	54	,	76	114	L	108	154	l
13	15	cr	45	55	-	77	115	M	109	155	m
14	16	so	46	56	.	78	116	N	110	156	n
15	17	si	47	57	/	79	117	O	111	157	o
16	20	dle	48	60	0	80	120	P	112	160	p
17	21	dc1	49	61	1	81	121	Q	113	161	q
18	22	dc2	50	62	2	82	122	R	114	162	r
19	23	dc3	51	63	3	83	123	S	115	163	s
20	24	dc4	52	64	4	84	124	T	116	164	t
21	25	nak	53	65	5	85	125	U	117	165	u
22	26	syn	54	66	6	86	126	V	118	166	v
23	27	etb	55	67	7	87	127	W	119	167	w
24	30	can	56	70	8	88	130	X	120	170	x
25	31	em	57	71	9	89	131	Y	121	171	y
26	32	sub	58	72	:	90	132	Z	122	172	z
27	33	esc	59	73	;	91	133	[	123	173	{
28	34	fs	60	74	<	92	134	\	124	174	|
29	35	gs	61	75	=	93	135	]	125	175	}
30	36	rs	62	76	>	94	136	∧	126	176	~
31	37	us	63	77	?	95	137	—	127	177	del

Appendix C

Modula-2 Standard Identifiers

ABS	HIGH
BITSET	INC
BOOLEAN	INCL
CAP	INTEGER
CARDINAL	NEW
CHAR	NIL
CHR	ODD
DEC	ORD
DISPOSE	PROC
EXCL	REAL
FALSE	TRUE
FLOAT	TRUNC
HALT	VAL

Appendix D

A Table of Listings and the Topics They Exemplify

237

A Table of Listings and the Topics They Exemplify (cont.)

A Table of Listings and the Topics They Exemplify (cont.)

Listing	*Title*	*Topics*
8.7c	MODULE WordArraysTest	a case study using WORD, enumerated types, and procedure types to perform limited generic sorting and displaying
9.1	MODULE PointerDemo	example of working with pointer types
9.2	MODULE StackWithPointers	using pointers to implement a stack data structure
9.3a	MODULE OddAndEven	
9.3b	DEFINITION MODULE StackOperations	
9.3c	IMPLEMENTATION MODULE StackOperations	
9.3d	DEFINITION MODULE StackOperations	
9.3e	IMPLEMENTATION MODULE StackOperations	
9.3f	IMPLEMENTATION MODULE StackOperations	
		a case study development using an opaque type and object-oriented design
10.1	DEFINITION MODULE Terminal	"standard" library module
10.2	MODULE Daisy	a simple coroutine example using objects from SYSTEM and Terminal
10.3	MODULE KeyboardPolling	a character entry interrupts a background computing routine; uses SYSTEM
10.4	MODULE EnterDataAndDoSearch	a case study using coroutines
10.5	DEFINITION MODULE Processes	"standard" library module
10.6	MODULE Daisy	a sequential processes example using objects from Processes
10.7	MODULE KeyboardPolling	a character entry interrupts a background computing routine; uses Processes
10.8	MODULE KeyboardPolling1	reactivation of a pair of sequential processes

Appendix E

A Short Bibliography

At this writing, there is precious little material to be found in the literature concerning Modula-2. This situation will soon be rectified due to the wide interest that Modula-2 has engendered. A few sources of information are listed below. A short comment is included with each source.

Additionally, there are a number of topics touched on, or merely mentioned, in the book which you may wish to pursue through further reading. A few titles concerning these topics are also listed below.

Modula-2

Wirth, N., *Programming in Modula-2*, Springer-Verlag, New York, NY, et al. 1982. *A book on Modula-2 by its designer.*

"Volition Systems Modula-2 User's Manual," San Diego, CA. *A good source of additional information concerning Volition Systems' implementation of the language.*

Journal of Pascal, Ada and Modula-2, Wiley, New York, NY. *An excellent publication concerning topics important to Modula-2 programmers.*

Ford, G. and R. Wiener, *Modula-2, A Software Development Approach*, Wiley, New York, NY, 1985. *An advanced book which formally details Modula-2 and associated topics.*

Data Structures

Kruse, R., *Data Structures & Program Design*, Prentice-Hall, Englewood Cliffs, NJ, 1984.

Tenenbaum, A. and M. Augenstein, *Data Structures Using Pascal*, Prentice-Hall, Englewood Cliffs, NJ, 1981.

Object-Oriented Design

Booch, G., *Software Engineering With Ada,* Benjamin/Cummings, Menlo Park, CA, 1983.

Wiener, R. and R. Sincovec, *Software Engineering With Modula-2 And Ada* Wiley, New York, NY, 1984.

Index